THE
HANDKNITTER'S
HANDBOOK

THE
HANDKNITTER'S
HANDBOOK

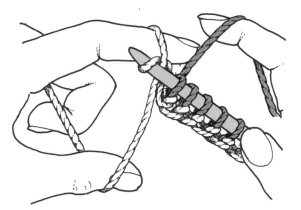

MONTSE STANLEY

With 656 two-colour line illustrations
by Elaine Franks

A David & Charles Craft Book

To my mother, the 'knitting Fittipaldi'

British Library Cataloguing in Publication Data
Stanley, Montse
    The handknitter's handbook.
    1. Knitting
    I. Title
    746.43'2   TT820

    ISBN 0-7153-8805-3

First published 1986
Second impression 1987
Third impression 1988
Fourth impression 1988

Phototypeset by ABM Typographics Ltd Hull
and printed in Italy
by New Interlitho, Milan
for David & Charles Publishers plc
Brunel House   Newton Abbot   Devon

Distributed in the United States by
Sterling Publishing Co, Inc, 2 Park Avenue, New York, NY 10016

Contents

Introduction

It has been said that handknitting is easy, just knit and purl. It could equally be said that writing is easy, just put one word after another; why all the fuss about Shakespeare? Like all things, **knitting is easy when you know how.** Techniques that ten years ago would have scared the wits out of me I now use without a second thought, simply because I have learnt their ins and outs. Conversely, first-timers left to discover by themselves that there are a few catches to 'just knit and purl', or 'just follow a chart', may give up knitting for good. Finding difficult what has been described as 'easy, anyone can do it', they may logically conclude that they are not cut out for the job.

Knitters can well do without patronising reassurances that no effort is involved, or that their little brains will not be unduly taxed. What they desperately need are hard facts about the how, the why and the when of each technique at their disposal; and these arranged so that a knitter can easily pick out the precise technique required at a given moment, and totally ignore the rest. Which is precisely what this book attempts to do.

Knitting is an extremely rich, wonderfully exciting craft, that can be experienced at as many levels as medicine – from learning a few first-aid routines to becoming a brain surgeon. All levels of hand knitting can be satisfying, but there is something magic about going higher and higher until you almost touch the clouds. The attractive results obtained with elementary techniques turn into the easy flow of the true masterpiece. And you discover that, if knitting a simple sweater is fun, being in full control of a really complex one is positively exhilarating.

So rich is hand knitting that no book, however comprehensive, can ever claim to be 'complete'. This one collects together all the techniques I have learnt to date, but with new avenues opening up even as the book was going to press, and considering that only a few countries were studied, it is plain that the subject is far from exhausted. I would be most interested to hear from readers who would like to share aspects I have missed. Please write c/o David & Charles, Brunel House, Newton Abbot, Devon TQ12 4PU.

My first intention was to mention by name every person and every publication that had helped to build the jigsaw. When I passed the hundred mark on books, let alone people and magazines, I started to have second thoughts! So, instead of filling up precious pages with endless names and references, may I be forgiven for just saying THANK YOU to ALL KNITTERS, past and present, who have made the craft grow through their work, their writings or their quiet dedication.

The task of comparing, coordinating and supplementing information produced some fascinating insights:

● Knitting can be approached from different angles: texture, colour, shaping, tailoring, innovation, tradition, technical ingenuity, no-nonsense practicality. Countries seem to develop preferences for particular approaches, so that the nationality of a publication is often given away by its content as much as by its language.

● There is a certain amount of cross-pollination, not always admitted. French, German and Italian books, for instance, have been translated into English but, at the same time, English text has been 'assimilated' into

Italian publications and large chunks of a French book have appeared under a Spanish needlecraft title.

• Nothing is new. Independently of cross-pollination, some of the cleverest tricks keep being discovered (or 'unvented' as Elizabeth Zimmermann, the British-born American, would put it with characteristic wit) time and again. A very slight variation of the famous 'slip, slip, knit' decrease that Barbara Walker gave to America in the late sixties, for example, had been published in France by 'Mon Tricot' in 1955 and, quite possibly, even earlier. (This is certainly not intended as a criticism of one of the authors who most deserves the respect and admiration she receives.)

• Non-Western cultures offered some surprises and food for thought. Why are patterns with diagrams, and tubular methods for casting on and casting off ribbing, popular in Japan (as well as Spain, Italy and France) – but not in England? Why do the Peruvians, the Egyptians (and the Portuguese) place the yarn around the neck instead of in one hand, like all the other countries studied?

• Large areas (casting on and off, holding two colours in one hand, finishes) did not seem to have been fully developed anywhere. Other areas (paired increases and decreases being a striking example) were somewhat chaotic. It was rather amusing, in fact, to see how much contradictory advice there was: casting off with a crochet hook would give a loose/tight edge, stitches should always be slipped knitwise/purlwise, garments should always/never be sewn before blocking.

• In Britain, Mary Thomas had reigned supreme, her words and illustrations (even the occasional slip-up) reverently echoed for over forty years by umpteen know-how books. This is not surprising, given the intellectual brilliancy of her work; but it has meant that today's knitters are still suffering from Mary Thomas's weak side. In sharp contrast with books from other countries and the refreshing breath of fresh air offered by Audrie Stratford, the two volumes she wrote show a curious detachment. As a clinical analysis of hand knitting her work cannot be faulted, yet the superficial advice she gives on such everyday matters as seams, buttonholes, darning, blocking, knitting up or holding the needles, puts her practical experience very much in question.

• • •

Finally, I must give a word of thanks to Tom, my husband. He read it all, changed 'ins' for 'ons', and 'thats' for 'thans', and never fell asleep – quite a feat, since a non-knitter is bound to find this book as enthralling as a telephone directory!

Montse Stanley

How to use this book

What to find where

The book has five parts.

Part One, **Basics**, will familiarise you with stitch structure, ways to hold the work, tools, yarns and other key elements of hand knitting.

Part Two, **Get clicking**, starts with a short look at terms and abbreviations, and then explores all the things that can be done with needles and yarn. Each chapter deals with one technique and, when appropriate, ends with specific applications. The chapter on **Casting on and off**, for instance, ends with the fascinating **picot knitting**.

Part Three, **Final touches**, deals with blocking, joining, cutting, adding ornament and other finishing processes.

Part Four, **Pattern instructions**, explains how to decode charts and row-by-row descriptions of stitch patterns and garments.

Part Five, **Help!**, is the knitter's rescue and recycling kit.

Finally, there are lists of **Publications** and useful **Addresses** (specialist booksellers, suppliers and organisations) and the real key to the book, the **Index**.

How much to read

I am tempted to say that Part One, **Basics**, should be compulsory reading. Some information may not be of immediate interest, but on the whole it will save you from wasting time, yarn and enthusiasm in projects only good for backs of drawers.

Have a quick look, if nothing else, then dip into the rest of the book as the need arises or the fancy takes you.

Glancing through

The staggered green strip at the edge of each page makes it an easy matter to turn to Part One, Part Two etc. The words inside the strip are chapter headings.

Colour is also used to spotlight the start and end of chapters, the working yarn in the illustrations, and the symbols that describe each technique as being:

ESSENTIAL: cannot knit without learning — E

USEFUL: to achieve good general standards — U

SPECIAL: for less common situations and/or highest levels of craftsmanship — S

Bold type is used when referring to techniques or information given elsewhere in the book. These can be easily located through the **Index**.

Finding a technique

Supposing you want to find the **tubular cast-on for single ribbing**. Look in the **Index** for either **tubular, cast-on** or **ribbing**. It is under all three headings, and there is also an entry for its other name, **invisible cast-on**. For this example there are three different methods. Assess which one suits you best by reading the text and by knitting samples.

Make sure not to miss the introductory paragraphs at the start of each chapter, where the general rules are set.

Selecting a technique

Suppose, for instance, you want to cast on but have no idea which method to use, or are not even aware that there is more than one method (in which case you are heading for a big surprise!).

Look up the general **Casting on** heading in the **Index**. Read the opening paragraphs, which here include a **choosing a cast-on** section. If more than one method seems suitable, start with the one marked **E** (essential), then continue with **U** (useful) and **S** (special) if you want to. If in doubt between methods, knit samples and compare.

Beginners in a hurry

If you have never knitted and are itching to get started:

● Choose something straightforward in thickish **yarn**, but do not buy this yet. The less fancy the yarn, the easier it will knit up.

● Get a practice ball of thick, plain yarn. Get also a pair of **standard needles** 35–40cm (14–16in) long (do not accept shorter needles), and a 60cm (24in) **circular needle**, of appropriate thickness for the yarn – ask the shop or look at the yarn **label**.

● Read **flat or circular** and the first few paragraphs of **Holding the work**. Get ready to try two ways of knitting, to see which will work best for you.

● **Cast on** 20 stitches on the standard needles with the **two-strand simplified** method. Practise the first version of the **knit stitch** (Fig 2.86) on all 20 stitches, working with

yarn in right hand – fixed needle. Read **flat knitting** and the start of **Stitch understanding**. Continue practising until you can knit confidently, then alternate one row of knit with one row of common **purl stitch** (Fig 2.90). When you can both knit and purl, close the stitches with a **basic cast-off**.

● Repeat what you have just done on the circular needle, but use the **German** version of the **two-strand cast-on** and work with **yarn in left hand**.

● Decide which type of needle you prefer and buy all you need for your chosen project. See **buying yarns, essential equipment** and **stitch size** (including **which needles?** and **tension**).

● Once you start work, the following may prove helpful:

a **What is what**, at start of Part Two
b Part Four: **Instructions**
c **using yarn** and **joining in yarn**, under **Yarns**
d introductions to **Casting on** and **Casting off**
e **common problems** under **Holding the work**
f **Mishaps**

● Once you decide that you are going to enjoy knitting, it is time to start reading all Part One: **Basics**, as suggested earlier in **how much to read**.

PART ONE

BASICS

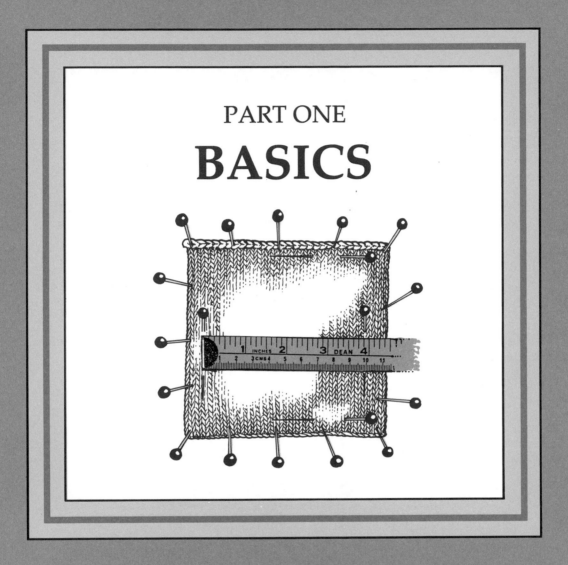

Stitch understanding

(See also **Yarns, Holding the work** and **Rows and rounds**)

The knitted stitch

Knitting is no more than a succession of yarn waves (Fig 1.1) which have been made to interlock. The trough of a new wave is interlocked with the crest of the previous wave, leaving the crest of the new wave free. To keep this in position, a needle is used. A second needle helps to interlock the following wave.

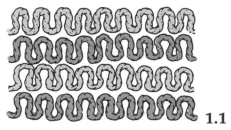

1.1

Each loop that is, or has been, on a needle is a **stitch**. A stitch has two **sides**:
knit side (Fig 1.2); smooth, looking rather like a V.

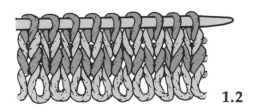

1.2

purl side (Fig 1.3); rugged, clearly showing how the two waves interlock. If the waves are in different colours or textures, the dividing line is a broken one.

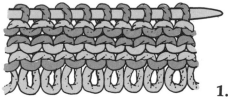

1.3

When interlocking, you decide which side of the stitch you want to show. You can also interlock two or more stitches with one new loop (**decreases**), and two or more new loops into one stitch (**increases**). You can make new loops without interlocking them with a previous stitch (**overs**), and do various other things. This all creates thousands of **stitch patterns**, used to make **fabrics**.

Stitch patterns also have two sides:
• **right side**; the one you want to show.
• **wrong side**; the one you do not want to show.

Some patterns look good from both sides, and can be used for reversible fabrics.

Whilst working, you may be turning the knitting. Either side of the stitch pattern can then be:
• at **front of work**, if you see it. Or,
• at **back of work**, if you do not see it.
You then have:
• **right-side rows** – lines of stitches made whilst the **right side** is at **front of work**.
• **wrong-side rows** – lines of stitches made with the **wrong side** at **front of work**.
This will only occur when you knit **flat** pieces. If you make tubes (**circular knitting**), the rows will become **rounds** and you will never turn the work. All rounds will be either **right-side** or **wrong-side**, usually the former.

Stitch and needle

Although there are exceptions, the normal position of a stitch on the needle is with its right arm at **front of work** (Fig 1.4). If right arm is at **back of work** (Fig 1.5) the stitch will become **twisted** when you interlock it.

To straighten a stitch going the wrong way, you drop it and insert the needle from the other side; or you pass it onto the other needle and return it straight; or you work into **back** arm instead of **front** arm (which, in either case, is the right hand arm).

Normal work progresses from **right to left**, with the yarn hanging from the right needle. The left needle merely holds the stitches from the previous row. If the last stitch made is a **knit**, the yarn hangs at **back of work**; if **purl**, it hangs at **front of work**.

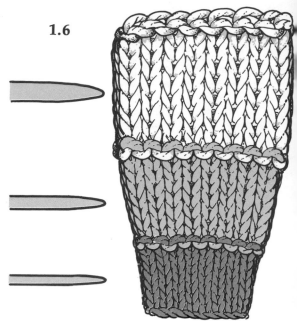

1.6

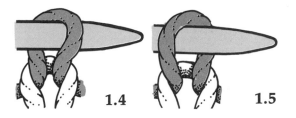

1.4   1.5

Stitch size

The size of a stitch is the direct result of **yarn thickness** and **needle size** (Fig 1.6), influenced by **stitch pattern**. If the needles are too fine for the yarn, working is difficult. The resulting fabric is stiff, has no 'give' and tends to felt – it is **tight**. If the needles are too thick, the fabric is **loose**. It may look appealingly soft, but it has no hold. It grows and grows and never recovers its original shape. It may also be uneven. If the needles are correct, the fabric is elastic and keeps its shape. It is not stiff, nor sloppy, but nicely firm. And it looks and feels more even.

Too abstract? Take a good selection of needles and a ball of medium-thick yarn. **Cast on** 15 or 20 stitches on the finest needles and work your way up the sizes allowing 10 or 12 rows on each. Work in **stocking stitch** with a **purl row** at each needle change, as in illustration. Feel and pull about each section.

Which needles?

No two knitters work alike, but we all think of ourselves as 'average', which is why so many people take the needle size mentioned on **ball bands** or in **instructions** as 'the' one for them.

The size of the stitches you get with a pair of needles depends on:

● **yarn tension**, or how much you pull the yarn. You may be a **tight knitter** (perhaps so tight that knitting is hard work and the stitches take some persuading to glide down the needles), or a **slack knitter** (perhaps so slack that the stitches keep **dropping** off the needles).

● **length of yarn drawn through**. We may think our stitches go all the way round the needle as in the previous illustrations, when in fact they only go half-way round (as a result of a **tight yarn tension**, of keeping the finger feeding the yarn too high, or of not pulling the needle far enough when drawing the new stitch). Fig 1.7.

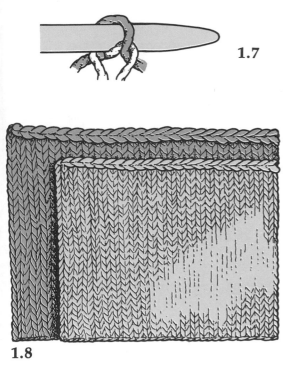

1.7

1.8

Fig 1.8 shows two pieces of knitting with identical numbers of stitches and rows, worked with the same yarn and needles by two knitters – both of which presumed to be 'average'.

If a certain pair of needles gives you a **loose fabric**, you need thinner needles. If they give you a **tight fabric** you need thicker needles. Sometimes you can successfully work certain areas with thinner or thicker needles than the rest, either for texture or for shaping. What you should never do is change the size of an entire project by altering needle size, instead of altering number of stitches and rows, because fabric quality and performance will be drastically affected.

Having established what needles give you the best fabric with a certain yarn, keep in mind that changing **stitch pattern** can alter stitch **size** and/or **shape** (see **stitch patterns** below). Do not be surprised if, as a result, you need a very different needle size.

Occasionally, you may choose the 'wrong' needle size intentionally – if you want something very stiff and sturdy which can only be achieved with fine needles, or you want to make use of the holes left by large needles when working **lace**. In this case you are likely to **block** the fabric well stretched, so no further stretching is likely to occur.

Tension

(See also **tension** under **garment instructions**)

The **stitch size** of a **fabric** is measured by the number of stitches and rows to a given square, normally 10cm × 10cm (4in × 4in). (Note that metric and imperial are not identical, and should not be interchanged.) In Britain, this is referred to as **tension**. The Americans call it **gauge**, probably a better choice as it cannot be confused with **yarn tension**.

Samples

Before you start a project, whether following instructions or designing your own, you must make sure that the fabric will be neither **tight** nor **loose**. To this effect you work a sample on which you measure the **tension** or **gauge**. For good results, the sample must be:
• off the needles, either **cast off** or with a length of yarn securing the free loops.
• larger than 10cm, or other intended measurement, so that you can check away from the distorted edges. If you are told to achieve, say, 28 stitches in 10cm, the **sample** should at least have 32. If working 'blind', use the following table as guidance for **stocking stitch**:

Yarn	Needle size (mm)	Number of stitches
2-ply	2	46
3-ply	2½	38
4-ply	3	32
Double knitting	4	28
Triple knitting	4½	22
Double-double	6	18
Extra chunky	9	14

(See **knitting needles** for needle size equivalents)

If the sample feels **tight**, try again with thicker needles; if it feels **loose**, try again with finer needles.

• pinned flat to reach its natural size, or **blocked**; **stretched** if the fabric is to be stretched. **Wash** if you want to perform a **shrinkage test** (see also **handle** and **resilience** under **Yarns**).

• worked in same **yarn colour** and quality as final fabric will be, and in same **stitch pattern**.

• worked **flat** or **circular**, but always as the intended project. To work a 'circular' sample, with **circular** or **double-pointed needles**, cut yarn at end of each row then, without turning, slide sample to the right end of the needle and **join in** yarn again.

Work one sample for each stitch pattern and each yarn involved.

When trying to achieve tensions stated in **instructions**, it may be impossible to achieve both **stitch** and **row** counts. Concentrate on the stitches and, if the row difference is large, avoid projects where the numbers of rows are crucial. In projects where length is checked with a tape measure rather than by counting rows, remember that you will probably need a different amount of yarn than the instructions say.

If you are designing, and do not need to know the row count from the start, you may only need to check the **stitches**. A 5–7cm (2–3in) deep sample is then usually enough. Check row count later, over the part-knitted project.

To measure the sample (Fig 1.9):

a Place edge of **tape measure** or ruler at least two stitches away from left edge, and mark with a **pin**.

b Keeping the tape totally horizontal, place another pin at 10cm (4in). With very fine yarns, you could make a smaller sample and measure only 5cm (2in). With extremely thick yarns you may need 15 or 20cm (6 or 8in).

c Count the number of stitches. (When following instructions, having more than

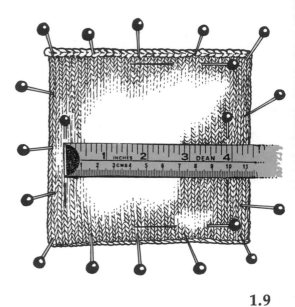

1.9

you should means that your stitches are too small – try again with thicker needles. Having fewer stitches means that they are too large – try again with finer needles.)

Repeat vertically to check **rows**. DO NOT DISMISS HALF, OR EVEN QUARTER, STITCHES OR ROWS. Another way of checking is with a **tension gauge**. You may then be asked to mark a certain number of stitches or rows on the sample. Placing the graduated gauge over the sample tells you how many there would be in 10cm (4in). This is of help when stitches are too small to be seen properly, or when the stitch pattern makes them difficult to count.

A way of counting complex stitch patterns is to measure one or more complete **repeats**. Knowing, as you do, the number of stitches in each repeat (see **stitch pattern instructions**), you can work out the number of stitches in 10cm (4in):

$$\frac{\text{stitches in repeat} \times 10\ (4)}{\text{width or length of repeat}}$$

Approximate the result to two decimal points. To help you identify a repeat, halfway up the sample attach a **safety pin** to the stitch before the start of the repeat you want to measure, and another to the last stitch of the repeat.

Calculating stitches and rows

Once you know the number of **stitches** in 10cm (4in), it is very easy to find out how many are required for a certain width. Simply divide:

$$\frac{\text{stitches in 10cm (4in)}}{10 \text{ (4)}}$$

Approximate the result to two decimal points, to obtain the stitches in 1cm (1in), multiply by the total number of centimetres (in) required, to obtain the total number of stitches. This is all there is to it, but if you would like to work from a table instead, there is one in my first book (see **Books**). You can also work directly from the width of one single repeat. If this is 4.5cm (1¾in) end the project, with 33cm (13in) you need 7.3 repeats plus a few extra stitches. Do the same with rows, if required.

Stitch patterns

Together with **yarn texture**, **stitch patterns** are the means of obtaining **fabric texture**. Yarn and pattern go hand in hand:

● A smooth yarn will emphasise a smooth pattern, and counter a rugged one.

● A delicate flower motif will look even more delicate in a soft, lightweight yarn, but positively coarse in a heavy, oiled yarn.

● A lace pattern will look light and airy in a very fine yarn, clumsy in a chunky yarn.

● A **bouclé** yarn will make a knobbly fabric if the pattern has many purl stitches, but will have little impact in a fabric with many knit stitches, because the 'bumps' will naturally stay on the purl side.

● A shiny yarn, on the other hand, will look shinier on knit and lose some sheen on purl. The message should now be clear. YARNS AFFECT THE CHARACTER OF STITCH PATTERNS. NEVER DECIDE ON A PATTERN WITHOUT FIRST KNITTING IT IN THE INTENDED YARN.

Fabric character

(See also **the Knitted stitch, Knit and purl – applications, Slip-stitch knitting, Crossing,** Raised patterns, All sorts** and **Colour knitting.**)

Character is basically determined by the structure of the **stitch pattern**. A knitted stitch pulls in a certain way. When all the stitches show the same side (**knit** or **purl**), the original pull is magnified; if some of the stitches show the other side, the pull is countered around those stitches. If you work a very small sample in **single rib** and pull the needle to free the loops, you will see how clearly the knit stitches come to the front and the purl stitches go to the back.

Interlocking in unusual or combined ways adds new dimensions to the interaction of knit and purl stitches. Even taking the yarn to the other side of work between a knit and a purl stitch has an effect. Not only the pull is reversed, but the yarn is made to travel further when, in fact, comparing the free loops of the **single rib** sample with the free loops of a **stocking stitch** sample you can see that the distance out of one stitch and into the next is now shorter. The result is a larger **stitch size** – the reason why ribbings are generally worked on fine needles. Further variations are determined by the way the fabric is used – vertically, horizontally or diagonally (a change in direction often dictates how a fabric drapes).

Fabrics can be roughly classified as: **wide** or **narrow** (Fig 1.10), depending on the width given by a pre-set number of stitches. **Cables, cross stitches, slip stitches** make

1.10

fabrics narrower. **Openwork, double stitch** make fabrics wider.

- **long or short** (Fig 1.11), depending on the length given by a pre-set number of rows. **Slip stitches,** consecutive knit or purl rows **(garter stitch), double stitch, pull-up stitch** make fabrics shorter. **Openwork, elongated stitch** make fabrics longer.

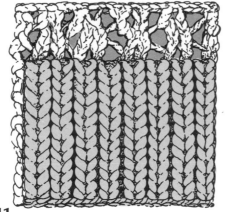

1.11

- **flat or curly**, depending on whether the edges lie flat or curl in. Fabrics with a **stocking-stitch** base are curly, an effect often emphasised by **slip stitches**. Fabrics with a **garter-stitch base**, and fabrics with close, balanced arrangements of knit and purl stitches (**moss stitch, ribbings** etc) are flat.
- **thin or thick**, depending on how deep the layer of fabric is, irrespective of **yarn thick-**

ness. Narrow and **short** fabrics tend to be thick. So do **ribbings, brioches, jacquard, mosaic, knitweave** and all the embossed and **raised-motif** fabrics.

- **elastic or inelastic**. Vertical arrangements of knit and purl stitches (such as **ribbings**) and **brioches** are very elastic. Fabrics with a **slip-stitch or cross-stitch** base are very inelastic. Most of the remainder fall in between.

All of these can, of course, be in combination.

In general, **narrow, short** or **thick** fabrics take a longer time to knit, and require more yarn.

Stitch shape

With so many types of fabric, a variation in the shape of the stitches is only to be expected. Square stitches are rarities. In fact, with the exception of **elongated stitch** and possibly some other obscure case, stitches are always wider than they are tall.

To know whether a stitch is **nearly square**, **medium** or **wide**, find out the **tension** in 10cm (4in). Divide:

$$\frac{\text{number of rows}}{\text{number of stitches}}$$

and examine the result:

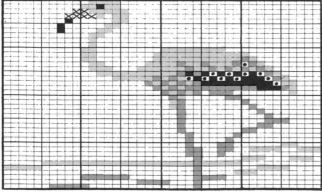

1:7 ratio

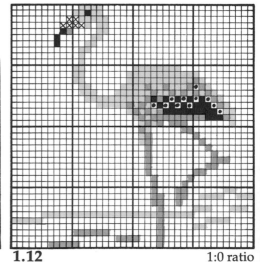

1.12

1:0 ratio

under 1	a rare **tall** stitch
1.0	**square**
1.1–1.2	**nearly square**
1.3–1.6	**medium**
1.7 and over	**wide**

Therefore a **chart** or **graph**, to give an accurate picture, needs to be drawn on **ratio graph paper**. An exception is **garter stitch**. This is so **wide** (around 2), that it can sometimes be successfully charted on square graph paper, if each square is made to represent one stitch and TWO rows. Fig 1.12 shows the impact a 1.7 ratio would have on a design intended for a 1.0 ratio, as might be the case when knitting designs intended for cross-stitch or canvas embroidery. See **Publications** and **Addresses**.

The **stitch shape** of a particular pattern is not fixed. **Yarn** and **fabric tension** can have dramatic effects. **Stocking stitch**, for instance, often shows a ratio between 1.3 and 1.4 but values going down to 1.15 and up to 1.6 are not unknown.

Measuring knitting

Length and width are totally interconnected. If you look only at one you can usually get any measurement you want!
For good results:
● Use a flat surface. Pin work down if necessary, or ask someone to keep it in place.
● Measure width at the very least 2.5cm (1in) below the needles, and away from **ribbings** and other gatherings.
● Measure for length on a vertical line, away from edges.
● Half-stretch ribbings, to about what they will be when in use.
● Measure on the true vertical, or the true horizontal, unless you have special reasons not to do so.
● Measure work often, especially if prone to uneven tension.
● With large, heavy pieces that may tend to drop, stop short of the required length and leave to hang for a couple of days before

deciding how much more to do.
● DO NOT CHEAT. To unravel half-way up is distressing; to discover that you have finished something useless is maddening.

To measure:
a If working **flat**, stop work at mid-row.
b Spread knitting on needle(s) until the last row is quite flat. With a **circular needle** and with short straight needles you will have to place some of the stitches on **holders** or spare needles.
c Spread the rest of the work to the required width (Fig 1.13) without pulling (unless you intend stretching it). If it is noticeably

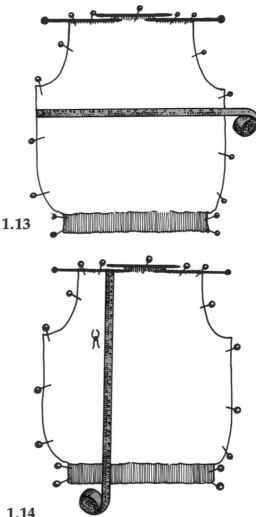

1.13

1.14

wider or narrower, admit that something has gone wrong. If it cannot be corrected, perhaps by altering the width of an adjoining piece, **unravel**.

d Keeping the work spread at full width, measure length from under the needle to the **cast-on**, or other appropriate place. Use **fabric markers** to highlight critical rows, such as the armhole in Fig 1.14.

Identical pieces

When matching the length of identical pieces, count rows instead of using a tape measure. (Two **identical pieces**, **flat** or **circular**, can be worked together to save you counting.) Some stitch patterns are very easy to count because they have very clear **repeats**. Count the repeats, then multiply by the number of rows in each one. On others you have to count every row. This is easier to do if you point at each row with something short and sharp like a **sewing** or a **cable needle** – when your eyes start seeing double, push the needle into the fabric and take a rest. If your eyesight is poor, or if you want to count the rows at a glance, work in a string of **bead markers**.

Stocking stitch is easy to count if you see each stitch as a V; but some people prefer to count ridges on the **purl** side.

Paper patterns

If working from a full-size paper pattern, spread it flat and place knitting on top – the edges should coincide exactly.

Problem fabrics

(See also **common problems** and **flat knitting**, Fig 1.35)

Slanted fabrics

This may be caused by a very high **twist** in the yarn, by continuously **twisting** or **plaiting** the stitches (Fig 1.15), by some other type of fabric construction that somehow stresses the fabric, or by a combination of these. It cannot be corrected but you should be able to

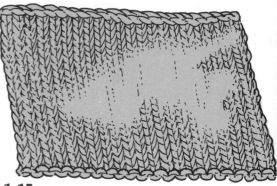

1.15

spot it on the tension **sample**, when there is time to prevent it.

If it is a fabric problem, use a different stitch pattern or see **close-bead knitting**.

If it is a yarn problem, look for a pattern that slants in the opposite direction (perhaps **twisted** or **plaited stocking stitch**).

Uneven fabrics

Something has gone wrong with the **tension**. Perhaps you changed it unwittingly because the weather made your hands numb or sticky, or because you had a row with a friend or were watching a thriller on TV!

Or perhaps the yarn was not evenly spun, or you keep poor control over yarn and needles and need to read **common problems**. Someone helping you might be another cause, because no two knitters work alike.

If the problem is that the last stitch of a group of two or more knit stitches in a **rib** or a **cable** pattern is consistently larger than the others (Fig 1.16), try this next time:

● on the **right-side row, knit-back** the offending stitch (Fig 2.87);

● on the return row, **purl** the stitch wrapping the yarn **under** the needle (Fig 2.93).

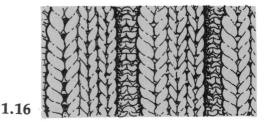

1.16

Holding the work

(See also **holding the yarns** under **Colour Knitting**)

Knitting illustrations tend to show only the tip of the needles and, occasionally, the hands. What is missing from needles and body, however, should not be dismissed because it has a very direct effect on your work, your comfort and, ultimately, your enjoyment.

The finest points of knitting posture are very individual and, once established, very difficult to change. Although nothing is intrinsically right or wrong if it achieves the desired results, there are certainly ways which are easier to learn than others, and ways which make it hard to work evenly. If you are learning to knit, read on carefully and get used to an efficient way such as shown in Figs 1.20 to 1.23 and Figs 1.27 to 1.30. If you learnt a long time ago, a quick read will do you no harm, and could lead to improvements without changing your basic habits.

There are three basic knitting positions: **yarn in right hand**, **yarn in left hand** and, less commonly, **yarn around neck**. All three methods make the stitches in exactly the same way, but because the yarn is held at a different angle, the impression is of the stitches being worked differently. **Left-handed knitters** add an extra dimension to the three basic positions.

General rules for all these methods are:
● Sit comfortably, without slumping.
● Have enough light to see without straining. If working with very dark colours, place a white cloth on your lap – the stitches show much better.
● Relax. Needles are not there to be clutched as if your life depended on them.
● Make both hands share equally in the work.

● Keep thumbs and fingers close to the needle tips, so that they only have to move short distances.
● Keep the stitches by the needle tips as close to the ends as they will go without **dropping**, so as not to stretch the work.
● In **flat knitting**, keep the work reasonably gathered towards the working ends. It will feel lighter than if spread evenly along the needles.

Common problems

(See also **problem fabrics** and **flat knitting** – Fig 1.35)
If you suffer from any of the following, it may be because of the way you hold your work:

Slow progress
If your work grows at snail pace, you may be:
● making your fingers travel too far to make each stitch.
● keeping the working stitches too far from the tips of the needles.
● not keeping the needles under full control.
● trying to keep one needle still whilst the other does all the work.
● using needles with very long, very blunt tips (Fig 1.41b).

Dropped stitches
These could be caused by:
● the working stitches being too close to the tips of the needles.
● you being a **slack knitter**.
● not keeping both needles in your hands all the time.

• holding the right needle **like a pen**, with the work tightly gathered into the crook of the thumb (Fig 1.25).

Left edge too long

A problem that creates havoc when trying to sew two edges together (Fig 1.17). The main cause is likely to be lack of control when starting to purl. Are you holding the yarn in your right hand but not **fixing** the right needle?

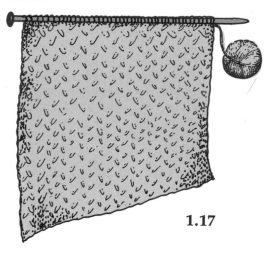

1.17

Try tightening the yarn more on the first purl stitches. It is not as easy as with knit stitches, but quite possible. If that fails, try a **double chain selvedge** on the over-long edge.

Stretched edges

You have problems both when starting to purl and to knit, perhaps made worse by a **slippery yarn**. Apply last paragraph to both edges.

Purl stitches too large

This gives a stripy look to **stocking stitch** (Fig 1.18). It is a fairly common problem amongst **yarn-in-left-hand** knitters, but can also happen to others. Possible solutions:
• Practise tightening the purl stitches and loosening the knit stitches (see **which needles?**).
• Purl with a finer needle than you knit. This only works with **stocking stitch**.

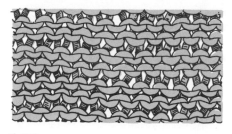

1.18

• When purling, wrap yarn under needle as in **plaited purl stitch** (Fig 2.93). On the next row, **knit-back** the resulting stitches (Fig 2.87) to straighten them up. Again, only for **stocking stitch** and a limited number of stitch patterns.
• Adapt to **circular knitting** and avoid **stitch patterns** with groups of purl stitches on the **right side** – the odd one is not likely to be a problem.

Uneven work

Invariably caused by poor control. It is not 'part of the charm of something done by hand'; it is plain lack of craftsmanship (Fig 1.19). Do you:

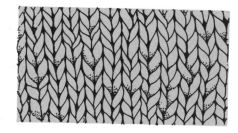

1.19

• hold the right needle **like a pen**?
• drop the yarn or any of the needles regularly?
• keep the yarn quite long between the work and the finger that wraps it around the needle?
• work some stitches well away from the tip of the needles, and others very close?
• hold the needles at a longish distance from the tip?

● use needles with very long tips (Fig 1.41b)?

Aches and pains

Arm or hand cramps, stiff shoulders, neck-ache, backache etc. If knitting gives you any of these, consult your doctor to make sure there is nothing seriously wrong with you. If there is not, the cause could well lie in the way you arrange yourself and use your muscles. Do you:
● keep your head permanently bent forward, or to one side?
● let your body slump in a heap?
● sit on something that does not give support to your back?
● get all tensed up?
● clutch needles or yarn?
● stick your elbows out?
● keep your two arms in constant movement?
● bend your right thumb up to hold the needle?
If you do, STOP IT. It is easier said than done, and your good intentions may only last a few minutes! Persevere.

If your problems persist, it might be worth trying relaxation techniques, acupuncture, manipulation or one of the other natural therapies. Ask your doctor. (Addresses from libraries and health-food shops.) Or, you could have Alexander technique lessons and learn how to use all your muscles correctly (see **Addresses**).

Yarn in right hand

Although most knitters in Britain hold the yarn this way, there is an invisible line half-way across the country that broadly determines what happens to the right needle. To the south, it is held like a pen; to the north, it is steadied under the arm or into a **sheath**. It may be that northerners mainly knitted to earn (or scrape) a living, whilst many southerners considered it a drawing-room pastime, requiring 'elegance' rather than efficiency. In Barcelona, where the knitting

tradition goes back many centuries (having had one of the first guilds in Europe), I learnt to hold the right needle as they do in the North of England and Scotland. Catalan knitters worried about 'elegance' rest the needle on the forearm, losing efficiency but not too badly.

In any case, the yarn is wound around the right hand in a number of possible ways, a few of which are shown in Fig 1.20. Use whichever you find more comfortable to get a steady flow of yarn. My favourite is the first one.

Fixed needle

An excellent way of keeping control of your work. The right hand is free to concentrate on wrapping the yarn, using the right needle merely as a rest. The shuttle movement of this hand automatically helps the new stitches to glide over the needle.

Double-pointed needles plus a **sheath**, or **standard needles** not shorter than 35cm (14in) are necessary – not very convenient if knitting on a train.

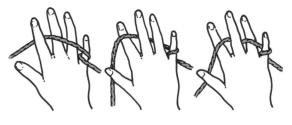

1.20

a Tuck needle under right arm (Fig 1.21) or into a **sheath** (Fig 1.22 – see also **double-pointed needles** under **Circular knitting**).
b Wrap yarn around right hand and place hand on top of needle.

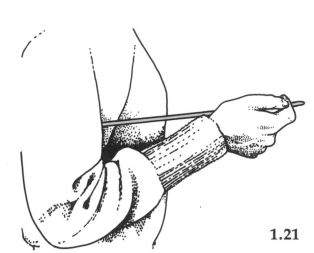

1.21

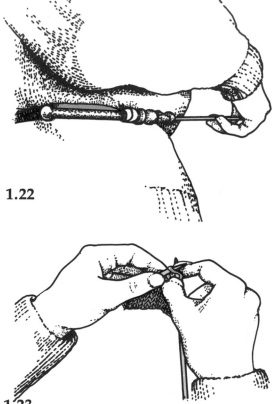

1.22

1.23

c Take needle with stitches in left hand.
d Push first stitch to tip of needle with left thumb and, at same time, flick left needle so that right needle gets inserted into the stitch.

e Wrap yarn, moving right hand as little as possible (Fig 1.23).
f Flick left needle with left hand to pass the old stitch over the new wrap and, at same time, push tip of right needle back through the old stitch with left thumb (purl) or left index finger (knit).

Take care not to tighten the right arm too much against the body.

Needle as pen

Work as before, but omit **a** and hold right needle as in Fig 1.24. Use the shortest needles that will accommodate all the stitches, either **standard** or **circular**.

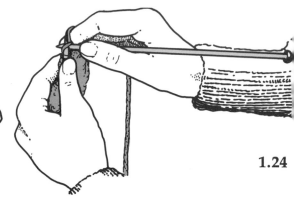

1.24

One problem with this method is that many knitters try to make the right hand do all the work, and there are so many things to be done that mastering them all is not easy, especially if the right thumb is bent up against its natural inclination.

Another problem is that, after a few stitches, a lot of fabric gathers at the crook of the right thumb. If you carry on gathering fabric, the stitches on the right needle may start to drop-off. So, you then put the thumb under the fabric (Fig 1.25), which does nothing to improve needle control. In either case, with so much pawing, the fabric may look grubby before you even finish, control over needles and yarn is lost and the work tends to be **uneven**.

Beware not to move your elbows about and not to bend your right thumb up as this can quickly cause cramp.

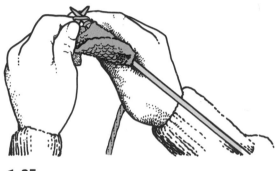

1.25

Hand on top

Half-way between the two methods just explained. Work as for **fixed needle** but omit **a**. Control will not be quite as good, but it will be better than in **needle as pen**.
Work with **standard** or **circular needles**.
Beware not to stick your elbows out and not to clutch the right needle.

Yarn or needle

A method often betraying a knitter who has learnt from books, or one who could not cope with **needle as pen**. After inserting the right needle into the stitch, the needle is dropped and forgotten. The yarn is then picked up, wrapped (Fig 1.26) and dropped, leaving the hand free to go back to the needle and draw the loop through.

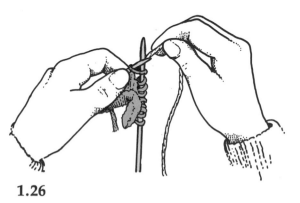

1.26

It is the slowest, most awkward, most tiring and least even way of knitting. Very little control over the work is maintained.

Yarn in left hand

Also called **German** or **continental** knitting. The last name should be discouraged, as many European countries do not hold the work in this way. Using **circular** or **standard needles**, just long enough to hold the work, it is a very fast method to knit, not so much to purl. **Purl stitches too large** (see **common problems** above) are far from infrequent.

a Wind yarn around left hand in one of the ways shown in Fig 1.27.

1.27

b Take needle with stitches in left hand and empty needle in right hand. Both hands should be on top of needles.
c Push first stitch to tip of needle with left thumb and insert right needle into it.
d 'Hook' yarn with right needle and pull through the stitch. To hook the yarn to knit is very straightforward (Fig 1.28). To

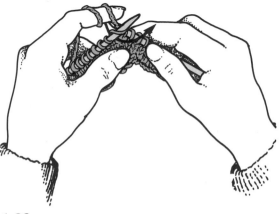

1.28

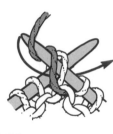

1.29   **1.30**

purl, it is less so (Fig 1.29), unless you work a **plaited purl** stitch (Fig 1.30). But, as explained in **common problems**, the new stitch needs to be untwisted on the next row.

Take care not to move your right arm more than necessary.

Yarn around neck

This is a less known way of holding the work, popular in Portugal, in rural Egypt and amongst the Peruvian Indians of Taquile Island. (If you know of any other places I would be interested to hear about them.)

This method makes purling easier than knitting, because the yarn lies in **front**, rather than at the **back**. So much so that traditional Taquile hats in very complex **jacquard** patterns (Fig 2.276), worked in **rounds**, are totally constructed with purl stitches. That is, the wrong side of the colour pattern is facing the knitter, who has to keep checking how the pattern forms on the right side.

Traditionally, knitting is done with **hooked needles** (like long **crochet hooks** with or without a knob at the end). Pointed needles may also be used.

a Wind yarn around your neck, or secure it with a **safety pin** on left shoulder. If working with two colours, wind them in opposite directions (Fig 1.31).

b Take needle with stitches in left hand and empty needle in right hand.

c Insert right needle into stitch, flick yarn with left thumb, and catch it with right needle (Fig 1.32).

1.31

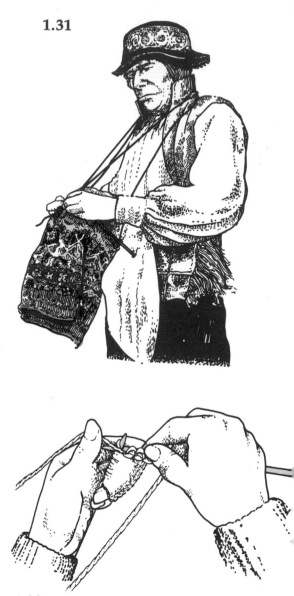

1.32

Beware of keeping your neck permanently bent forward.

Left-handed knitters
(See also **from left to right** under **Picking up stitches**)

There are two approaches:

● Hold illustrations next to a mirror, and

follow their reflection. Reverse any non-symmetrical instructions.

• Consider knitting as the two-handed craft it really is. Use either the **fixed needle** or the **yarn in left hand** approach, whichever you prefer, and forget that the instructions are for right-handed knitters.

The second system would seem clearer, because reversing instructions could create confusion. Some people, however, seem to feel happier if they work the rows from **left to right**. Next chapter explains how right-handed knitters work in this way, which may be of help even if it is not a true reversal. If not happy, use the mirror approach.

The only book I have found on the subject suggests a total reversal of the **yarn in left hand** method. The rows now go from **left to right**, but the yarn is being held by the right hand (Fig 1.33). For a total reversal, would it

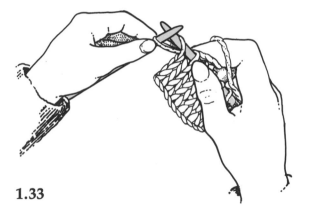

1.33

not make more sense to use **fixed needle** and have the yarn in the left hand? (See **Books**.)

I would greatly appreciate any information left-handers can give me. Being right-handed, it is difficult to appreciate all the subtleties.

Rows and rounds

Almost all knitting is done from **right to left**. It is worth remembering, though, that going from **left to right** without changing yarn position is equally possible. In fact, it has some very interesting applications.

Flat or circular

Whichever direction you work in, you can produce either an open flàt fabric, or a tube. Each has advantages and limitations. Personal preference is likely to be a result of the sort of things you knit.

If you are interested in **odd-row stripes**, round mats, seamless garments, gloves, hats, socks, or **jacquard**; if you hate sewing (or find it difficult because of eyesight problems)

then **circular knitting** is for you. If you love **intarsia**, open collars, edgings, wall hangings, shawls, bedspreads, pieces that require very accurate **blocking**; if you hate transcribing **instructions** and do not want to design your own; then go for **flat knitting**. If you want to add a **round** yoke or **border** to something worked **flat**, use first one method and then the other. When changing methods, **tension** may be altered; check beforehand.

Having made your decision, you have a further choice between straight (**standard** or **double-pointed**) and **circular needles**.

Circular needles have some clear pluses:

• The stitches can be slipped onto the cord so that they do not **drop** when you put the work away, or **set** into a slant if left for any length of time.

- They are good for working in a tight space.
- You can make very wide **flat** pieces that would not fit on standard needles.
- You can never lose the 'other' needle.

They also have some drawbacks:

- They are not so easy to store as straight needles.
- There is no size indication on the needle itself.
- They are difficult to keep dead straight when spreading the work for **measuring**.
- The work gets heavy if you knit as you walk.
- The stitches have to be pushed more often because not many can be crowded on the stiff points, and the ones on the connecting cord keep slipping back. If working in circles you also have to make the stitches go all the way round.

But the decisive question is, are they good to work with? If you hold the **yarn in left hand**, yes, circular needles are excellent. You have no right needle swinging around, that can be quite heavy if full of stitches. If you hold the **yarn in right hand**, circular needles do not give nearly the same control as a straight **fixed needle**, although people used to work with **hand on top** find them quite satisfactory. The fact that the weight of the fabric is now on the lap will not impress fixed-needle knitters much, because they have already taken care of the weight problem. In fact, they might get worried about having to bend their neck because their hands are now much lower. Non-fixed-needle knitters, though, might welcome resting the work on their lap.

To sum up. Try the different methods and decide for yourself which one works best for you. Under no circumstances let anyone, and that includes me, tell you that one way of knitting is better than all the others.

Flat knitting

Use a pair of **standard needles** or one **circular needle**.

Each line of stitches is called a **row**. At the end of a row, the left needle is empty and the right needle full. Turn the work, so that if you were first seeing the **right side**, you now see the **wrong side**. Swap hands and start again.

To use a **circular needle**, work in exactly the same way. Think of each point as a separate needle, and forget that they are joined with a cord (Fig 1.34).

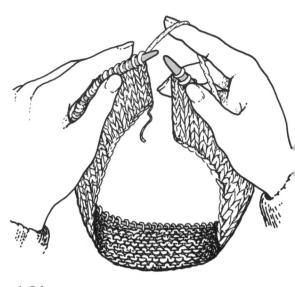

1.34

When working very wide pieces that do not fit onto standard needles, consider having several of these, one after the other, if you do not like circular needles. **Stops** might be advisable to prevent stitches from dropping. For **measuring**, stop at mid-row.

Identical pieces

In flat knitting it is very easy to work two symmetrical or **identical pieces** (such as two sleeves or two jacket fronts) at the same time. Two balls of yarn are obviously necessary (Fig 1.35). This saves much time checking **shapings** etc. It also ensures identical results. If your **tension** is not very stable, this is a good way of compensating for it. If the two pieces were worked separately, one might end up much longer than the other. To avoid

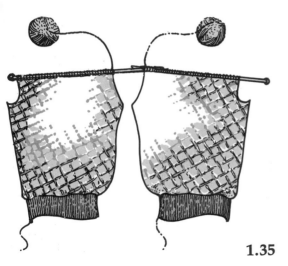

1.35

twisting the two yarns, turn the work clockwise at the end of one row, anti-clockwise at the end of next row.

Circular knitting
(See also **casting on circles**)

Each circle of stitches is a **round**. Rounds are arranged like a spiral, and they are worked without any breaks. As a result, a 'step' forms on the pattern when changing from round to round. Use a **needle marker** to see where the rounds start.

Because the work is never turned, you are always facing the same side. This is usually the **right side**. If you want to work from the **wrong side**, your hands will be at the far end of the circle (see **yarn around neck**).

With circular knitting it is possible to produce totally seamless projects, including whole sweaters. These are garments of undoubted appeal, deeply rooted in tradition. Remember, however, that they:
- are very heavy and cumbersome in their final stages, both to work and to cart around;
- show a step at the start of the rounds;
- restrict shape experimentation;
- make certain types of **blocking** awkward, if not impossible;
- are better than badly put together,

'homemade' **flat knitting**, but not necessarily better than good flat knitting;
- are not so easy to adjust as garments worked in pieces, if something goes wrong with the sizing.

Circular knitting can use a **circular needle** or a set of **double-pointed needles**. The sets can be used for any size of circle, from glove fingers to huge round rugs, although it is not too comfortable to work very small circles with the longer needles; if the stitches grow too crowded, extra needles can be added. Circular needles must be smaller than the circle, otherwise the stitches are stretched out of shape and work is slow and awkward; if the project changes width, you might need to change needle length.

The shortest circular needle usually available is 40cm (16in) long; shorter ones are very difficult to work with. Smaller circles, therefore, cannot be worked adequately with circular needles. If changing from sets to circular needles, your **tension** may alter; check it.

Circular needle
Simply work round and round (Fig 1.36). **Measuring** always requires additional needles, as it is impossible to lay the work flat.

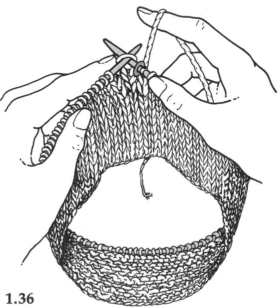

1.36

Double-pointed needles

These can be used with or without a **sheath**. Fig 1.21 shows the conventional sheath position, but if the needle fits snuggly rather than loosely into the hole, the sheath can also be tucked under the right arm – like a **standard needle** in the **fixed needle** way of knitting. Needles 35cm (14in) or more in length can be tucked directly under the arm, without a sheath.

One needle is kept free, and the stitches divided amongst the other needles, equally if possible. Having worked the stitches off one needle with the free needle, a new needle is released. If the needles are crowded, use **stops**.

Use as many needles as make sense for a particular shape. Trying to work a square on three needles is nonsense. You will not see how work progresses, and the join stitches will get distorted.

It is essential that an even **yarn tension** is kept when changing needles. Loose stitches often appear but are quite simply avoided – always start a new needle on top of the old one (Fig 1.37); pull first stitch tight. Changing needle position by two or three stitches each time is only partly helpful. You could end up with a spiral of loose stitches instead of a vertical line of them, and unless you have many needles it could be awkward.

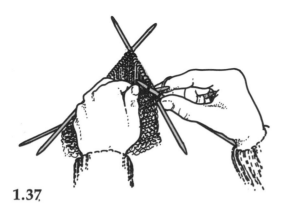

1.37

Identical pieces

Although two identical tubes (such as sleeves or socks) are generally worked inde-

pendently, it is quite possible to work them at the same time, one inside the other. The advantages would be those outlined in **flat knitting** above.

With two balls of yarn:

a **Cast on**, alternately, one stitch from each ball, until you have enough stitches for both tubes. Make sure that the two yarns do not get tangled.

b Work each stitch with the yarn it was cast-on with. You can either work all rounds with two yarns (use second or third methods of **holding yarns** explained in **jacquard**), or work one round with one yarn and the next with the other – each time **slip purlwise** the stitches not being worked. If the two tubes are in **stocking stitch**, knitting the outside tube and purling the inside one helps to differentiate the two layers.

Tension is likely to be looser than in one-layer work. Check it, and use finer needles if necessary.

Adapting instructions

Most instructions, including those in this book, are intended for **flat knitting**. When adapting them to circular knitting, whether you are working from **row-by-row** instructions or from **charts**, the stitch pattern must flow continuously. That is, you need complete **pattern repeats**, which in written instructions are the stitches between **asterisks**. If the number of odd stitches at either side of the asterisks varies, a repeat is probably split between the two ends. **Chart** the pattern, or knit a sample with at least two repeats, to find out the relevant stitches. Then, reverse all **wrong-side** rows:

● Read them from the end, in order to reverse the sequence.

● Work knit for purl and purl for knit. Rows instructing 'knit the knit stitches and purl the purl stitches' take care of themselves.

● Work **increases** and **decreases** from the other side. The instructions in this book mention shapings **on knit** or **on purl**, but say nothing about **right** or **wrong** sides. If a wrong-side row has an increase on knit (purl), work the same increase on purl (knit) when you are working rounds.

• Work **with yarn in front** instead of **with yarn at back**, and vice versa.

To avoid mistakes, it is best to transcribe the instructions before starting to work. If there are armholes or other openings, divide work and shape as required. Either change to **flat knitting**, or make a **bridge** and continue in circles.

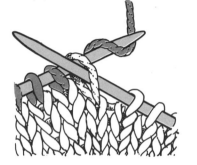

1.38

From left to right

This is a way of working **flat** without turning the work, although it is not the complete reversal that **left-handed knitters** may want. Some people work large pieces in this way, back and forth from end to end. But, even if you do not want to go this far, you will find it useful for some **raised patterns** (which, of course, can also appear in **circular knitting**), for **sculptured knitting** and for working with **ribbons**.

Keep yarn in right hand. To **knit**:

a   Insert left needle into back of stitch.

b   Wrap yarn down front and up back of needle (Fig 1.38).

c   Draw new stitch through.

To **purl**:

a   Insert left needle into back of stitch.

b   Wrap yarn up back and down front of needle (Fig 1.39).

c   Draw new stitch through.

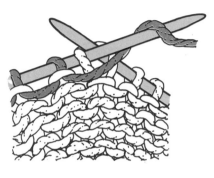

1.39

Equipment

Compared with other crafts, the equipment necessary for hand knitting is inexpensive and can be built up slowly. The most expensive items are often not essential, and a look around the home could well supply you with free alternatives.

Arthritic and physically handicapped knitters can work with one hand only by using a leather knitting belt or a special needle-holder (see **Publications** and **Addresses**). Knitters with visual handicaps may also be interested in the information given under **Books**. Knitters with these or any other disabilities may find the Disabled Living Foundation of assistance (see **Addresses**).

Knitting needles E

(See also **Holding the work** and **Rows and rounds**)

Fig 1.40 shows three types of needles: **standard, circular** and **double-pointed**. **Hooked needles** are not unknown, but seem restricted to **yarn around neck** areas. All needles should be kept well protected when not in use.

The needle tip should taper to a blunt point (Fig 1.41a). If the tapering is very long and/or the point is too blunt (Fig 1.41b), work will be slow and awkward.

What a needle is made out of will also affect the speed at which you work, apart from some materials being more pleasant to handle than others. Modern needles are

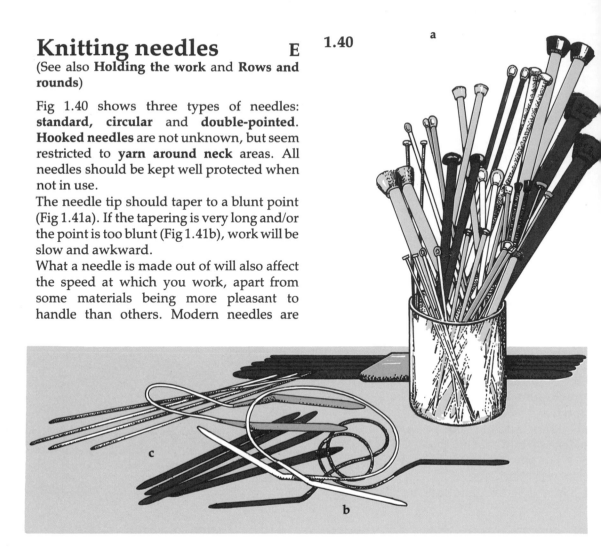

1.40

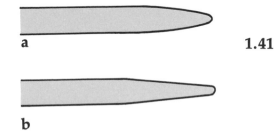

1.41

made out of aluminium, plastic, wood or bamboo. In the past you could find steel, tortoiseshell, celluloid, bone, ivory, silver and even glass!

The more polished the surface, the faster the stitches glide. Some people go as far as painting needles with gloss, or nail varnish, obviously changing the thickness in the process. Be careful, though, when working **slippery yarns** with high-gloss needles; whole rows could drop off.

The thickness range varies between countries. To have as wide a selection as possible, search for foreign needles if you go abroad. The following table shows approximate, if not always perfectly exact, equivalents between ranges. Metric and British equivalents to American sizes vary wildly from author to author, not surprisingly since American needles often fall between sizes of the other two ranges.

European metric	British metric	British old sizes	American
2	2mm	14	0
	2¼mm	13	1
2½			
	2¾mm	12	2
3	3mm	11	
	3¼mm	10	3
3½			4
	3¾mm	9	5
4	4mm	8	6
4½	4½mm	7	7
5	5mm	6	8
5½	5½mm	5	9
6	6mm	4	10
6½	6½mm	3	10½
7	7mm	2	
7½	7½mm	1	
8	8mm	0	11
9	9mm	00	13
10	10mm	000	15

Needles finer than 2mm are difficult to find, although in the past they used to be the norm. See **Addresses** for **suppliers** of British size 16 needles.
British needles saying 2½ or 3½mm are not always what they claim to be. Check them with a **gauge**.

Standard needles (Fig 1.40a)

Also called **pins**, they can only be used for **flat knitting**.
They come in pairs, and in several lengths. Choose length according to how you **hold the work**. Difficulty in finding certain lengths is a reflection of how most knitters hold the work in that area.

Circular needles (Fig 1.40b)

(See also **circular knitting**)
Can be used for **flat** or **circular knitting**, and consist of two very short needles connected by a strong, flexible cord. The short stiff ends must be long enough to span your closed hand; otherwise you will not get a good grip. Before buying, inspect the joint between needle and cord; it must be absolutely smooth.

Double-pointed needles (Fig 1.40c)

Used alone or with a **sheath** (Fig 1.22). In the past, they were sometimes curved.
They come in sets of four or five, and are used for **circular knitting**. Two of them with a **stop** at one end can be used for **flat knitting**.

Essential accessories   E

Markers (Fig 1.42a)

Indispensable for trouble-free knitting.
Needle markers. Closed or coil rings that are slipped around the needle to highlight changes in **stitch pattern**, the start of **rounds** in **circular knitting**, lines of **increases** or **decreases** etc. Also, in complex **stitch patterns**, to establish check points every so many pattern **repeats**.
ALTERNATIVES: loops of contrast yarn, **safety pins**, paper clips.
Fabric markers (see also **bead markers**) These are attached to the fabric, to pinpoint **increases** or **decreases**, row 1 of **stitch pattern** etc. Use coil rings, **safety pins**, short lengths of contrast yarn.

Pins (Fig 1.42b)

Use for pinning, measuring **tension samples**, **blocking**. Unless working extremely fine knitting, 5cm (2in) glass-headed pins are by far the best. Get chrome rather than black shafts if given a choice.

Safety pins (Fig 1.42c)

Use as **markers**, as **stitch holders**, to secure **dropped stitches**, to pin **seams**.

Sewing needles (Fig 1.42d)

Known as 'yarn', 'knitter's', 'heavy embroidery', or 'tapestry' needles. They must have a blunt point, or you will split the yarn. Use the size most appropriate to the yarn, as this can be ruined if forced through too small a

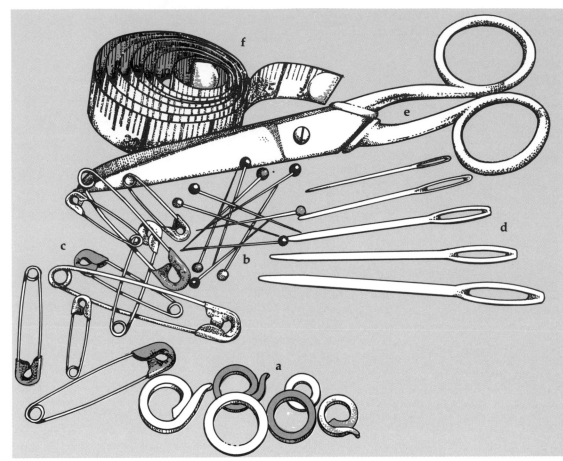

1.42

needle. See **suppliers** for jumbo needles (24cm/9½in) for very heavy decorative work.

Scissors (Fig 1.42e)
If you are using conventional yarn, they do not need to be very big, but they must be sharp.

Tape measure (Fig 1.42f)
Use an accurate dressmaker's tape, or a rigid ruler if you prefer. Take all measurements consistently in either centimetres or inches.

Blocking board
Use anything large, flat and pinnable – mattress, carpet, foam pad etc. Ironing boards are usually too small.

Covering with a checked cloth will help you keep straight lines. On surfaces such as carpets, covering with a clean cloth is essential.

Sprayer
An ordinary plant sprayer giving a fine mist will do for **blocking**. If you prefer **pressing** or **steaming** to **cold water spray**, you will need an iron instead of a sprayer.

Work bag
Large bag or basket for storing the work in hand. It must be easy to carry, have a flat base so that it can be left on the floor without falling on one side, be large enough to hold the nearly finished work, and be 'organisable' so that small things do not keep disappearing under the rest.

Filing system

Use whatever type suits you best, but find a way of keeping a record of what you have made: instructions, your own sketches or alterations, **samples, ball band**, record of needle size and amount of yarn, any difficulties and comments.

Useful accessories   U

Sheath (Fig 1.43a)

(See **fixed needle** and **circular knitting – double-pointed needles**)

Tie around waist or tuck under right arm. It has one or more holes into which to insert the free end of the right needle when working with sets of **double-pointed needles** (Fig 1.22).

Not widely available, having gone out of fashion, but see **Addresses**. Wooden sheaths or 'sticks' may be found in antique shops or may be commissioned from a craftsman. The Shetland knitting belt (a stuffed leather pouch), can be obtained by mail order.

ALTERNATIVES: tie around the waist anything a needle can be inserted into; or catch the needle into the top of your skirt or trousers.

Needle gauge (Fig 1.43b)

To check needle size, especially of **circular** or **double-pointed needles** that have no indication of size. The needle is the size of the smallest hole it can go through.

Cable needles (Fig 1.43c)

Straight or angled (so that the stitches do not drop off). Straight ones look like very short **double-pointed needles**. Apart from their obvious use for **cables**, they are good for poking stitches into place when **blocking, counting** stitches etc.

Stitch holders (Fig 1.43d)

To keep stitches from unravelling when they are not needed. They come in various shapes; buy the ones least likely to unfasten when knocked about.

ALTERNATIVES: spare **needles** with **stops** at both ends, **safety pins**, a length of contrast yarn.

1.43

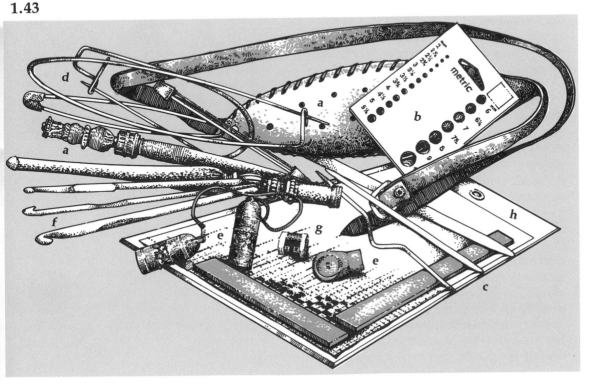

Stops (Fig 1.43e)

Used either to protect the point of the **needles**, or to prevent crowded stitches from dropping off.

ALTERNATIVES: corks, wooden beads, elastic bands wrapped over and over. Avoid Plasticine and the tacky stuff used for fixing posters – they can stain.

Crochet hooks (Fig 1.43f)

Apart from being used in a number of techniques, they are very good for picking up **dropped stitches**. Keep at least one or two at hand.

Tension gauge

A graduated ruler that, placed over a certain number of stitches or rows, gives an immediate reading of the **tension** in 10cm (4in). See **Addresses** if you cannot find one.

ALTERNATIVES: **tape measure** (or ruler) and calculator (or paper and pen).

Row counter (Fig 1.43g)

To keep a tally of **rows** and **repeats**. Some can be attached to a **standard needle**, others are left on a table.

ALTERNATIVES: pocket abacus, strokes and dashes on a piece of paper, or pencil marks by each row.

Line finder (Fig 1.43h)

The best type for charts is a metal sheet with two magnetic strips. Place **instructions** and **charts** over the metal sheet, and move the magnets, row by row, as you work (see **Addresses**). Simpler, much smaller ones, are sometimes combined with **tension gauges** – a popular design is a card or plastic strip with a long slit. The strip can be moved up and down the page, masking the text or chart except for one line that shows through the slit.

ALTERNATIVES: Go over the rows already worked with a fluorescent pen, either directly on the instructions or on a piece of see-through plastic placed on top. If you have to follow the instructions several times, change the plastic after each repeat.

White cloth

To protect your lap when working with yarns that shed hairs, or improve your vision when working with black or dark yarns.

Other accessories   s

Devised for very specific purposes, some of these accessories are priceless, others are downright gimmicky.

Swift or skein holder

Expanding frame that turns on an axis. Holds **skeins** of yarns for **winding**. If you cannot find one in hand- or machine-knitting shops, see **Addresses**. Or buy an antique one; they are expensive but very beautiful.

ALTERNATIVES: chair back, a friend's hands.

Ball winder

Invaluable used with a **swift** (Fig 1.44), if much of your yarn comes in **skeins**. It makes cylindrical 'balls' that can be left flat on the floor, and can be started at the centre. Avail-

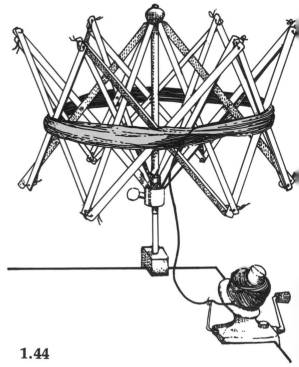

1.44

able from machine-knitting shops (see also **Addresses**).

Needle case
To keep **needles** in safely when not in use.

Bobbins
Card or plastic shapes used in **colour knitting** for wrapping small amounts of yarn around. The yarn is unwound in short lengths and passed through a slit to stop it from unwinding any further (Fig 1.45).

ALTERNATIVES: take a square piece of card, or fold a piece of paper, and cut a slit in one side.

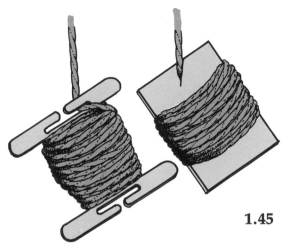

1.45

Knitting mill
A little machine made out of plastic that has four mobile latch needles (like those on knitting machines), at the top of a central 'chimney'. At the turn of a handle the needles go up and down, quickly producing long lengths of **bobbin knitting**.

Thimbles
For **stranded jacquard**. Several yarns are threaded through a guide at the side of the thimble, and can then be carried on one single finger.

Ratio graph paper
Graph paper in varying width/height ratios, to accurately represent the **stitch shape** of

particular fabrics in **graphs**. The long side is usually the horizontal one; if in doubt, remember that counting up the number of rows in 10cm (4in) and counting sideways the number of stitches in the same measurement should give you a square. A full set first appeared in **Knitting Your Own Designs for a Perfect Fit** (see **Publications** and **Addresses**).

Teasel brush
Small wire brush used for fluffing up **mohair** and other **brushed yarns**.

ALTERNATIVES: wild or cultivated teasel; weaver's fine flick carder; suede brush, very stiff brush.

Yarn gauge
To check **thickness** when substituting yarn (see **Addresses**). The most sophisticated versions show the metres (yards) in a certain weight of yarn. They come with instructions.

ALTERNATIVE: see **thickness test**.

Wool-box
Spherical or cylindrical container, with a hole at the top and a cord for hanging. Used to keep balls of yarn fully protected.

ALTERNATIVES: jam jar, snug plastic bag secured with elastic band.

Magnifier
The type that hangs from the neck with a cord, and rests on the rib-cage. Good for very fine work or for knitters with vision difficulties. Available from needlecraft or general craft shops, and from opticians. (See **Addresses** for pattern holder with built-in magnifier. For serious visual handicaps, see **Books** and Disabled Living Foundation).

D-fuzz-it
A patented knitting and fabric 'comb' that effectively removes the little balls that appear when a garment **pills**. Available from haberdashers or department stores.

ALTERNATIVES: strips of Sellotape, which are not very efficient; shaving with a razor, which can cause irreparable damage.

Yarns

What follows is a few notes on a vast, fascinating subject. If you want more than very basic advice, see **Books**.

Yarn character varies in the extreme. Not all yarns suit the same designs, even if they knit to the same **stitch size**. When following printed **instructions**, tread carefully if planning to use a yarn other than the recommended one (see **Books** for guides to yarn substitution and **Addresses** for suppliers of **yarn gauges**).

Fibres

There are basically two types:

NATURAL FIBRES: either animal (**wool, mohair, angora, cashmere, alpaca, llama, vicuña, silk**) or vegetal (**cotton, linen, raffia**).

MAN-MADE FIBRES: either made out of regenerated natural fibres (**viscose rayon, acetates**) or synthetic (**polyamides, polyesters, acrylics**).

For decorative knitting, rougher fibres are sometimes used: **jute, sisal, cowhair, horsehair, leather**, amongst the naturals; **polypropylene, PVC**, amongst the man-mades. **Dog** owners brushing, spinning and knitting their pet's hair are not unknown either!

Each fibre has its own characteristic **handle, resilience**, strength, inflammability, resistance to dirt and/or **moths** and **mildew**, resistance to heat and water etc. In general, **man-made fibres** are easier and cheaper to produce, attract fewer pests, and are easier to clean than untreated natural fibres. These fibres do not shrink, although they can stretch in hot, humid conditions, such as hot **washing**. **Natural fibres** generally breathe and are absorbent; they are still comfortable in the rain or if you perspire. They **pill** less, if at all, take dyes better and do not attract dirt so readily.

Many **blends** try to make the most of both natural and man-made fibres by mixing them. It is a sound practice, but do not expect miracles. A cheap mohair blend may only have 10 or 15 per cent mohair. Even if the name 'mohair' appears quite prominently on the **label**, the yarn will have very little in common with 85 per cent mohair blends, and even less with pure mohair.

Natural fibres may **shrink**, even when washed at low temperatures. Cotton and linen are amongst those prone to shrinking. Wool may either shrink or 'plump up'. It is sometimes treated to make it **shrink resistant** and/or **machine washable**. These types need to be worked slightly tighter than ordinary wool, and have a somewhat different **handle**.

Shrinkage test
a Work a **sample**.

1.46

b Either cut a piece of paper to the exact shape, or take a photocopy – yes, knitting photocopies beautifully.

c **Wash** the sample.

d **Block** and, when dry, compare with original shape (Fig 1.46).

Handle

This is how a yarn 'feels' to the touch. It varies from very harsh to incredibly soft.

Very smooth and shiny yarns tend to be **slippery**. They glide through your hands and along the needles. But just as they make for easy work, they also make for easy **unravelling** and easily **dropped stitches**, especially when worked **loosely**. This, though, is an advantage in techniques such as **provisional cast-on** where a contrast yarn is used as a foundation to be unpicked at a later stage. Silk is possibly the most slippery of all yarns. Others are mercerised cotton and some viscoses.

Slippery yarns also make the project 'drop'. A point to remember, especially with heavy projects. **Tension samples** and work should be stretched horizontally and compressed vertically when **blocking**.

Resilience

This is the elasticity or 'give' a yarn has. Some yarns (wool, for example), will immediately recover their original length if stretched and released. Others (silk, some man-mades and all vegetal fibres) either cannot be stretched, or remain stretched if pulled. Elastic stitch patterns such as **ribbings** can only be successfully knitted with resilient yarns. In, for example, silk or cotton, they widen and widen until totally useless. Therefore, garments in these fibres should never have ribbings as **borders**. If you want to follow printed instructions and can only find garments with ribbings, use **knitting-in elastic**.

Resilience test

a Accurately cut a 20cm (8in) length of yarn.

b Stretch it as far as it will go, and measure to check how much it has lengthened.

c Release and measure again (Fig 1.47).

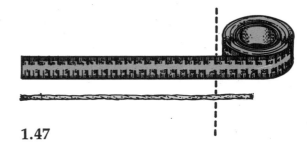

1.47

A yarn that does not lengthen at **b**, or that remains stretched at **c**, is not resilient. When working with non-resilient yarns, always **block** the **tension sample** and the work well stretched, especially if the yarn is also **slippery** (see **handle** above).

Twist

Totally **untwisted yarns** (such as the Icelandic lopi of Fig 1.48) are very warm, because air is trapped between the fibres. They are also very weak and break easily.

lopi

high-twist cotton

1.48

High-twist yarns are strong and give a much clearer **stitch pattern** definition, but are not so warm.

Sometimes, a very high-twist yarn combined with a certain stitch pattern will produce a **slanted fabric**.

Thickness

Although there are some very sophisticated and accurate methods of describing the thickness, or 'count', of yarns, the common names used in Britain are loosely based on the concept of **ply**. A ply (also called **fold**) is one of the twisted strands that make a yarn. The more plies there are, the thicker the yarn is, provided ply thickness is maintained.

From thin to thick, common names are: **1-ply, 2-ply, 3-ply, 4-ply, double knitting (DK), triple knitting** (or **Aran**), **double double-knitting (or chunky), extra chunky** (Fig 1.49). The first three are not very readily available, 1-ply being the cobweb yarn used in fine **lace knitting**. In reality plies vary in thickness, and it is possible to read '2-ply, knits as 4-ply'! Thickness within each category also varies; not all DK yarns are the same by any means. Some years ago, **3-ply** yarns were found to vary from 113 to 187 yards in 1oz – the shortest ball being a mere three fifths of the longest! This result was a combination of yarn thickness and fibre **weight**

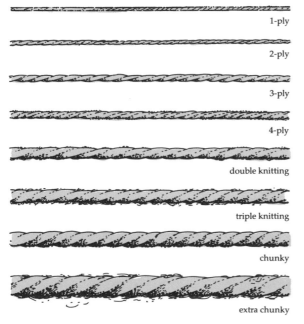

1-ply

2-ply

3-ply

4-ply

double knitting

triple knitting

chunky

extra chunky

1.49

variations. Keep this well in mind when substituting yarns.

Colour introduces yet another factor. Dark colours use more dye and this makes the yarn both thinner and heavier. Two large, identical items knitted in a very light and a very dark colour of exactly the same yarn, might require different needles, different **stitch sizes** and different amounts of yarn!

Thickness test

To check whether two yarns are of the same thickness, consult a yarn substitution guide (see **Books**), use a **yarn gauge** or:

a Cut one short length of each.
b Link the two lengths.
c Twist both yarns well (Fig 1.50).

1.50

d Run your fingers along. If you feel a 'step', they are of a different thickness.

Texture

(See also **the knitted stitch** and **stitch patterns**)

Yarn texture must always be matched to **stitch pattern**. Remember:

• The **knit** side of the stitch is smooth. If teamed with a smooth yarn, the effect will be emphasised. With a highly textured yarn, one will counter the other.

• The **purl** side of the stitch is rugged. Any bumps or loops will naturally stay on that side, showing many times better than from the knit side.

• Complex stitch patterns in highly textured yarns are a waste of time, because they do not show.

• Some yarn textures make certain techniques awkward. Brushed and hairy yarns get caught when passing one stitch on top of another, as in **basic cast-off** and certain **decreases**.

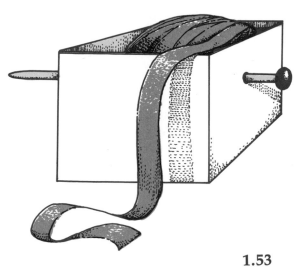

Brushed yarns (such as most mohair) and **hairy** yarns (such as angora) may shed hairs and cause choking, especially in young children. Placing the yarn, wrapped in plastic, in the fridge for one or two hours is supposed to help the problem; and placing a cloth on your lap to protect yourself is a well-tested and good idea. Work these yarns loosely, letting the hairs fill the gaps, or work tightly for a furry effect. **Brushing** after making up gives extra lift to the hairs. Projects in plain yarn can also be brushed, either in parts or all over, to achieve a brushed-yarn effect.

Bouclé, in common parlance, is applied to three types of yarn: real **bouclé**, **gimp** and **loop** (Fig 1.51). Another popular term for these is **poodle yarn**.

1.53

ball and let the ball hang free until the ribbon has lost all the twists.

In **flat knitting**, working the return rows **from left to right** helps to keep ribbon untwisted. Ribbons give extraordinary depth to purl stitches.

bouclé

gimp

loop

1.51

Chenille (Fig 1.52) is a yarn with many short hairs, rather like velvet.

chenille

1.52

Ribbons require special treatment because they should be knitted without any twists. Try threading a knitting needle or similar object first through one side of a box, then through the ball or spool of ribbon, and then through the other side of the box (Fig 1.53). Some twisting will still occur, but less. To get rid of it, remove ball from box, pin ribbon to

Colour

(See also **thickness** above)

Yarns can be dyed in many ways, apart from in **solid** colours (Fig 1.54).

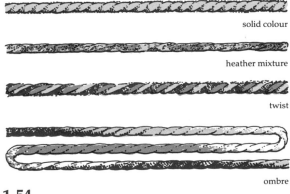

solid colour

heather mixture

twist

ombre

1.54

Heather mixtures are very subtle combinations of fibres – dyed and blended before spinning.

Twists are combinations of **plies** of different colours.

Ombré yarns have different shades of the same colour appearing at regular, or irregular, intervals.

Although colour-running when **washing** is not very common nowadays, it is not a bad idea to check fastness beforehand, especially when using unbranded yarns.

Colour-fastness test

a Take a small piece of white cloth – 10cm (4in) square will do unless you are testing many colours.

b Fold the cloth and wrap 20–30cm (8–12in) of yarn tightly around it (Fig 1.55).

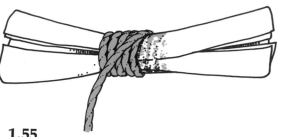

1.55

c Repeat **b** with all the colours to be tested.

d **Wash.**

e When dry, unwind yarn. If the cloth is still white, the yarn is fast.

Buying yarn

(See also **yarn required** below)

Much of the yarn used by hand knitters is manufactured by large- and medium-sized spinners, and sold through wool shops and department stores. But you can also spin your own yarn, or use small, specialist suppliers.

Addresses of mail-order yarn retailers can be found in knitting and craft magazines (see also **Books**). Some offer superb qualities that are not viable for the mass market, or ordinary yarns at a reduced price because they are selling direct. Others offer mainly weaving qualities, not always suitable for knitting. And others have very inferior yarns that is best to keep away from; cheap does not always mean a bargain.

Cobweb yarns for **lace knitting** can be difficult to find. A local lacemaker may be able to tell you of a source of cotton; try asking your library for any lacemaking courses or for a branch of the Lace Guild. Cobweb wool is available from the Shetlands; the manufacturers advertise regularly in magazines.

Yarn is dyed in batches, called **dye-lots**. Mixing dye-lots can add subtlety to **colour knitting**, but in general it should be avoided. If you have no option but to mix, change dye-lots every couple of rows, to give an all-over effect.

Some wool shops 'lay by' yarn. You buy part of what you think will be needed, and they keep the rest for a few weeks. Other shops take back untouched balls in pristine condition, provided that you return them within a reasonable time (say, whilst stocks of the dye-lot last), and that you can show the sales ticket. These services are rarely offered by mail-order suppliers. Do remember that, in any case, they are unique services to be treasured and never abused, because they are exclusively for your benefit and could easily be discontinued. All the shop gets out of them, apart perhaps from increased good will, is headaches. The lay-by system ties up much capital and may be the cause of lost sales – if putting 10 balls aside for you leaves only 15 balls on the shelf, another customer needing 16 balls will have to go elsewhere (if you turn up an hour later saying that you only want 2 balls after all, the retailer will be hard put to keep a smile!). Returned yarn, on the other hand, may prove unsaleable because it has taken on a smell (tobacco smoke and deep frying are two common nasties), or because an unscrupulous customer has used part of the ball. Please remember this when a shop does not offer either service – they might have had one abusing customer too many.

Labelling

Yarn bought from shops (except sometimes yarn on special offer), always carries a **label** or a **ball band**. Mail-order yarn sometimes does not. Information on the label will include some, or all, of the following:

- Fibre content.
- Weight.
- Cleaning instructions.
- Approximate length in metres (yd).
- Suggested **needle size** and **tension**. Symbols such as those of Fig 1.56 should be read:

1.56

'The manufacturers recommend a tension of 24 stitches and 32 rows in **stocking stitch**; an average knitter will obtain this with 4mm needles, then use 3¼mm needles for the **ribbings**. Use 4mm needles to work your first **tension sample**, and assess how average you are; if necessary, change needles until the correct tension is achieved. For patterns other than stocking stitch you could need a totally different tension and possibly different needles too.'

Using yarn

Do not let yarn roll free on a dirty floor. Keep inside the **work bag** or in a **wool-box**. **Slippery yarns** should always be kept in a wool-box.

Most hand-knitting yarn comes in **balls**, but some is sold in **skeins (hanks)**. There are also occasional **spools** and, if you want to use machine-knitting or industrial yarns, **cones**.

Commercial balls

These are easier to start from the outside, but it is better to start them from the inside to avoid twists.

To get to the inner tail, remove the **band** and poke a couple of fingers right into the centre of the ball. If the tail is difficult to find, pull out a small bundle. Replace the band if it is not broken.

Skeins

These need to be wound into a soft ball. Tight balls put the yarn permanently under stress. The yarn then weakens, becomes thinner and loses its **resilience**, but perhaps only until it is **washed**. Then, if washing restores the yarn to its original non-stress length, the knitting will shrink.

Whilst winding, the skein must be kept stretched. Use a **swift**, a chair back, or ask someone to hold it for you (Fig 1.57). Undo the tie and start winding the end that hangs from the outside. Wind carefully and slowly. NEVER cross any strands or take the ball to the other side. Knots must be eased out by gently turning the skein.

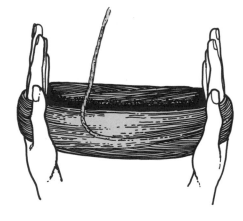

1.57

Either work with a **ball winder** or by **hand**:

a Leaving an end at least 20cm (8in) long, wrap yarn around thumb and little finger of left hand in a figure of eight, say 10 to 20 times (Fig 1.58).

b Slip the little hank off your fingers, without disturbing it, and fold in half.

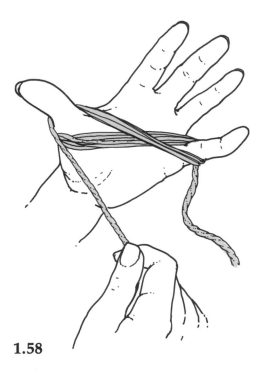

1.58

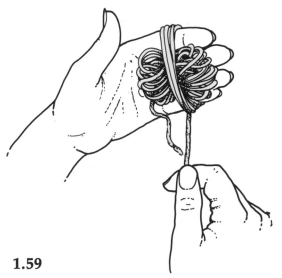

1.59

c Keeping the free end to the left, place the hank against the left fingers and wind the yarn over both the hank and the fingers, some 20 to 30 times (Fig 1.59).

d Turn the ball and wind 20 or 30 times more over ball and left fingers, at right angles from **c**.

e Wind again between **c** and **d**.
Always keeping the free end loose, repeat **c** to **e** until the skein runs out.

f Tuck the end of the skein into the ball. You now have a ball of yarn that can be started from the centre (Fig 1.60).

1.60

If you want a ball that starts from the outside, wind the start of the skein around the fingers of the left hand, instead of **a** and **b**. Do not leave a tail.

Spools and cones

To avoid twisting, place inside a box as explained for **ribbons** (Fig 1.53).

Yarn required

Instructions always tell you how much yarn you are going to need, but if you change **tension, stitch pattern**, style or indeed yarn, you will need more or less.

When designing your own project, try to find guidance in instructions using the same yarn, and ask the shop assistant. This will give you only the roughest of ideas, but it is a start. Try to make use of the 'lay-by' or return system (see **buying yarn** above).

Having worked part of the project, you can guess the final amount more exactly:

a **Measure** what you have knitted so far and calculate its surface area.

b Divide this area by the number of balls used.

c Calculate the surface area of the finished project.

d Divide **c** by the answer to **b** and you have the total number of balls required.

Remember that areas such as **borders** may take more yarn than others. In a sweater, you may be able to ignore this if you take necklines, shoulder slopes, armholes etc as being fully worked.

Always approximate in excess. A ball too much is infinitely preferable to a tenth of a ball too little.

Joining in yarn

In **flat knitting**, unless you are desperately short of yarn, or cannot face unpicking a nearly finished row, try to **join** yarn only at **seam edges**. Otherwise, join in at mid-row but NOT at a **free edge** unless extraordinary circumstances force you to do so. **Darning** the yarn ends could easily spoil the edge.

When joining at mid-row, try doing it at a change in stitch pattern, near a solid area in **lace** patterns, or at any other place that will make darning easy. If the two tails can lie on the wrong side, so much the better.

Always treat knots and imperfections in the yarn as if they were breaks. Cut them and re-join.

When nearing the end of a ball, to know whether you have enough yarn to complete two rows:

a Fold what is left of the yarn in half.

b Make a **slip knot**.

c Knit first row.

If you have reached the knot before the end of the row, there is not enough left for the second row.

To assess whether the yarn is enough for one single row, make the **slip knot** one fourth of the length away from the needle, and see whether you can knit a quarter of a row. If

you cannot, you will have to **unravel** the part-row.

If a join leaves you with a long length of yarn that could be used for **seaming,** do not cut it. To stop it from getting in the way, tie it into a **little bundle**:

a Starting with the free end, wrap yarn around a couple of fingers, until a short distance away from the work.

b Make a loop and place wrapped yarn inside it (Fig 1.61).

c Pull to fasten loop.

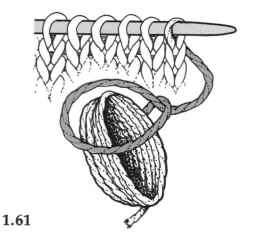

1.61

Of the following methods, I would recommend **drop and take** for self-coloured knitting and **woven join** for **colour knitting**. Methods that work a few stitches with double yarn have not been included because they alter fabric thickness and are always detectable.

Knots

These are generally far best avoided, but if you ever need them (for instance, to leave the two ends on the right side as decoration when working with **ribbon** or **leather**), make them properly.

The ordinary, 'granny', knot can come undone. When joining yarns of the same **thickness**, use a **reef** or **square knot** (Fig 1.62). This is best done (see **drop and take**), when you can control exactly where you want it; if done in advance you may have difficulties

1.62

passing it through a stitch. Work as for granny knot, but tie first left over right, then right over left.

For yarns of different thickness, use a **weaver's knot** (Fig 1.63). This has to be done in advance.

1.63

Drop and take

Simply, drop the old yarn, take the new yarn, and continue knitting. Leave tails not shorter than 15cm (6in), and **darn** them later (or tie into a **square knot**). If you find it difficult to keep an even **yarn tension** on the next row, work the first stitch after the join with the two yarns. Unpick one of the two strands before darning.

Woven join

Weave in the old tail for not less than ten stitches when you start knitting with the new yarn, as in **jacquard**. On the next row, weave in the new tail in the opposite direction. In **circular knitting**, weave in the two tails together. Cut tails after **blocking**.

With **slippery yarns** and **chenille**, it is safer to weave in the tails on two rows, changing direction, or to weave them in for a longer length.

Splicing

This can only be used with straightforward, twisted yarns. Its main problem is that there are always thin ends of yarn finding their way onto the right side.

a If, say, the yarn has four **plies**, cut two some 5–7cm (2–3in) away from the end of the old yarn (or one there and the other at mid-way).

b Repeat with the end of the new yarn.

c Roll the ends together to mimic the original twist (Fig 1.64).

1.64

d Work as usual, taking any free ply tails to the wrong side.

e After **blocking**, cut the ply tails.

Aftercare

General care
(See also **cleaning** below)

A few thoughts to help you get the most out of your knitteds:

- **Dust** is a great destroyer of textiles. Closed wardrobes and drawers make better storage areas than open shelves. Mats, curtains, bedspreads etc should be cleaned regularly. Wall-hangings with drapings in which dust tends to accumulate should be vacuumed often.

- **Starch** is another destroying agent. Do not store starched items. Wash them first.

- **Dirt** can also cause damage. Cleaning lightly and often is highly advisable. The drastic action required by heavy soiling could well cause irreparable damage to the fabric. Shaking, brushing and airing outdoors helps to lengthen the time an item can go without cleaning.

- **Stains** (see **Books**) require swift action; once set they often prove impossible to shift. Washing without treating them first, or trying to remove them with the wrong agent, may cause them to set. Many stains respond to cold water if quickly applied; dab, sponge or soak, but do not rub. Avoid water, however, on oil-based stains such as paint, ball-point ink, grease and lipstick; these should be treated with a solvent – applied from the wrong side to drive the stain out of the fabric and onto a clean white cloth placed against the right side. To soften a dry stain, dilute equal parts of glycerine and warm water, dab onto stained area and leave for one hour. Rinse or sponge with lukewarm water, then wash or use a solvent as appropriate.

- **Pilling** (those annoying little balls that form on the surface of some fabrics) can easily be removed with **D-fuzz-it** (Fig 1.65).

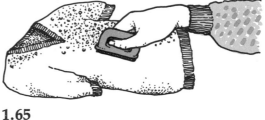

1.65

- **Snags** must never be cut. If possible, ease the yarn back where it belongs with a **cable needle** or a blunt **sewing needle** (Fig 1.66).

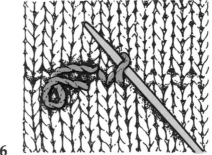

1.66

Otherwise, take the loop to the wrong side with a **crochet hook** (Fig 1.67).

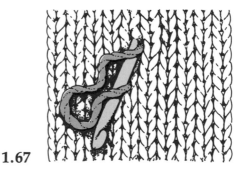

1.67

- **Knitwear** stays fresher if you change it often, rather than wear it for weeks on end, even if altogether you wear it for the same number of days. To give it a chance to 'breathe', do not put it away as soon as you take it off. Instead, leave flat on a chair overnight. If it has taken on a smell (perfume, tobacco smoke, cooking) air it outdoors for a little while, away from direct sun. Fold and put away. DO NOT HANG.

• If **storing** knitted items for any length of time, either dry-clean and air outdoors to remove chemical fumes, or wash. If cleaning does not seem necessary, shake, brush and air outdoors away from direct sun. Fold carefully – acid-free tissue paper between the folds helps to avoid creasing. Wrap with more tissue paper, a clean cloth or a plastic bag with plenty of holes; textiles need to breathe. Use a moth deterrent if necessary (see **under attack** below).

Cleaning

Look at the **yarn label** for instructions. Unlabelled yarns should be treated with caution. Carry out a **shrinkage test** and a **colour-fastness test**, preferably before starting to knit. Dry-cleaning can also be tested on samples if you are not sure.

Cleaning instructions often adopt the symbols of the International Textile Care Labelling Code:

Washing:

 Hand wash only

 Wash at stated temperature

 Machine wash at stated programme

 Do not wash at all

Bleaching:

 Household bleach may be used

 Household bleach must not be used

Drying:

 Tumble drying beneficial but not essential

 Line dry

 Drip dry – hang whilst wet for best results

 Dry flat – do not hang

Ironing:

 Cool iron

 Warm iron

 Hot iron

 Do not iron

Dry-cleaning:

(A) Dry-clean in any solvent

(P) Dry-clean in perchloroethylene, white spirit, Solvent 113 and Solvent 11 only

(P) Professional dry-clean only – do not 'coin op' clean

(F) Dry-clean in white spirit or Solvent 1 only

 Do not dry-clean

FOLLOW CLEANING INSTRUCTIONS STRICTLY. Clean mixed-fibre articles as required by the most delicate fibre.

Washing

Use a washing machine only when specifically mentioned in the label. Only **machine-washable** or **shrink-resistant wool** should be put into a machine, and then only if the machine has a special wool programme.

Non-washable trimmings, such as untreated wooden or leather buttons, should be removed or tightly covered with aluminium foil.

To **hand wash**:

a Dissolve a little powder or solution specially formulated for delicate fabrics (NOT ordinary washing powder), into enough lukewarm to cold water to cover the knitting.

b Immerse the item to be washed. Do not wash more than one item at once unless really small.

c Leave to soak a few minutes if the product you are using recommends soaking, otherwise omit this step.

d Squeeze the fabric gently with your fingers to release dirt. Do not rub. Just squeeze (Fig 1.68).

1.68

e Rinse several times until water becomes clear, at the same temperature used for washing. Keep squeezing gently. If you lift the knitting from the water, do not let it hang; support it with both hands.

f Squeeze as much water as you can, but do not wring.

g Place knitting flat over a dry, clean towel and roll the two together (Fig 1.69). Press to absorb as much water as possible with the towel. Repeat if necessary. Natural fibres may be put in a spin drier on short cycle.

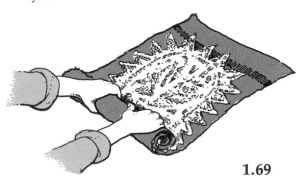

1.69

Lace and unstructured articles may need extra care when lifting them from the water. You may want to place them on top of a piece of glass or plastic so that you can lift them safely when rinsing.

Wool and **silk** can have a little vinegar added to the last rinse. This removes the last traces of soap and brightens the colour.

Delicate knitwear is best turned inside out, with fastenings done up.

Drying

DO NOT TUMBLE-DRY NATURAL FIBRES, ESPECIALLY WOOL. Man-made fibres, even when tumble drying is recommended, should be carefully watched. Take them out before they are quite dry and leave them flat to finish drying. Use a cool setting only.

DO NOT HANG ANY KNITTING TO DRY. It would lose its shape, and a bad crease would form. The best way to dry knitting is flat. Ideally, you should draw the outline on a piece of thick paper or, even better, interface, when it is brand new. You then have a guide to its correct shape. Second best is to take the main measurements.

Start by removing any wrinkles from the back with the palm of your hand. Lay the item on its back on a flat, pinnable surface covered with a dry towel. Remove the wrinkles from the front, check the measurements and ease into correct shape if necessary. Use pins to keep sharp lines if required (Fig 1.70).

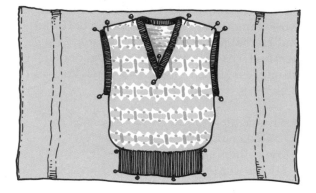

1.70

For items that need **stretching** or adapting to a less straightforward shape, use the guidelines followed when **blocking**. If that is now difficult because the item has been made up, consider dry-cleaning instead of washing.

Yarns that 'plump up' when washed, such as Shetland wool, need stretching into shape. This is why in Scotland they use special **frames** for drying sweaters. If you do not have a frame, shake the knitting and gently pull small areas of fabric to open up the fibres and re-trap the air that has been expelled. DO NOT TUMBLE-DRY.

Dry away from direct heat and direct sun, but in a warm atmosphere. Long drying periods are best avoided.

Ironing

Knitting should NOT be ironed, but **pressing** is often recommended. The difference between the two is that whilst ironing you move the iron up and down the fabric, but whilst pressing you rest it gently on the surface, then lift it, then rest it again (Fig 1.71).

1.71

Pressing is done **wrong side** up, on a well-padded surface. Despite the process's name, pressure should not be applied. Steam, though, is essential. Either use a steam iron, AT THE INSTRUCTED SETTING FOR THE FIBRE, with a dry cloth over the knitting, or a dry iron and a wet cloth. Do not press **ribbings** or elastic fabrics.

Personally, I never let an iron get anywhere near knitting, hand or machine. Drying flat as just explained, or **reblocking**, gives immaculate results and totally avoids accidental scorching or texture flattening.

Under attack

Knitting can be irreparably damaged by both **mildew** and **moths**.

Mildew

This develops in moist conditions. Silk is easily attacked. Mildew stains cannot be removed.

Your main lines of action are:

● Store only thoroughly dry items.

● Dry freshly washed knitting in a warm atmosphere. If you have to do it in a cold room, use a window screen or one of those wire driers that can be placed on top of the bath. Then air circulates more freely than with the method explained earlier.

● If your storage area is cold, avoid wrapping in plastic bags and keep the area well aired.

Moths

Moths love **animal fibres**, oiled yarns, food particles and human perspiration; which is why only clean knitting should be stored for any length of time.

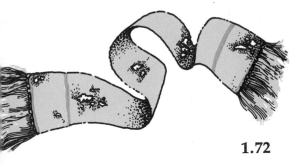

1.72

The damage to the fabric (Fig 1.72) is not done by the moth itself but by the little hungry larvae that come out of the one or two hundred eggs each moth lays. Sunlight and fresh air, as well as a good shaking, are good ways of getting rid of the eggs.

Moth deterrents work best in enclosed environments, such as sealed boxes or bags. Commercial moth flakes and crystals, however, give out a lingering smell nearly as repellent to humans as to moths!

Many things are said to repel moths. Some are proven, some not, but people go on using them. cedar wood (it might lose its effectiveness after a few years), sealed paper bags, newspaper, conkers, lavender, scented toilet soap, and many others. To find out for certain, I asked Dr Malcolm Stuart, world famous for his **Encyclopedia of Herbs and Herbalism**. He had never heard of conkers and was rather scornful of lavender. But he suggested the following as good, natural deterrents (see **Addresses**):

Artemisia absinthium	wormwood
Artemisia vulgaris	mugwort
Chrysanthemum cinerariifolium	pyrethrum flower
Chrysanthemum balsamita	costmary
Ruta graveolens	rue
Santolina chamaecyparissus	cotton lavender
Tanacetum vulgare	tansy

PART TWO

GET CLICKING

What is what

Common terms

Full explanations to all knitting terms and expressions can be located through the **Index** on page 281.

Fig 2.1 merely maps out some common terms to give new knitters a quick, visual reference.

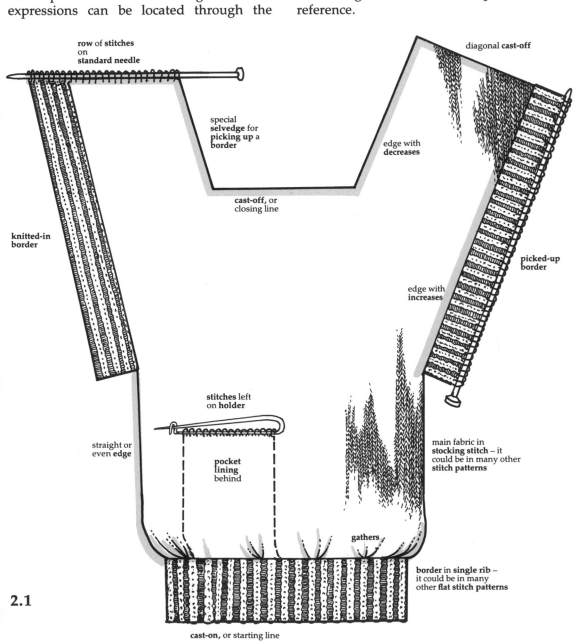

row of **stitches** on **standard needle**

diagonal **cast-off**

special **selvedge** for **picking up** a **border**

edge with **decreases**

cast-off, or closing line

knitted-in border

picked-up border

edge with **increases**

stitches left on **holder**

straight or even **edge**

pocket lining behind

main fabric in **stocking stitch** – it could be in many other **stitch patterns**

gathers

border in **single rib** – it could be in many other **flat stitch patterns**

2.1

cast-on, or starting line

Abbreviations

To a greater or lesser extent, all knitting instructions contain abbreviations. Used in moderation, abbreviations make the text shorter and sharper and are a great help. Taken to the extreme, they can make the instructions difficult to follow.

There is no universally agreed set of abbreviations for English speakers. Differences between authors can be staggering, and very confusing when two or more books are consulted simultaneously. However, each book or leaflet carries a list, and this should always be checked.

If the amount or type of abbreviations used bother you, transcribe the instructions in your own 'shorthand'.

All abbreviations used in this book can be found in the **Index**, but here is a complete list of those used in instructions:

k	**knit**
k2 tog	**knit** two stitches together
k-b	**knit-back** (insert needle through back of loop)
k-b2 tog	**knit-back** two stitches together
kwise	**knitwise**
p	**purl**
p2 tog	**purl** two stitches together
p-b	**purl-back** (insert needle through back of loop)
p-b2 tog	**purl-back** two stitches together
psso	**pass slip stitch(es) over**
pwise	**purlwise**
sl	**slip**
sl st	**slip stitch**
ssk	**slip, slip, knit** (see **knit decrease**)
st, sts	**stitch, stitches**
st st	**stocking stitch**
wyab	**with yarn at back**
wyif	**with yarn in front**
yb	**yarn back**
yf or **yfwd**	**yarn forward**
yo	**yarn over** or **over**
yrn	**yarn round needle**
(...)	Repeat instructions inside brackets as many times as indicated after brackets
...	Repeat instructions between asterisks to end of row

Casting on and off

When it comes to starting (**casting on**) or finishing (**casting off**) a piece of knitting, it is very tempting to learn one method and then stick to it whatever the circumstances. Many knitters actually boast of ALWAYS using such-and-such. How utterly boring! Have you ever heard of a cook who ALWAYS starts with bringing water to the boil and ALWAYS ends by adding a knob of butter?

Any knitted edge (cast-on, cast-off or **selvedge**) is as important to the end result as the main fabric. Chosing one or another might have a decisive effect. Therefore, always keep an open mind, read carefully the opening paragraphs not forgetting the **choosing** sections, and be ready to experiment – at your own pace, of course, or you could end up with a bad case of indigestion!

CASTING ON

(See also **Edges and selvedges** and **Seams and joins**; extra stitches may have to be allowed for these)

A cast-on is a foundation row of stitches – without it, you cannot knit. **Samples** are a must. A cast-on may have a **stitch size** far greater or far smaller than that of the pattern to follow. If necessary, cast on a different number of stitches than required by the pattern, and adjust on the first row. Or consider using different needle sizes.

Do not take anything for granted. One side of the cast-on may blend in better with a particular pattern than the other side. Make two very small samples, starting one with a **right-side** row, the other with a **wrong-side**. Experiment with **colour**:

• use a contrast to cast on, or
• in methods requiring two strands, use two colours instead of one, or
• cast on one stitch in one colour and the next in a second colour.

Watch the **tension**. A tight cast-on will not make a firmer edge – just the opposite. An edge that pulls will soon snap. To avoid this try one of the following:

• do not overpull yarn
• cast on with thicker needle(s)
• cast on a few extra stitches and **decrease** evenly on the first row
• cast on the stitches on two needles held together.

A loose cast-on will wave and look awful. To avoid it, try one of these:

• pull yarn tighter
• cast on with finer needle(s)
• cast on a few stitches less than necessary and **increase** evenly on first row.

Always leave a 15cm (6in) tail of yarn. Shorter tails are difficult to **darn**. If it can be used for **seaming**, make the tail much longer and tie up into a **little bundle**.

When casting on many stitches, a **needle marker** after every tenth stitch (or after the stitches required for each pattern repeat) helps with the counting.

Casting on circles

The first stitch of the first **round** will close the circle. Before working it check that the cast-on is not spiralling over the needle(s) as happens in Fig 2.2.

2.2

If the first round has any **decreases**, try to work one of them over the first and last cast-on stitches, either at start or end of the round.

If your circle joins are untidy:

• pull yarn firmly at the join, or
• cast on an extra stitch and **decrease** as just indicated, or
• cast on an extra stitch and **decrease** over the first and second cast-on stitches.

With a **circular needle**, slip a **marker** around the needle before closing the circle.

With sets of **double-pointed needles**, distribute the stitches evenly on the holding needles. Pull yarn firmly when changing to a new needle. If in trouble, cast on with straight needle(s), then **slip** or work the stitches onto the set.

Slip knot   E

The starting point of many methods (Fig 2.3).

a Loop the yarn into a full circle.
b Draw the short end through the circle with a needle.
c Tighten first the long end, then the short one.

2.3

Choosing a cast-on

It is amazing how, with so many cast-ons to choose from, the selection offered to knitters is usually very poor. My suggestion is to start with a good all-rounder: **two-strand cast-on**. Follow with three methods to improve common situations: one for adding on stitches – **double-twist loop** or **buttonhole**; one for **single rib** – **tubular** or **Channel Islands**; and one for **lace** – **chain** or **twisted loop**.

The following guidelines will help you graduate to the whole range (within each group, methods are in the order in which they appear in the book).

ORDINARY EDGES
two-strand
twisted two-strand
cable
Peruvian

BUTTONHOLES
(See **end of rows** below)

CROCHET EDGINGS to be added
cast-off

DECORATIVE EDGES
Use either for contrast or to blend in with the main pattern:
alternate loop
twisted two-strand
combined two-strand

double two-strand
multi-strand
Channel Islands
knotted
cast-off
twice knitted
Peruvian
tubular
frilled
edging

END OF ROWS
For firm edges:
double-twist loop
cable
buttonhole
For lace and soft edges:
loop for softest results
twisted loop
alternate loop
chain

FRINGED EDGES
chain
twice knitted
provisional

HEMS
loop
twisted loop
chain

LACE AND SUPPLE EDGES
loop for softest results
twisted loop
alternate loop
chain
edging
As a last resort, **two-strand** probably on a thicker needle.

MEDALLIONS
If worked in **short rows**:
provisional when the medallion is to be grafted. If it is to be sewn, any cast-on that will either make a bold line, or blend in with the pattern after sewing (see **decorative edges** above).

If worked from the centre out:
pinhole
centre line

REINFORCED EDGES
twisted two strand
double two-strand
multi-strand
Channel Islands
knotted

RIBBINGS
two-strand, starting pattern with a **wrong-side** row
Channel Islands
alternate cable
tubular
tubular for double rib
provisional, for **single rib** only. Once unravelled, the work will not ladder.

TEMPORARY EDGES
Eventually to be **unravelled**, so that another piece of work can be **grafted** on. To avoid errors, cast on·with a contrast colour. For greater ease use a **slippery yarn**.
loop
twisted loop
double-twist loop
provisional
(See also **two-way edges** below)

TUBULAR FABRICS
For an **open end**, cast on half the stitches on one double-pointed needle and half on another needle. Use appropriate cast-on for fabric. Fold, so that the last stitch faces the first one (Fig 2.4). On first row, work one stitch from each cast-on needle.
For a **closed end**:
two-strand
Channel Islands
alternate cable
tubular

TWICE-KNIT FABRICS
twice knitted

TWO-WAY EDGES
After completing work in one direction, **pick up stitches** from the cast-on and work in the opposite direction. Check the number of stitches after picking up.
loop
chain
Some **decorative cast-ons**, for example an **edging cast-on** such as **picot cord** or **slip cord**. As a very last resort, **two-strand** loosely knitted.
Or, after completing work in one direction, **unravel** the cast-on, pick up the free loops and work in the opposite direction. Check the number of stitches; you could be one short. **Increase**, if necessary, as discreetly as possible. For yarn and methods, see **temporary edges** above.

Loop cast-on U

One needle; one strand (Fig 2.5).
Very easy. First row can be tricky because the

2.4

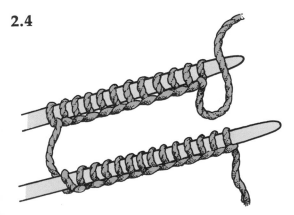

2.5

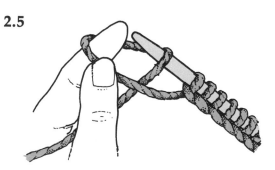

stitches sometimes tend to drop off the needle.

Gives a very understated and soft edge, without much strength. For extra softness, it can be worked on two needles held together. One needle is removed before the first row. This makes it easier to work the loops – and even easier to drop them.

a Make a **slip knot**.
b Lift yarn with left index finger, moving away from you.
c Catch strand behind index finger, as shown in illustration.
d Tighten loop.

Twisted loop cast-on U

One needle; one strand (Fig 2.6).
Slightly firmer than **loop cast-on**, but just as easy.
Work first row through front of loops, even if the stitches seem to ask to be worked through the back. This is what gives the twist to this method.

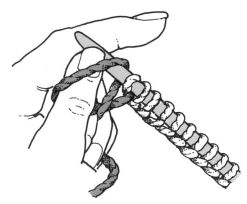

2.6

a Make a **slip knot**.
b Lift yarn from behind with left thumb, moving from left to right.
c Catch strand in front of thumb, as shown in illustration.
d Tighten loop.

Alternate loop cast-on S

One needle; one strand (Fig 2.7).
A soft, decorative edge.
● Alternate one stitch from **loop cast-on** with one stitch from **twisted loop cast-on**.

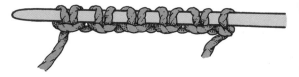

2.7

Double-twist loop cast-on U

One needle; one strand (Fig 2.8).
Very easy. Somewhat firmer than **twisted loop cast-on**. Easier to knit first row.

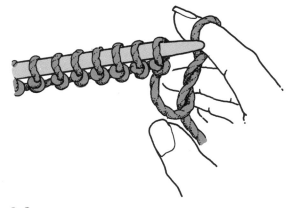

2.8

a Make a **slip knot** and take needle in left hand.
b Lift yarn from behind with right index finger.
c Twist yarn twice with your finger and place on needle.
d Tighten loop.

Two-strand cast-on E

Generally one needle; two strands.
Strong, elastic and the most versatile of all methods. Structure like **loop cast-on** (it may face the other way) plus a first knit row, but performance radically altered by the base loops being tightened.

In **flat knitting** it is best to start most patterns with a **wrong-side** row. Exceptions are **reverse stocking stitch** and other patterns with purl rows on the right side.

There are many versions. The **thumb cast-on** is the most popular in Britain, but beginners may find **Italian cast-on** (and, even more, **simplified cast-on**) easier and less painful – no thumb prodding! **Yarn-in-left-hand** knitters are likely to prefer **German cast-on**. The Swedish **two-needle cast-on** is the least common.

Notice that the twist is sometimes to the right and sometimes to the left. This can be reversed by wrapping the yarn around the hand in the opposite way (see **combined two-strand cast-on**). Make sure not to over-tighten the stitches.

All versions start with:
a Make a **slip knot**, leaving a tail at least 3 times the width to be cast on.

Thumb cast-on
Fig 2.9.
b Take needle and long strand in right hand.

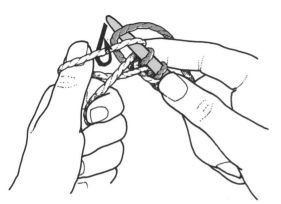

c Holding short strand in left hand, catch a loop with left thumb, moving clockwise.
d Catch loop around thumb with needle.
e Wrap long strand under needle.
f Pass loop over tip of needle and pull short strand.
g Tighten long strand.

Italian cast-on
Fig 2.10.
b Take needle and long strand in right hand.
c Holding short strand in left hand, catch yarn from underneath with both thumb and index finger.
d Catch yarn with needle, from left to right. This makes a loop around index finger.
e Wrap long strand under needle.
f Pass loop over tip of needle and pull short strand.
g Tighten long strand.

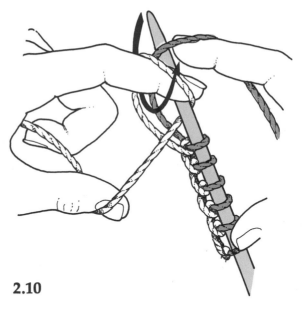

2.10

Simplified cast-on
Fig 2.11.
b Take needle and long strand in right hand.
c Holding short strand in left hand, catch yarn with index finger moving backwards.

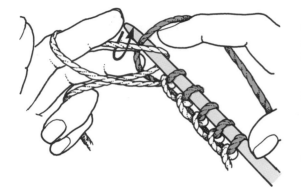

2.11

d Catch yarn behind index finger with needle. This creates a loop.
e Wrap long strand under needle.
f Pass loop over tip of needle and pull short strand.
g Tighten long strand.

German cast-on
Fig 2.12.
b Take both strands in left hand and needle in right hand.
c Catch short strand with left thumb, moving clockwise.
d Lift long strand with index finger.
e Catch loop around thumb with needle.
f Catch strand going to index finger with needle and draw through thumb loop.
g Let go thumb and pull short strand.
h Tighten long strand if necessary.

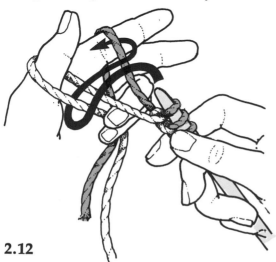

2.12

Two-needle cast-on
Fig 2.13.
b Take needle with **slip knot** in left hand and free needle in right hand.
c Take short strand behind long strand (it will already be there once you have 2 or more sts) and wrap around needle, up the back and down the front.
d Take long strand in front of short strand and wrap in same way.
e With right needle pass the 1st wrap over 2nd one.
f Pull, first, short strand, then long strand.

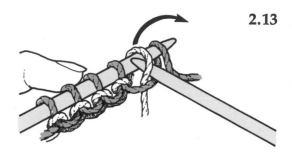

2.13

Twisted two-strand cast-on   U

Giving an extra twist to the **two-strand cast-on** results in an edge of great strength and elasticity. The **Italian** version is the better known.

Twisted thumb cast-on
Fig 2.14. Like **thumb cast-on** but:

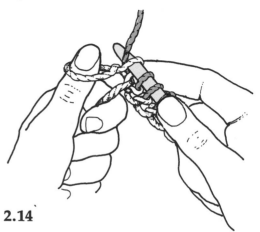

2.14

d Pass needle in front of short strand and catch back of loop around thumb, from behind.

Twisted Italian cast-on
Fig 2.15. Like **Italian cast-on** but:
d Catch back of strand around index finger, from behind.

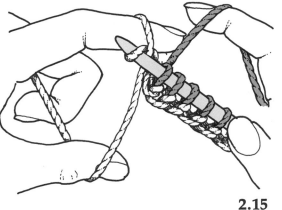

2.15

Twisted German cast-on
Fig 2.16. Like **German cast-on** but:
f Catch strand at the back of index finger with needle, from behind, and draw through thumb loop.
g Let go thumb and pull long strand.
h Tighten short strand.

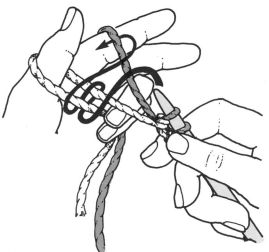

2.16

Combined two-strand cast-on U

An interesting edge is obtained by alternating the way of winding the short strand of the **two-strand cast-on** around the left hand (Fig 2.17).

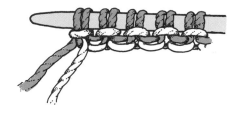

2.17

● Make the first stitch in the usual way. For second stitch:

Thumb and German methods
Loop short strand around thumb by moving thumb anticlockwise instead of clockwise. Catch loop from inside thumb (Fig 2.18).

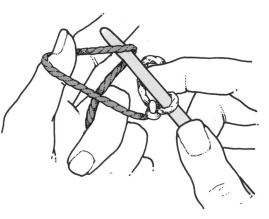

2.18

Italian method
Catch yarn with index finger from the top. With needle catch yarn behind finger (Fig 2.19).

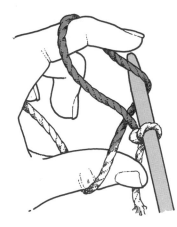

2.19

Simplified method
Catch yarn with index finger moving forward. With needle catch yarn in front of finger (Fig 2.20).

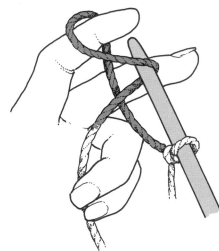

2.20

Double two-strand cast-on   U

Fig 2.21. To strengthen a **two-strand cast on**:
• Wrap yarn twice around thumb (**thumb** and **German**) or index finger (**Italian** and **simplified**), and insert needle into the double loop.

2.21

The same idea can be applied to **twisted** and **combined** versions of **two-strand cast-on**.

Multi-strand cast-on   U

Fig 2.22. Another way to strengthen and give body to **two-strand cast-on** and its many variations:

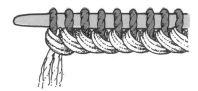

2.22

• Use one strand for the actual sts and two or more for the foundation.
A variation is to use two or more strands in both hands, and even continue in **multi-strand** for the first few pattern rows. In this case, other cast-ons such as **loop**, the **knitted** version of **chain**, or **cable** could be used.

Channel Islands cast-on   S

A combination-plus of **two-strand** or **multi-strand,** and **double two-strand**! Far easier than it sounds. Strong and very well suited to **single rib**. Knit the **overs** and purl the stitches on first row.
Work a **two-strand cast-on** but:
• use two strands of yarn in left hand (one strand for a softer edge).
• wrap the two strands twice around thumb or index finger – in the usual way if using

implified method, the other way round (see combined two-strand cast-on) if using humb, Italian or German methods.

after each stitch, wrap yarn under and up he front of needle to make another stitch Fig 2.23).

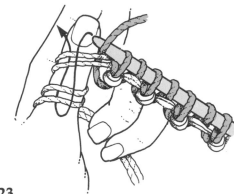

.23

Vrapping the yarn in the usual way around humb or finger gives a somewhat different esult, unsuitable for ribbing (Fig 2.24).

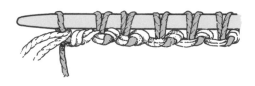

.24

Knotted cast-on   S

et another method based on two-strand ast-on. Strong and decorative.

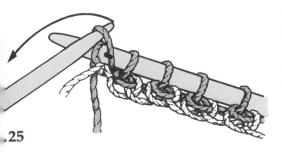

25

a Cast on 2 sts.
b Take 2nd needle in left hand and insert into 1st st.
c Lift 1st st over 2nd and off the needle (Fig 2.25).

A finer, less strong variation uses twisted loop cast-on instead (Fig 2.26).

2.26

Chain cast-on   U

The first two versions give a loose cast-on, good for soft edges. It can be made firmer by working the first row twisted. Another way is to twist the loops before placing them on the needle (knitted version), or picking them up with the needle (crochet version). But even these tricks fail to make it ideal for firm patterns.

The knitted version is very popular in Britain, where it is often used for the wrong purpose. The crochet version is much faster if you can handle a hook (not that difficult). Always work the first stitch of the first row, whatever the selvedge.

The third version (Peruvian) is much firmer because of the way the stitches are tightened. It also looks different: the chain is back to front and faces the other way. To compare chains, cast on ten stitches with the knitted version, followed by ten more with the Peruvian; fasten the last loop and pull the needle.

Knitted cast-on

Two needles; one strand.
a Make a slip knot.
b Take needle with slip knot in left hand, and free needle in right hand.

2.27

c K into slip knot (Fig 2.27) and place new st onto left needle (Fig 2.28).

Repeat **c,** always knitting into the last made st.

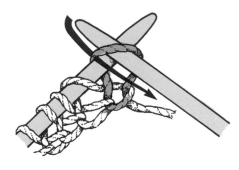

2.28

Crochet cast-on

One thick hook; one strand.

a **Crochet** a very loose **chain** (Fig 2.51), 1 link for each st required.

b Draw a long last loop to stop any unravelling.

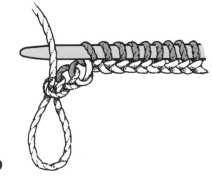

2.29

c Turn the chain back to front if you are right-handed.

d Pick up top of each link with a knitting needle, starting with the 1st link (Fig 2.29).

e Tighten last loop.

Peruvian cast-on

One needle; one strand. I was shown this by an Indian from Taquile Island (Lake Titicaca).

a With needle in left hand, loop yarn as for **slip knot**, but draw short end through circle with right thumb; place circle on needle; grasp the two yarn ends firmly in left hand and pull loop on right thumb to tighten the knot (Fig 2.30).

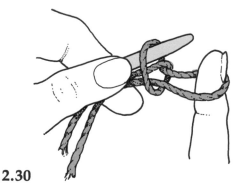

2.30

b With right hand, wind non-slipping end of the long, loose loop up back of needle (omit this step first time round).

c Draw free end of yarn through loop.

d Keeping free yarn firmly in left hand, pull it through loop with right hand (Fig 2.31).

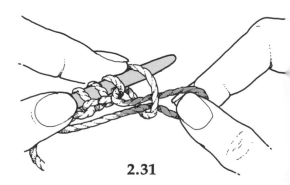

2.31

This will tighten loop around needle and form a new long loop.

Repeat **b** to **d**. Place last loop on needle and tighten.

Cast-off cast-on   S

Another chain method, but this time it is the back of the link that makes the stitch. Popular in Japan.

Looks exactly like **chain cast-off**. If the loops are not taken off the hook and reversed, the resulting chain is **twisted**.

a Take needle in left hand and **crochet hook** with **slip knot** in right hand.

b Place needle over long strand, held in left hand.

c With hook, draw a loop over needle and through slip knot (Fig 2.32).

d Place yarn again under needle.

e Remove hook from its loop and insert it again from the other side.

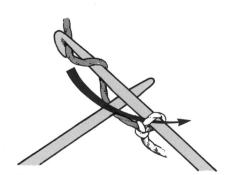

2.32

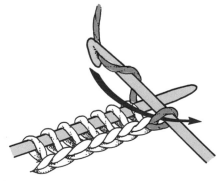

2.33

Repeat **c** to **e** (Fig 2.33) until 1 st short from number required. Transfer last loop from hook to needle after **d**.

Twice knitted cast-on   S

Two needles; one strand.

Originally devised for **twice-knit knitting**. A good decorative cast-on. Useful for edges to be **fringed**.

Work loosely on very-thick needles. Whatever the **selvedge**, always work the first stitch of the first row.

a Make a **slip knot**.

b Cast on 1 st following **knitted** method.

c Continue as for **knitted cast-on** but always **k2 tog** (insert right needle into the last 2 sts made, from left to right – Fig 2.34).

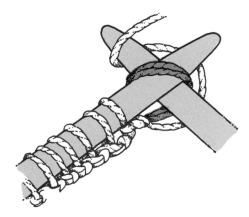

2.34

Cable cast-on   U

Two needles; one strand.

A firm, cord-like edge. Not very elastic.

Work loosely or progress will be slow and uneven. Whatever the **selvedges**, always work the first stitch and **twist** the last stitch of the first row.

a Make a **slip knot**.

b Cast on 1 st following **knitted** method.

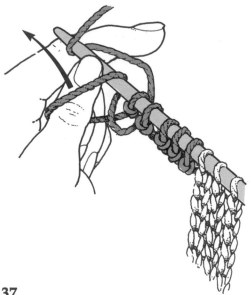

2.35

c Continue as for **knitted cast-on** but insert needle behind last st (Fig 2.35).

Alternate cable cast-on   S

Two strands; one needle.
A **cable cast-on** variation. Good for **single ribbing**, although **tubular** and **Channel Islands cast-ons** are even better.
● Proceed as for **cable** but **k** behind one stitch, then **p** behind following stitch (Fig 2.36) – as a rule, **k** if the yarn is at **front of work**, **p** if it is at **back of work**.

2.36

If last cast-on st was purl, start 1st row of ribbing with **p.** If it was a knit, start with **k.** On this 1st row, the **k** sts must be worked through back of loop.

Buttonhole cast-on   U

One needle: one strand (Fig 2.37).
Like a series of **slip knots** worked from one single end. Best used for **buttonholes** and for adding stitches at the end of rows in firm fabrics.
Avoid gaps between knots. The instructions

2.37

give the hand position that minimises gaps.
a With yarn in right hand, lift yarn from behind with left thumb, moving clockwise.
b Catch strand in front of thumb with needle, as in **twisted loop cast-on.**
c With right hand pass yarn under and up front of needle.
d Pass left-thumb loop over tip of needle.
e Remove thumb from loop and place on top of needle, securing new st.
f Pull yarn with right hand to tighten st. Make sure that final loop goes all the way around needle.

Provisional cast-on   U

Sometimes called **invisible.** Three methods, all using a contrast, preferably **slippery yarn** as foundation. This is later **unravelled** to free the loops for **grafting** or **picking up** – either for a **fringe**, for an **edging cast-off**, or to work in the opposite direction. One stitch may need to be **increased** in the last case.
Stocking stitch will show no break if cast on

at mid-height, but most patterns will. **Provisional cast-on** is best used at a change-of-pattern line.

The **looping** method sometimes uses the main yarn as foundation; this can later be pulled to gather the edge if desired. In the other two methods, if the edge is to be gathered with the same colour yarn, this has to be threaded later – leave a long end.

Once you master it, **looping** is fastest. **Two-strand** will give neat results first time without having to learn extra tricks. **Crochet** is very cunning, faster than **two-strand** and very easy if you can **crochet** a **chain** (Fig 2.51).

Two-strand provisional cast-on

Cast on in a contrast yarn. Continue in main yarn and main pattern. When appropriate, snip the cast-on, stitch by stitch, and pull to free the loops.

Methods other than **two-strand** can equally be used. One of the **loop** methods would be easiest to unpick.

Crochet provisional cast-on

This is popular in Japan.

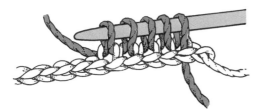

2.38

a With contrast yarn, **crochet** a **chain** – 1 link for each st required plus 1. Cut yarn and pull last loop.

b With main yarn, **pick up** a st from each link. This must be done from the loop at the back of the link. Do not pick up any sts from last link made (Fig 2.38). One **k** row made.

When required, pull back of last link. Chain will unravel leaving loops free.

Looping provisional cast-on

a Make a **slip knot** at one end of a foundation yarn, of a length over twice the required width.

b Make another **slip knot** in main yarn. Leave a long end only if of use later.

c Take needle in right hand and yarn in left hand as in **German two-strand cast-on**, with the foundation yarn around thumb. Taking one strand in each hand is possible but slower.

d With a flick of right wrist, catch main yarn from underneath, working from centre out (Fig 2.39a).

e With another flick of the wrist, go under foundation yarn, from the front (still Fig

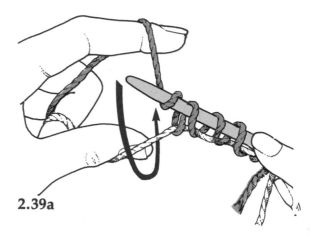

2.39a

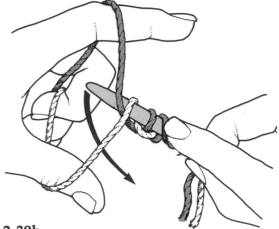

2.39b

2.39a); catch main yarn from the top and bring it up from under foundation yarn (Fig 2.39b).

Repeat **d** and **e**. The main yarn must make a full loop around needle. If it only goes halfway, use a thicker needle or two needles held together.

Drop the contrast slip knot at end of 1st row. Tie the 2 foundation ends.

Tubular cast-on   U

Sometimes called **invisible**. It can be applied to a wide range of patterns, but is best known for the beautifully rounded edge it gives to **tubular stocking stitch** and **single rib** (Fig 2.40).

2.40

In edges expected to stretch and recover (cuffs, waistbands etc) it may tend to wave. Always work with needles two or three sizes finer than for the pattern to follow, but do not work it too tight. Try a **sample** first.

It can be achieved in a number of ways.

Two-strand tubular cast-on
One needle; two strands.

The fastest method, once you have the knack. The wrist movements are NOT as in **looping provisional cast-on**.

a Make a **slip knot**, leaving a free end 4 times the desired width (shown here in contrast colour for clarity).

b Keep both yarns in left hand as in **German two-strand cast-on**, with the free end around thumb. Taking one strand in each hand is possible but slower.

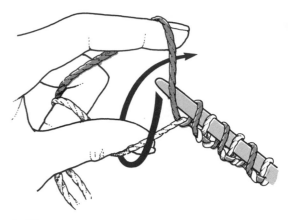

2.41

c With a flick of right wrist, go over and behind the long strand, catch free end from the top and bring it up from under long strand (Fig 2.41).

d With another flick of the wrist, go over and in front of free end, catch long strand from the top and bring it up from under free end (Fig 2.42).

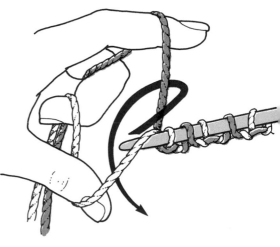

2.42

Repeat **c** and **d**, making sure the sts go all the way around the needle.

e Tie the 2 strands under the needle after the last stitch.

f Work 2 or 4 rows in **tubular st st** – **k** the **k** sts, **sl** the **p** sts **pwise wyif**. The 1st st of the 1st row will be **k** if last cast-on st was a

c, it will be **sl** if last cast-on st was a **d.** On 1st row only, **k-b k** sts.

g Continue in chosen pattern, with ordinary size needles.

For softest results, **single rib** can be started directly after **e.**

Yarn-over tubular cast-on

Not as fast as **two-strand**, but no new tricks to be learnt. Gives an odd number of stitches. For an even number increase one stitch at the end of the first **c** row.

a With a contrast, **slippery yarn**, cast on half the required number of stitches – if the total is an odd number (for example, 101) cast on half a stitch in excess (51). Use **two-strand provisional cast-on** or **crochet provisional cast-on** (combine the picking-up step with **b** below).

b With main yarn, **k1** row, **increasing** after each st (except the last) by wrapping yarn under, then up front of needle (Fig 2.43).

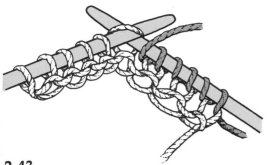

2.43

c Work 2 or 4 rows in **tubular st st** – **k1, sl1 wyif** on 1st row; reverse order on 2nd row.

d Continue in chosen pattern with ordinary size needles.

e Unpick contrast cast-on.

A variation, not so easy to work evenly, casts on the required number of stitches with the **looping provisional cast-on**, then continues from **c.**

Another variation, somewhat tighter, changes **b**: **k** 1 row, then work 1 row in **single rib**, knitting the sts on the needle and purl-ing the horizontal strands between every 2 sts. The 1st row of **c** then starts with a **sl st**. A loose loop may appear at one end after un-picking the contrast yarn (see **neatening loops**).

Stocking-stitch tubular cast-on

The slowest method, but not to be dismissed (see also **tubular horizontal hems**).

a With a contrast, **slippery yarn**, cast on half the required number of stitches. Deduct half a stitch if total is an odd number (if total is 101, cast on 50). Use any cast-on method.

b **P** 1 row, then **k** 1 **elongated** row – wrap the yarn twice around the needle for each st.

c With main yarn, work 4 rows in **st st**, starting with a **p** row.

d With a fine needle, pick up the loops of main yarn showing through the elongated sts.

e Work 1 row in **single rib**, alternating **p1** from original needle and **k1** from fine needle (making sure sts are not twisted) (Fig 2.44). **Increase** 1 st at end of row if an odd total is required.

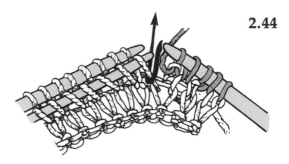

2.44

Continue in chosen pattern with ordinary size needles. Snip the elongated row at one end and pull it from the other end. This will free the edge.

It is possible to omit **b**. Simply use one of the **provisional cast-on** methods and unravel it before **d**.

It is also possible to omit **d**, and knit the loops of main yarn in **e** without the help of a third needle.

Tubular cast-on for double rib   S

A perfect edge for **double rib** has proved elusive. This **tubular** variation is slanted, but at least has been designed with **double rib** in mind (Fig 2.45).

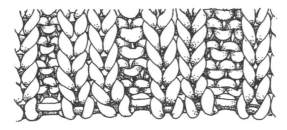

2.45

• Proceed as for **stocking-stitch tubular cast-on**, but **p** 2 sts from the ordinary needle, then **k** 2 sts from the finer needle.

If total number of stitches is a multiple of 4, the resulting rib will start with **p2** and end with **k2**. If it is a multiple of 2, but not of 4, **cast on** 1 st extra in contrast, then **decrease** 1 st at each end of last **st st** row. The resulting rib will start and end with **p2** (**k2** if other side is used).

A variation uses one of the other two methods, but at the end of the **tubular stocking stitch** continues in **double rib**, dropping every other **k** st and picking it up again after the **p** st next to it has been worked (Fig 2.46).

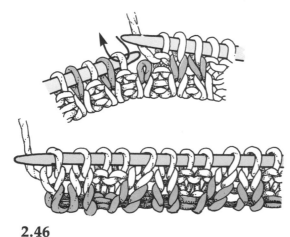

2.46

Frilled cast-on   S

A clever trick for a frilly edge.
a Cast on twice the required number of sts, either with a **decorative** or a **lace** method
b **K2 tog,** or **p2 tog** all along 1st row.
Fig 2.47 shows the results in **knotted cast-on** and **reverse stocking stitch**.

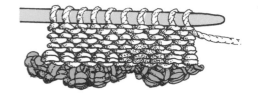

2.47

Edging cast-on   S

Strictly for fun lovers.
a Knit anything long and narrow that would make a good trim, such as **pico cord, slip cord, picot-point chain,** or one of the many **edgings** to be found in pattern dictionaries (see **Books**).
b **Pick up** the necessary stitches from the most convenient place along the trim, and work from there.
Do not rely on the number of rows required for the **edging** as being the same as the number of stitches to be cast on. You may need more, or less, rows. You may even want to make the edge twice as long and gather it when picking up the stitches. Work **samples**.
It might be possible to carry the edging up

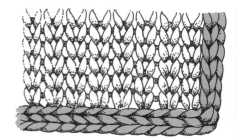

2.48

the side as **selvedge** (Fig 2.48, showing a **slip cord**). To turn the corner in narrow edgings, start picking up a few rows below the last row. In wide edgings you may need a **mitred corner**.

The first row can add to the decoration. The loops of the **picot cord** in Fig 2.49 have been picked up from the back with the second needle, working from left to right. The right needle was at the right end, holding the last two stitches. The first row is a line of **eyelets**.

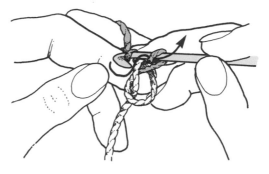

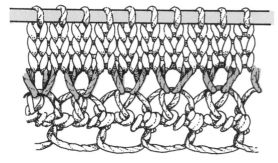

2.49

Pinhole cast-on   S

For any work that starts from one central point.

Avoid casting on directly on a set of needles. It is too awkward for good results. **Crochet-hook** methods are best.

Tiniest hole cast-on

a Wrap yarn around index finger of left hand.

b Draw through a loop with hook.

c Remove finger from circle. Secure circle between finger and thumb.

d Draw a new loop through loop on hook (Fig 2.50a).

Repeat **b** and **d** until you have enough sts for 1st needle. Transfer sts from hook to needle. Continue on sts for 2nd needle (Fig 2.50b). When work is completed, pull free end tight and **darn**.

2.50b

Larger hole cast-on

a Make a crochet chain, 1 link for each st (Fig 2.51).

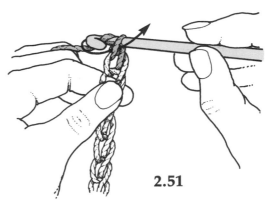

2.51

b Close chain by drawing a loop through 1st link.

c Draw a loop through each link until you have enough for 1st needle (Fig 2.52).

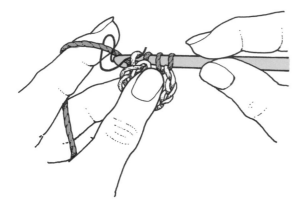

2.52

d Transfer sts from hook to 1st needle and repeat **c** for each of the other needles.
To tighten up hole, sew inside edge of links with the yarn tail using a **running stitch**. Pull, then **darn** free end.

Centre line cast-on   s

Oval and rectangular work often starts from a line across the centre. There are two solutions, using whatever cast-on blends in best with the pattern – either by disappearing or by creating a bold line.

Sewn cast-on

a With a **circular needle**, or a **set of needles**, cast on twice the number of sts required for the centre line.

b Close the circle and work in **rounds**. **Cast off**.

c Spread the work flat and **seam** the 2 sides of the cast-on (Fig 2.53).

Two-way cast-on

More fiddly, but easier to check progress.

a Cast on the centre-line sts, plus 1, on the 1st needle of a set of 5.

b **Pick up** the same number of sts from the cast-on edge, with the 2nd needle.

c Work in rounds. The short sides are worked on the other 2 needles, from the extra cast-on st (Fig 2.54).

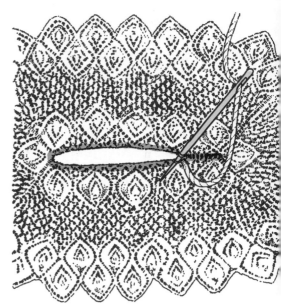

2.53

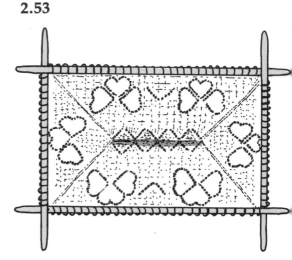

2.54

CASTING OFF

A cast-off is the row that closes the free loops, so that they cannot **unravel**. Most of the comments on **casting on** apply, with obvious adaptations, to casting off.

Tension samples are not so essential. Check the cast-off as you go along, and **unravel** if it pulls or waves. But samples may still be needed to compare methods and decide whether to cast off on the **right** or the **wrong** side.

If **increases** or **decreases** are necessary, work them discreetly and evenly on the actual cast-off row.

If the last few stitches tend to be untidy, watch the way you **hold the needles**. You may be stretching these stitches by moving the left needle too much (see **neatening loops** for how to deal with a long last loop). Before trimming the yarn, check that the cast-off does not pull and make sure that the work has no major errors. Leave a yarn tail long enough for **darning** or sewing.

Choosing a cast-off

Chain cast-off is essential to know.
Provisional and **diagonal** are both easy and very useful.
Tubular requires some effort, but is worth it. All the others are covered in the following guide (within each group, methods are in the order in which they appear in the book).

ORDINARY EDGES
chain

BUTTONHOLES
chain

CROCHET EDGINGS
chain

CROSSED FABRICS
chain, working in pattern
decrease variation

DECORATIVE EDGES
Working in pattern sometimes will spoil the effect. Maintain tension with **increases** and **decreases**. Choose either for contrast or to blend in.
double crochet
decrease
picot point
edging

cast-on
frilled
tubular
backstitch
stem stitch
long chain

FRINGED EDGES
two-row
provisional
long chain

GATHERED EDGES
two-row
one-over-two

HEMS
provisional

JOINS
seam

LACE
suspended
edging
long chain

REINFORCED EDGES
double crochet

RIBBINGS
chain as a last resort
two-row
decrease
tubular
tubular for double rib

SLOPED EDGES
diagonal

TEMPORARY EDGES
provisional

TUBULAR FABRICS
For a closed edge:
basic, slipping every other stitch
two-row
one-over-two

tubular
seam
For an open edge:
Slip stitches onto two needles and cast off
according to required style.

TWICE-KNIT FABRICS
one-over-two

Chain cast-off E

The most widely used cast-off (for a perfect
match, see **cast-off cast-on**). It is often knitted too tight. For best results the working
loop should be loosened up each time; this is
preferable to using a thicker needle or hook.
Always cast off in pattern, following **knit,
purl, slip stitches, overs, decreases** etc. If
any stitches are dropped to create **ladders**,
bridge the gaps with **long chain cast-off** unless you want to gather the top of the ladder.
Cast off free edges of **stocking stitch** and **garter stitch** on the **wrong side**, to hide the chain
(Fig 2.55).

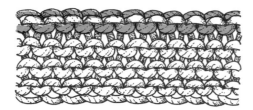

2.55

This cast-off can be worked in three ways.
Use **basic** unless you prefer to **crochet** rather
than knit. Use **suspended** if the yarn is not
resilient, or you cannot loosen the tension
enough.

Basic cast-off

a Work 2 sts.
b With left needle pull the 1st st over 2nd st
and off the needle (Fig 2.56).
c Work another st and pull previous one
over it.

2.56

Repeat **c** to the last st. Trim yarn and pull
loop.
If casting off purl stitches, either lift the st
from the other side of the needle, or take
yarn to back of work before lifting the stitch.
If instructed to cast off a certain number of
stitches, what count are the times that you
pull a stitch over another stitch. The loop on
the right needle after casting off a group of
stitches is not considered cast off. If you may
have to 'pattern 5', that loop is the first of the
five. **Lace** patterns might not follow this convention.

Crochet cast-off

Hold yarn in left hand and keep at back.
a **Sl** 1st st p'wise onto hook.
b Insert hook into next st and drop the st
from left needle.
c Catch yarn with hook and draw through
the 2 sts (Fig 2.57).
Repeat **b** and **c**.

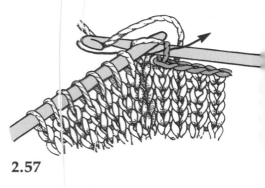

2.57

spended cast-off

rk as for **basic**, but keep lifted stitch on
needle. Work the next stitch on left nee-
(Fig 2.58) and drop them both together.

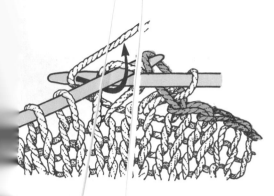

8

ouble crochet
st-off   S

variation of **crochet chain** – a row of
ble crochet is worked directly onto the
loops. Strong and elastic. Quite decora-
on the **wrong side** if worked with a con-
t yarn (Fig 2.59). Good base for **crochet
ings** (but not necessarily for **crab stitch**).
d yarn in left hand and keep at back.

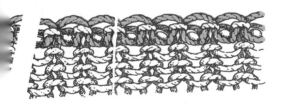

59

K 1st st with hook: insert hook into st,
catch yarn from **underneath** and draw it
through the st.
Drop st from left needle.
K next st with hook and drop from needle.
Catch yarn with hook and draw through
the 2 sts on hook (Fig 2.60).
peat **c** and **d**.

2.60

Two-row cast-off   S

Good for **tubular** fabrics (Fig 2.61). Not bad
for **ribbings**, but not as good as **tubular**. Useful for **fringed** edges.

2.61

a Work 1st row in **single rib**, pulling the
 knits over the purls as in **basic cast-off**,
 but not the purls over the knits. Half the
 original sts left.
b Trim yarn.
c Cast off remaining sts on a 2nd row, but
 without working them – simply **sl pwise**
 onto right needle, one at a time, and pull
 the previous one over.
d Sew down last st.

For a gathered edge on any fabric, **k** all the
sts on the 1st row.

In **ribbings**, work both the cast-off and the
row before it very loosely if you want an elastic edge. If necessary, use a thicker needle.

Decrease cast-off   U

Decorative. Much better than **chain** for ribbings, but not as good as **tubular**. Try alter-

nating knit with purl: **k** if 2nd st on left needle is a **k** st, **p** if it is a **p** st.
a **K2 tog,** through front.
b **Sl** new st back onto left needle without twisting.
Repeat **a** and **b** (Fig 2.62).
Variation: **k-b** the 2 sts to give a **chain cast-off** with a **twisted** last row.

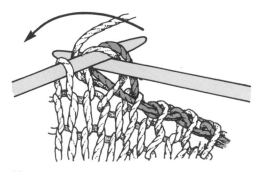

2.62

One-over-two cast-off S

Normally used in **twice-knit** and **tubular knitting**. In ordinary knitting it gathers the fabric, especially when it is a naturally spreading fabric (Fig 2.63).

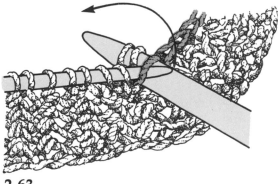

2.63

Work as for **basic chain cast-off** but:
● work 3 sts onto right needle and pull 1st st over the other 2.
You might need an extra thick needle, especially for **twice-knit knitting**.
Always **k** if gathering the edge whatever the pattern. Alternate **k** and **p** in tubular fabrics.

Picot point cast-off S

Very pretty.
● Work a **picot point chain** but **k** and **cast off** each time 1 st more than you **cast on**.

2.64

The picots can also be spaced. The stitches in between are cast off in **chain** or decrease. Fig 2.64 shows a **picot and chain cast-off**.

Edging cast-off S

Bold decoration, on the same principle as the non-spaced **picot point cast-off**. Good for matching an **edging cast-on**.
a Take needle with sts to be cast off in left hand.
b Cast on a few extra sts for an edging: **moss stitch, garter stitch** or other border; **slip cord, lace edging** etc.
Invert **a** and **b** if casting on with needle in right hand.
Knit the edging, working together one of the stitches to be cast off with the first edging stitch whenever needed to keep the edging

2.65

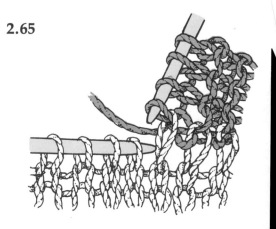

flat or suitably gathered. Do this on a back row, a front row, or on both (Fig 2.65). See **decreases** for best method for a particular case.

Cast-on cast-off S

Another decorative method. To be used in its own right or to reflect a **decorative cast-on** (see also **cast-on selvedges**).
● Join a 2nd yarn at front of work and use it to cast on an extra st for every st you cast off. Then, unless you want a frilled edge, cast off the new st together with the st next in line.

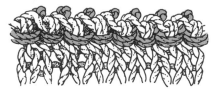

2.66

Possibilities are endless, although not all cast-on methods are adaptable. Results will also be affected by the cast-off used. Experiment to find cast-on/cast-off combinations that work for you.
Fig 2.66 shows a **multi-strand cast-on** teamed with a **decrease cast-off**. Both the new stitch and the stitch already on right needle are transferred to left needle. Three stitches are then knitted together.

Frilled cast-off S

More fun and games.
● Work any of the cast-offs described so far, but **increase** 1 st after every st. The increase may, or may not, leave a hole.
Fig 2.67 shows a **frilled decrease cast-off**. The increases are made by knitting into 1st st on left needle without dropping it. Transfer the 2 sts now on right needle to left needle, **k2 tog** as in **decrease cast-off**. Transfer the new st to left needle and **k2 tog** again.

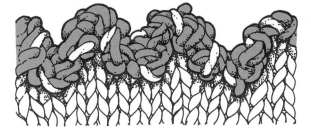

2.67

Provisional cast-off U

The easiest of them all. Use when stitches are to be left in waiting for any reason: **grafting, fringing, measuring** etc.
● With a **sewing needle**, thread a piece of yarn through all the sts, dropping them off the knitting needle (Fig 2.68).

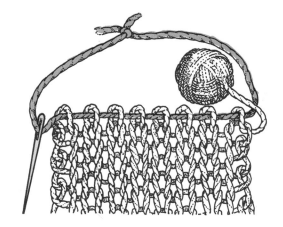

2.68

Use the main yarn if you want to gather the work. Otherwise a contrast, **slippery yarn** is best. Use a long piece that can be tied in a huge loop without drawing in the knitting.

Tubular cast-off U

Also called **invisible**.
A sewn cast-off that makes a perfect match for **tubular cast-on** (Fig 2.69). Ideal for

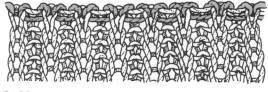

2.69

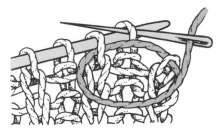

2.71

neckline **ribbings**, but work very loosely or your head will not go through.

Learn **knit grafting** before you tackle it.

a Work at least 2 rows in **tubular st st**. In **single rib** this is not strictly necessary, but it makes life easier. Remember that 2 tubular rows equal 1 ordinary row.

b With working yarn trimmed to about 4 times the length to be cast off, **graft** the front (1-row deep) layer of **st st** to the back layer.

To practise, **slip** the front stitches onto a **double-pointed needle**. Do the same with the back stitches. **Graft** with a contrast yarn. You should obtain a series of Vs on the top edge. When confident, try the one-needle approach. Starting with a front (**k**) stitch:

a Insert sewing needle **kwise** into 1st st. Drop st (Fig 2.70).

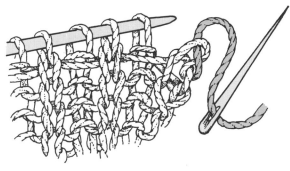

2.70

b Insert sewing needle **pwise** into 3rd (**k**) st. Do not drop st. Pull yarn through, not too tight.

c Insert sewing needle **pwise** into 2nd (**p**) st. Drop st (Fig 2.71).

d Insert sewing needle **kwise** into 4th (**p**) st. Do not drop st. Pull yarn through (Fig 2.72).

Repeat **a** to **d**.

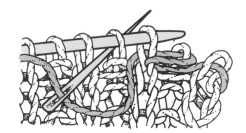

2.72

With practice, all four stitches can be dropped as soon as the sewing needle has gone through them, and the process can be cut down to two movements: **a** and **b**; **c** and **d**.

Tubular cast-off for double rib s

For masters of **tubular cast-off** on one needle. The cast-off has a slant, like **tubular cast-on for double rib**.

For the tubular rows:

● k 1st **k** st and **sl** 2nd **pwise wyab**;
● p 1st **p** st and **sl** 2nd **pwise wyif**.

Graft loosely. Assuming that the first two stitches are **k**:

a Insert sewing needle into 1st st **pwise**. Pull yarn.

b Working round back of **k** sts, insert needle **kwise** into 1st **p** st. Pull yarn. (Similar to Fig 2.77 below.)

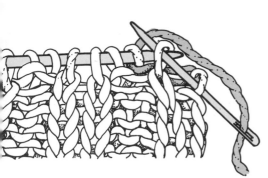

73

Insert needle into 1st **k** st **kwise**. Drop st and go **pwise** into 2nd **k** st. Pull yarn (Fig 2.73).

Working round back of **k** sts, insert needle into 1st **p** st **pwise**, then into 2nd **p** st

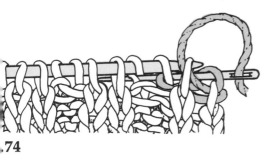

74

kwise. Pull yarn (Fig 2.74).

Insert needle into 2nd **k** st **kwise**. Drop st and go **pwise** into 3rd **k** st. Drop 1st **p** st. Pull yarn (Fig 2.75).

75

Insert needle into 2nd **p** st **pwise**. Drop it. Pull yarn (Fig 2.76).

2.76

g Working round back of 3rd and 4th **k** sts, insert needle **kwise** into 3rd **p** st. Pull yarn (Fig 2.77).

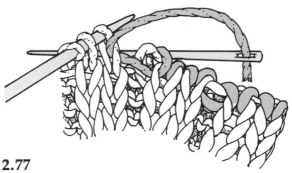

2.77

Repeat from **c** to **g**, reading 3rd st where it says 1st, etc.

Straighten up the loops as they come off the needle. The grafting should make a clear line of Vs. With practice, the stitches at the tip of the needle can be dropped as soon as the yarn has gone through.

Backstitch cast-off   U

A subtle, decorative method also achieved with a sewing needle (Fig 2.78). Also called

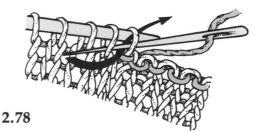

2.78

sewn cast-off or cast-on cast-off.

Will stretch the edge of fabrics that draw in, such as **ribbing**. This is used to advantage in a related technique: **free-loop backstitch seam**.

Use a length of yarn 4 to 5 times the width.
a Insert needle into 1st 2 sts **pwise**. Pull yarn.
b Insert needle into 1st st **kwise**. Drop st and pull yarn.

Repeat **a** and **b**.

Stem stitch cast-off   U

Another subtle, sewn cast-off, reminiscent of **loop cast-on**.

Use a length of yarn 4 to 5 times the width.
a Insert needle into 2nd st **kwise**.
b Insert needle into 1st st **pwise**, drawing the needle under cast-off strand (Fig 2.79).
c Drop 1st st and pull yarn.

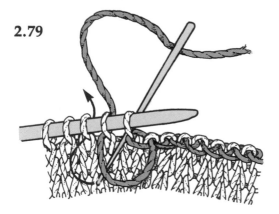

2.79

Repeat **a** to **c**. Ease cast-off up to the edge.

Or, from the **wrong side**, work as for **backstitch cast-off** but, in **a**, insert needle **pwise** into the 2nd st only, working round back of 1st st.

A variation, working from left to right, is known as **outline stitch cast-off**.

Long chain cast-off   S

A very decorative crochet cast-off.
Traditionally used in knitted **lace** mats,

where it greatly helps **stretching** when blocking or drying. It can be used for solid fabrics too.

a Sl last st onto hook.
b Crochet a **chain**, long enough for a picot loop when work is stretched (as in Fig 3.22).
c Insert hook into a group of sts (at least 3). Catch yarn with hook, from underneath, and pull through sts (Fig 2.80).

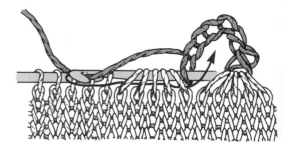

2.80

d Catch yarn again and pull through the 2 loops on hook (Fig 2.81).

Repeat **b** to **d**.

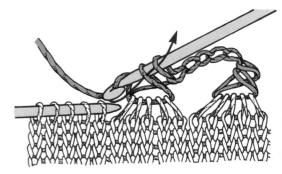

2.81

Diagonal cast-off   U

For sloping edges, such as sweater shoulders.

Cast off the sts in groups, every other row. For 2 symmetrical slopes, cast off the right slope on the **right side** and the left slope on the **wrong side**.

Two ways of avoiding 'steps'. Work a **dart** and cast off all the stitches in one go. Or, be cunning:

a Having cast off 1st group, do not work last st on return row. Turn work, 1 st on right needle.
b **Sl** 1st st on left needle **pwise** (Fig 2.82).

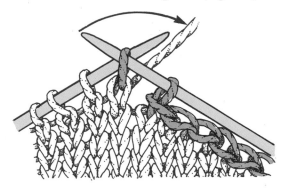

2.82

c Pass 1st st on right needle over **sl st**. First st of the new group is now cast off. Continue in usual way.
Adapt this method if using a cast-off other than **chain**.

Seam cast-off U

(See also **Grafting** and **Seams and joins**).
For **tubular** fabrics or to join two pieces without sewing them up.
Done from the **wrong side** (the two right sides facing), or from the **right side** (wrong sides facing). Two symmetrical cast-offs (for example, shoulders) must be started from the same end if worked on the **right side**. **Tubular** fabrics must be divided onto two needles.
● Proceed as for **basic cast-off**, but keep working together 1 st from each needle (Fig 2.83). If you want the cast-off chain to sit astride the top edges, and look the same from both sides, work in **single rib** (**k tog** the 1st st from each needle, **p tog** the 2nd st from each needle, etc).

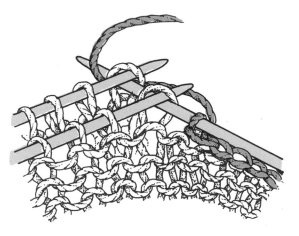

2.83

Many of the other casting-off methods explained could be adapted.

APPLICATIONS
(See also **cast-on cast-off cords**)

Picot point knitting S

(See also **edging cast-on**, **picot-point cast-off**, **picot-point selvedge** and **picot-point fringe**)
A truly ingenious way of knitting lacy structures.

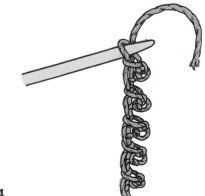

2.84

To make a **picot** you need one stitch on the left needle (a **slip knot** for the first picot):

a **Knitted cast-on** 2 (or more) sts.

b **Basic cast-off** same number of sts. One st left.

c **Sl** st onto left needle, without twisting.

Repeating **a**, **b** and **c** gives a **chain** (Fig 2.84). Chains can be made into circles by **knitting on** between two previous picots. Small circles can be made into larger circles, and so on (Fig 2.85).

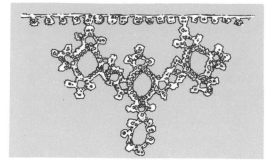

2.85

Knit and purl

Knit stitch

The basic **knitted stitch** worked from the smooth side. Fig 2.86 shows the most popular (**plain**) version (**k**):

2.86

a With yarn at back, insert right needle into 1st st on left needle, from front to back.

b Pass yarn under and up the front of right needle.

c Draw yarn through st with right needle.

d Drop original st from left needle.

If, instead, the needle is inserted through the back of the loop (**knit-back** or **k-b**), the original stitch becomes **twisted** (Fig 2.87). That is, unless the yarn is wrapped over the needle rather than under it, as in the second version of the plain stitch (Fig 2.88). Inserting the needle through the front of the loop will now produce a **plaited** stitch (Fig 2.89). This is like a **twisted** stitch going the other way.

Note that the stitches look different on the needles depending on whether the yarn is wrapped over or under.

2.87

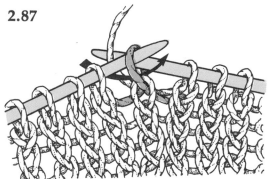

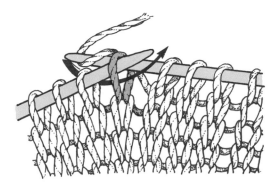

2.88

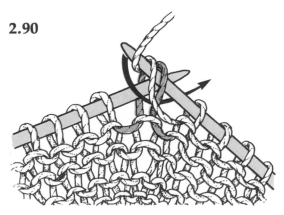

2.89

Purl stitch   E

The basic **knitted stitch** worked from the rugged side. The common version (**p**) is shown in Fig 2.90:

a With yarn in front, insert right needle into 1st st on left needle, from back to front.

2.90

b Pass yarn over, down the back and under needle.

c Draw yarn through st with right needle.

d Drop original st from left needle.

For a **twisted** stitch (Fig 2.91), insert needle through the back of the loop (**purl-back** or **p-b**).

2.91

Wrapping the yarn under the needle gives an untwisted stitch if the loop is worked from the back (Fig 2.92), and a **plaited** stitch if worked from the front (Fig 2.93).

2.92

2.93

APPLICATIONS

(See also **fabric character**)

Knit and purl can be combined into a huge range of fabrics, but remember:

● Knit stitches are smooth; the yarn is at the back.

● Purl stitches are bumpy; the yarn is at the front.

● To knit after purling, or vice versa, take yarn to the other side under the needles (see **yarn under**).

● Knit stands up from purl in vertical arrangements, it recedes in horizontal ones.

● Fabrics may 'draw in' (**ribbings**), 'draw up' (**welts**), look embossed (**brocades**) or wave all over (see **pleats**), depending on how knit and purl are combined.

● Fabrics may **curl** in or out. They may also be **flat**.

● A firm **tension** will give best results.

● **Twisting** or **plaiting** increases elasticity, texture and firmness. If extra firmness is not required, use thicker needles.

● Non-twisted stitches are easier to work.

● To work in **rounds**, read knit for purl, and purl for knit, on **wrong-side** rows.

Garter stitch E

A **flat**, slow growing fabric (Fig 2.94). It 'draws up' so much that one stitch and two rows can sometimes produce a perfect square (see **stitch shape**). Often used for **borders**.

2.94

Each bump equals two rows. Both sides are alike: a succession of horizontal ridges with vertical elasticity. Worked sideways it can sometimes replace **single rib**.

All rows: k (or **p**).

Stocking stitch E

'The' knitted fabric; taken as norm when assessing width and height of other fabrics. Top and bottom **curl out**. Sides **curl in**. The **knit** side (**st st**) is smooth (Fig 2.95). The **purl** side (**reverse st st**) is very lumpy (Fig 2.96) and curls in the opposite way. On the knit side, each V is a row.

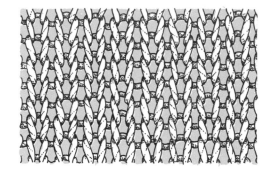

2.95

2.96

Row 1: k.
Row 2: p.
Yarn-in-left-hand knitters sometimes **knit-back** then wrap the yarn under the needle when **purling**. Easier and more even (see **purl stitches too large**).

Knitting as in Fig 2.87 and purling as in Fig 2.91 gives **twisted st st** (Fig 2.87).

Knitting as in Fig 2.87 but purling in the ordinary way gives **half-twisted st st** – one row is twisted and the next not.

Knitting as in Fig 2.89 and purling as in Fig 2.93 gives **plaited st st** (Fig 2.89).

Knitting as in Fig 2.89 and purling as in Fig 2.92 gives **half-plaited st st** – one row is plaited and the next not.

Twisted and **plaited st st** sometimes slant to right or left. If this happens, it cannot be totally corrected, but **blocking** straight might help. See also **close-bead knitting** and **slanted fabrics**.

Half-twisted and **half-plaited st st** keep every other row straight and are less prone to slant.

Moss stitch U

A **flat**, thickish fabric that grows fairly slowly (Fig 2.97). Very good for **borders**.
Row 1: *k1, p1* to end.
Row 2: k the p sts, p the k sts.

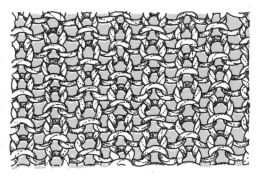

2.97

Ribbings U

(See also **planning for seams, choosing a cast-on** and **choosing a cast-off**)
Vertical combinations of knit and purl; also called **ribs**. Very strong 'drawing in' tendency.

Ideal for cuffs, waistbands etc because of their great elasticity.

Work tightly. Needles one, two, or even more, sizes finer than for **stocking stitch** are standard practice, because the vertical arrangement of **yarn unders** increases the **stitch size** (see **fabric character**). **Knitted-in borders** will often require you to pull the yarn firmly in order to increase the **yarn tension**, or to place the border stitches on short double-pointed needles of the appropriate thickness; change from border needles to main needles as for **circular knitting**.

Firmness and elasticity are increased by **twisting** or **plaiting**. They are lost by using yarns, such as cotton or silk, with little **resilience**.

Ribbings can be **regular** (same number of stitches are first knitted, then purled) or **irregular** (more, or fewer, stitches are knitted than purled). If the last stitch of a group of two or more **knit** stitches looks too large, see **uneven fabrics**.

● Two **rows**. The 1st sets the sequence. The 2nd is always: **k** the **k** sts, **p** the **p** sts. Most common ribbings:

Single (1 × 1) rib
Fig 2.98.
Row 1: *k1, p1* to end.
Row 2: see above.

2.98

Double (2 × 2) rib
'Draws in' more than **single rib** (Fig 2.99).
Row 1: *k2, p2* to end.
Row 2: see above.

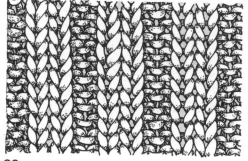

2.99

Welts U

Combinations of knit rows and purl rows, resulting in **garter stitch** or **reverse stocking stitch** raised stripes on a **stocking stitch** background. Strong tendency to 'draw up'. **Reverse stocking stitch** welts have deepest furrows. Do not try to **block** them flat; you will waste your time and ruin a dramatic effect in the process.

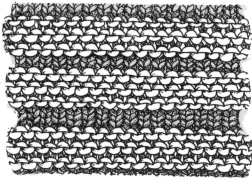

2.100

Any combination of rows is possible. Fig 2.100 shows:
Rows 1, 3, 5, 6 and 8: k.
Rows 2, 4 and 7: p.

Brocades S

Purl stitches forming simple or elaborate designs and motifs on a knit background. Work from a **chart** (Fig 2.101).

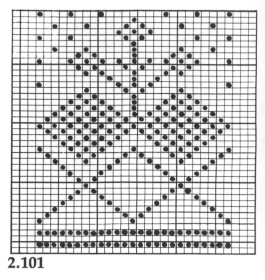

2.101

Other patterns U

Triangles, checkerboards, diagonals, chevrons, basketweaves, diamonds, crosses, pyramids etc can be worked in knit and purl. Get yourself a good pattern dictionary (see **Books**). Or, better still, a thick pad of **ratio graph paper**.

Spiral knitting S

A **circular-knitting** variation of **ribbing**. Useful for down-to-earth purposes (heel-less socks, hats), but also good for having fun (Fig 2.102).

2.102

Work a **regular rib**, say, 3 to 6 sts **k** and the same **p**. At regular intervals, say, every 4 to 10 rows, move rib 1 st over. Move either to the right or to left, but always in same direction. Move often for greater twist.

Short rows

Also called **turning**.

Rows, or **rounds**, do not need to be worked from end to end. You can stop anywhere, turn and work backwards.

If only a few stitches are involved, consider working **from left to right** on the return rows.

Avoiding holes   U

Merely turning the work leaves a hole. Depending on the pattern, the hole will be an asset or an eyesore.

There are three ways of avoiding holes. **Over** is the loosest, **catch** is very neat, **tie** is easier and also neat. The instructions given are for **stocking stitch**. Other fabrics may require adaptations.

Tie

a Before turning, take yarn to other side of work.

b Sl next **st pwise**.

c Return yarn to original side of work.

d Sl st back to left needle (Fig 2.103).

2.103

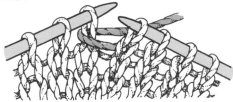

e Turn; work back; **sl** 1st st **pwise** if desired. If the **tie** interferes with your pattern, on the first long row work it together with the stitch it wraps. Insert needle first into the loop lying on the right side of work, from underneath, then into the stitch.

Over

a Turn work.

b Make an **over**.

c Work the short row – **sl** first st **pwise** if desired.

d On 1st long row, work **over** and next st together (Fig 2.104). If this is a **p** row, reverse order of **over** and st: drop **over**, **sl st**, pick up **over**, return st to left needle and **p2 tog**.

2.104

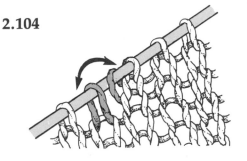

Catch

a Turn work.

b Sl 1st st **pwise** and work short row.

c First long row:
On **k**: pick up strand shown in Fig 2.105 and work it together with next st.

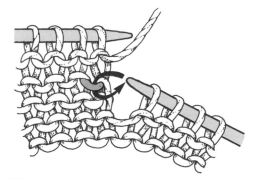

2.105

2.106

On **p:** pick up strand shown in Fig 2.106 and work it together with next st after reversing their order (see **d** in **Over** above).

APPLICATIONS

Horizontal darts   U

A series of increasingly shorter, or longer, rows. They smoothly lengthen one side of the fabric.

Long to short rows (Fig 2.107a) can be combined with short to long rows (Fig 2.107b), to form a **double dart** (Fig 2.107c). Each line in the diagrams is a row.

If working two **symmetrical darts**, one will be turned on **right-side** rows and the other on **wrong-side** rows (Fig 2.107d).

Use **needle markers** to highlight the turns.

To **calculate**, consider the depth of the dart in rows and the width in stitches. Half the

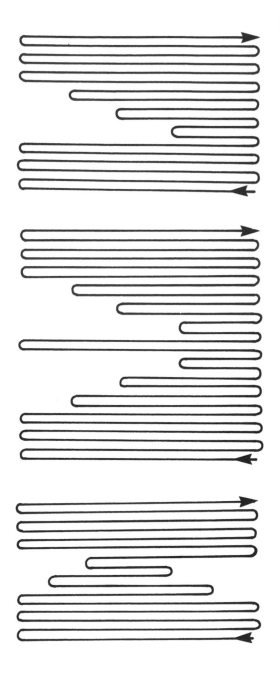

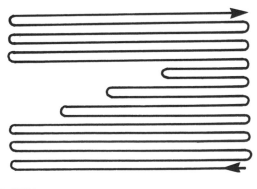

2.107a

number of rows gives the number of turns. Dividing the stitch total by the number of turns tells you by how many stitches each row will be shorter, or longer, than the previous row. If the result has a decimal point, make a few of the turns one stitch shorter, or longer, than the others.

Mitred corners S

(See also **mitred corners** under **Increases and decreases**, under **Hems and casings** and under **Edgings**)
Mitred corners can easily be achieved with a **double horizontal dart** (Fig 2.108).

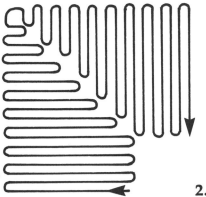

2.108

● For a right angle, leave 1 st unworked each time (and work 1 st extra later on) if the sts are **nearly square**; 2 sts if they are very **wide**; alternate 1 and 2 sts if they are **medium**. For obtuse/acute angles, leave fewer/more sts. Do not use any of the methods explained to avoid holes, but **sl pwise** the 1st st after turning. A neat row of holes will mark the mitre; for no holes, when lengthening the rows, work together **sl st** and head of st below next st.

Row adjustments U

When working vertical or diagonal blocks in different patterns, unless all the patterns have the same row depth, some areas will pull (see **long or short fabrics**). Avoid this by working extra pairs of rows on the shallower patterns as required (Fig 2.109).
● Either keep checking and adding short rows until a sequence is established, or calculate the sequence beforehand from **samples**: if Pattern One has 30 rows in 10cm (4in), and Pattern Two has 34 rows, add 2 rows to Pattern Two every 15 rows.

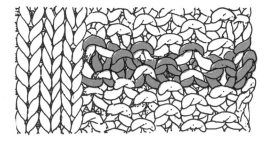

2.109

Usually, no need to **avoid holes**. They disappear after a few rows.
Use **fabric markers** to keep track of the extra rows.

Vertical gathers S

● To gather an insertion, work frequent pairs of short rows (Fig 2.110a).

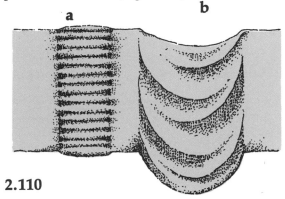

2.110

Frequency depends on patterns used and amount of gathering required. An extra pair of rows every other main row will double the length of the insertion.
Very wide insertions will **drape** (Fig 2.110b). The effect can be emphasised by lengthening the centre with **symmetrical darts**.

Ruffles S

Like **vertical gathers** but at one end of work, or forming a separate edging (Fig 2.111).

2.111

The illustration shows how the pattern (a **reverse st st welt**) can help accentuate the ruffling effect. The straight edge is in **garter stitch**.

Curves s

(See also **curves** under **Increases and decreases**)

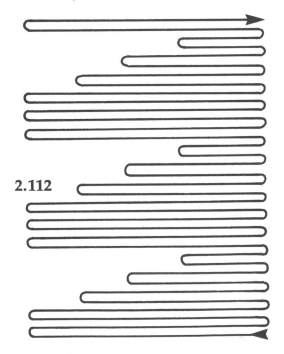

2.112

Placing one **dart** after another will shape the work into a curve (Fig 2.112). This is a technique often used in decorative knitting and in garment making – collars, yokes, skirts etc.

● **Calculate** the number of **rows** needed at either side of the curve, and the number of **stitches** across. If, for example, the outside needs 30 rows more than the inside, you can have 3 darts 10-rows deep, or 5 darts 6-rows deep. The rows needed for the inside edge are evenly distributed between darts and worked from end to end.

Many shallow darts give a smoother edge than fewer deep darts.

Medallions s

Individual geometric shapes. Only **circular** medallions can be achieved with short rows. For all other shapes, and for other circular medallions, see **Increases and decreases**.

● Same idea as for **curves**, but the inside edge has no rows between darts. The outside edge is as long as the circle. Medallions usually have between 6 and 16 darts, defining a similar number of sections (Fig 2.113).

2.113

The main drawback is that they need a **seam**. In solid patterns this can often be solved by **grafting** the last row to a **provisional cast-on** – remember that grafting will create a new row, so make the last section one row short.

lace work, however, even a grafted join is
nwelcome and invariably ruins the work. If
ou insist in using shorts rows to work circu-
r medallions, try to incorporate two plain
ows to match the grafting at the end of each
ection, on the principle that 'if you cannot
eat them, join them'. Or make a feature of
e join – use a **decorative cast-on** or **cast-off**
nd hide the seam under it.

pheres

haping a medallion over half the stitches,
nd a second medallion over the remaining
itches, gives a casing for a sphere.
ood for a ball (Fig 2.114).

.114

ylinders

straight piece between two edge medall-
ns gives an enclosed cylinder. Good for
olsters and decorative work.

2.115

Removing one of the end medallions gives a
cylinder with an open end. Good for baskets
and hats (Fig 2.115).

Sculptured knitting S

An unexpected use for **double darts** (Fig
2.116 – top view, and Fig 2.117 – side view).
Necessarily time and yarn consuming, but
worth every minute and every gramme; and
not that difficult.

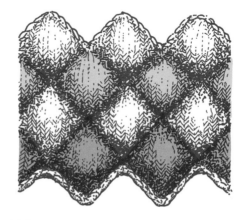

2.116

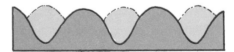

2.117

It can be used to literally 'raise' many standard patterns, or to create new ones. In some
cases, it might be best not to **avoid holes**
when turning.

For anchorage, leave at least one stitch between units, and work at least one row across
between unit lines.

Chart units and anchorage stitches
beforehand, to make sure that they can be
staggered.

Because each unit is worked individually,
different **colours** can be worked without any
difficulty.

a **Cast on** all the sts required for total width. It is absolutely essential to make a **sample** first.

b Work 1 or more rows across.

c First unit: work back and forth in increasingly shorter rows until only the centre, or 2 centre, st(s) remain (more sts for a less pointed unit), then work increasingly longer rows at the same, or at a different rate. In the illustration, 1 st has been left, then added, at the end of each row.

d Work the anchoring st(s), and then the next unit.

Repeat **d** to end of unit line.

e Work at least 1 row across.

f Start next unit line. If working **flat**, this will start and end with a half unit.

Special effects S

In combination with other techniques, short rows are the means of achieving some stunning three-dimensional effects.

See **sculptured knitting** above, and **Raised patterns.**

Slip stitch

A stitch that is passed from left to right needle without being worked (**sl st**).

The result is an elongated stitch with a bar across it on the side the yarn is held. If instructions do not say **with yarn in front (wyif)**, or **with yarn at back (wyab)**, leave yarn where it is.

There are two ways of slipping stitches. Unless otherwise instructed, do it **purlwise** but do not change yarn position.

Purlwise (pwise) E

a Insert right needle into st as if to **p** it.

b Drop st from left needle.

c Work next st without pulling yarn too tight.

Note (Fig 2.118) that the stitch does not become **twisted**.

Knitwise (kwise) E

a Insert right needle into st as if to **k**.

b Drop st from left needle.

c Work next st without pulling yarn too tight.

Note (Fig 2.119) that the stitch is **twisted** by the action.

2.118

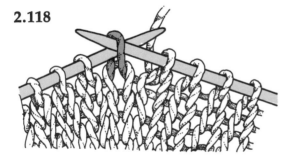

2.119

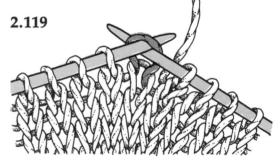

APPLICATIONS

Innumerable techniques make use of slipped stitches. The two dealt with here show how their properties are exploited in fabric construction.

Slip-stitch knitting U

A vast field to be explored with a good pattern dictionary (see **multicolour slip stitch** and **Books**).

Fabrics either emphasise the **elongated loop** (Fig 2.120), sometimes slipping it over several rows, or the **bar** across the loop. Across one stitch, a bar can produce intriguing 'woven' effects (Fig 2.121). Across several stitches, bars become quite dramatic (Fig 2.122), but are prone to snagging.

General notes:

- Thickness tends to increase.
- Elasticity tends to decrease.
- Fabric width may decrease; more stitches may be needed.
- Fabric length may decrease, more rows may be needed.
- On a **st st** base tendency to **curl** increases, especially if the stitches are slipped over several rows.
- Curling is only partially corrected by **blocking**.
- Slipping for several rows, or fairly tightly over two or more stitches, can create deep three-dimensional textures, of interest from both sides of work (Figs 2.123 and 2.124).
- Unless specified, yarn should not be pulled tightly after slipping.

2.120

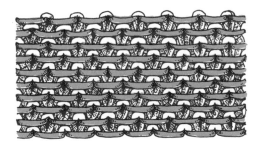

2.121

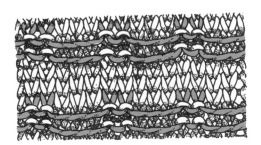

2.122

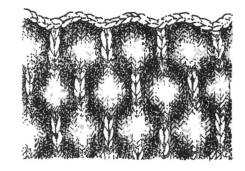

2.123

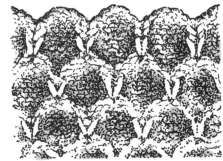

2.124

Tubular knitting S

(See also **tunnels**, **tubular pockets**, **tubular two-colour knitting**, **tubular selvedges** and **tubular cords**)

By slipping every other stitch, two layers of fabric are worked at the same time. The instructions below are for **stocking stitch**, which gives a firm, very thick and **flat** fabric. Many other patterns are possible, even different ones on each layer. Pull yarn tight after slipping and/or use fine needles.

Top and lower edges can be **closed** or **open**. See **choosing a cast-on** and **choosing a cast-off**.

For **closed sides**, on an even number of stitches:

Row 1: *K1, **slip 1 pwise wyif***, to end.
Row 2: k the **sl sts**, **sl** the **k** sts from previous row.
Repeat row 2.

For **open sides**, use two balls of yarn:
Row 1: with 1st ball, *k1, **slip** 1 **pwise wyif***, to end.
Row 2: with 1st ball, **p** the **k** sts of row 1 and **sl** the **sl sts pwise wyab**.
Row 3: with 2nd ball, **p** the **sl sts** of rows 1 and 2 and **sl** the others **pwise wyab**.

Row 4: with 2nd ball, **k** the **p** sts of row 3 and **sl** the **sl sts pwise wyif**.
Repeat rows 1 to 4.

Alternatively, use **double-pointed needles**, and work row 1, row 3, row 4 and row 2, in this order. Because two independent layers result, this work cannot strictly be called **tubular**. The sides, though, can be closed by twisting one yarn around the other every two rows if working with double-pointed needles. It is then possible to work the two layers of a truly tubular piece in two colours (Fig 2.125).

Tubular bands placed horizontally on ordinary knitting may, or may not, need exactly twice the number of stitches. Try **samples**.

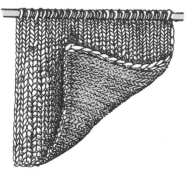

2.125

Increases and decreases

Also called **shapings**. Stitches added or subtracted (most often one or two at a time) to shape the work or to create texture – in which case the stitches increased in one place have to be decreased in another. To add or subtract three or more stitches at start or end of rows, **cast on** or **cast off**.

Increases and decreases are instantly spotted when a **fabric marker** is placed next to each one. Fabric markers are essential when working the shapings every so many rows, together with a **needle marker** next to the **guide stitch** – the stitch that aligns the shapings vertically.

To keep pattern correct whilst shaping, use **needle markers** at start and end of the block of complete repeats. Move marker(s) a whole repeat in or out as soon as possible.

Some shapings pull the fabric. One may be immaterial, ten in line may not.

Shapings worked at the edge are often placed one stitch in; a few stitches in for a fully fashioned effect. Beware, though, of shapings interfering with pattern (see **shaped edges**).

Shaped edges are longer than vertical, un-shaped ones. Work them loosely and keep checking that they do not pull.

Choosing shapings

The first **increase** to learn is **strand** (either left or right); the first **decrease** is **knit** (if not looking for symmetrical shapings, learn only **k2 tog**).

Otherwise, choice depends on fabric and whether or not a decorative effect is wanted. Look at the illustrations and knit **samples**. Points to remember:

• Most methods of shaping show a **slant**: they either point to the right or to the left. This is especially clear in **decreases**.

• Two similar methods, pointing in opposite directions, make a pair. Use pairs for symmetrical shapings.

• Unless pattern suggests otherwise, use only one type of slant when working many shapings along a row.

• Shapings slanting with the fabric may not show (Fig 2.126a).

2.126a

• The same shapings slanting against the fabric will stand out (Fig 2.126b). Try samples – there is no room to illustrate all possible combinations!

• **Double** shapings are shown in central positions. They could also be worked at the

2.126b

edges. The marker(s) should then always be kept to one side.

• To adapt **single** shapings to central positions, (Fig 2.127a), alternate one shaping be-

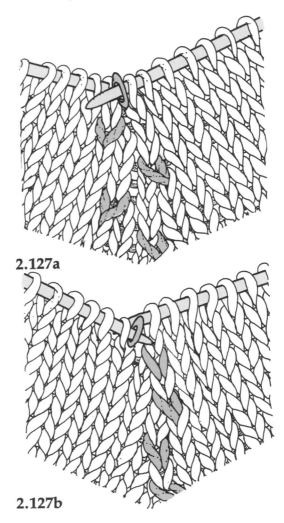

2.127a

2.127b

fore marker and one shaping with opposite slant after marker. To maintain the slant (Fig 2.127b), always shape before marker to **decrease** or after marker to **increase**; move marker one stitch to left after 1st, 3rd, 5th etc shapings. The effect will be slightly off centre – try on **samples** before deciding best marker position.

- For other ways to adapt single shapings to central positions, see **double increases** and **double decreases**.
- Do not feel restricted to use knit shapings only on knit fabrics. Try them on purl, or any other fabric.
- **Double** shapings can be chosen for their decorative value: five doubles instead of ten singles make a bigger impact.

Calculating shapings

Suppose you have to add 10 stitches in 60 rows. A straight division tells you to **increase** 1 stitch every 6 rows. Had the result been 5.8 rows, you would have had a choice: work the first or last increase only 4 rows away from the edge, or add 2 more rows to the total.

If using **double** or **paired increases**, halve the number of rows first.

Decreases are calculated the same way. (See also **calculating stitches and rows**).

Notes

Instructions are given for both knit and purl situations, so that shapings can be an odd number of rows apart. However, only the knit side is shown because this is where differences really show.

On **wrong-side** rows the left shaping is worked first.

Unless otherwise instructed, **needle markers** are slipped as follows:

RIGHT
On **knit**: before shaping
On **purl**: after shaping
LEFT
On **knit**: after shaping
On **purl**: before shaping

Paired single increases

Work right-hand increases after the **guide stitch**, and left-hand increases before the guide stitch.

Pinhole increase U

The simplest, but leaves a hole (Fig 2.128). (See **strand increase** for ways to avoid the hole.)

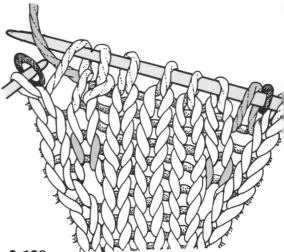

2.128

RIGHT
On **knit**: k into horizontal strand between last st and next st.
On **purl**: p strand.
LEFT
On **knit**: k strand.
On **purl**: p strand.

Eyelet increase S

Very decorative (Fig 2.129). Structure similar to **pinhole**, but leaves a larger hole one row later.

RIGHT
On **knit**: **front-to-back yo.**
On **purl**: **back-to-front yo.**
LEFT
On **knit**: **back-to-front yo.**
On **purl**: **front-to-back yo.**

DO NOT **twist** the **overs** on next row. Work them through back of loop if necessary.

2.129

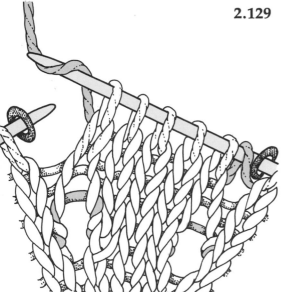

Closed eyelet increase U

To avoid the hole in **eyelet** (Fig 2.131). Same structure as **strand** but looser and one row later.

2.131

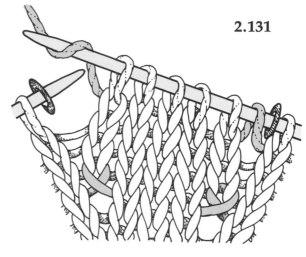

RIGHT
On **knit**: **front-to-back yo.**
On **purl**: **front-to-back yo.**
LEFT (sometimes called **garter increase**)
On **knit**: **back-to-front yo.**
On **purl**: **back-to-front yo.**
Twist the **overs** on next row.

Cast-on increase U

Also same structure as **strand**, but even more loose than **closed eyelet** (Fig 2.132).

2.132

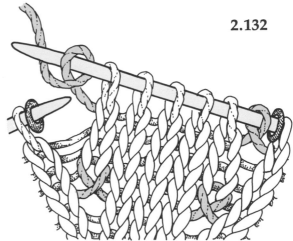

Strand increase E

Same principle as **pinhole**, but **twisting** the strand to avoid the hole (Fig 2.130).

2.130

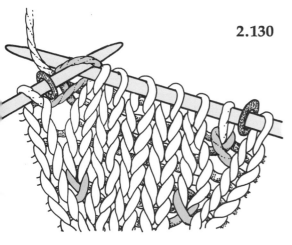

RIGHT
On **knit**: with left needle, pick up horizontal strand between last st and next st, from the front, and **k-b**.
On **purl**: pick up strand from the front and **p-b**.
LEFT
On **knit**: pick up strand from the back and **k**.
On **purl**: pick up strand from the back and **p**.

RIGHT
On **knit**: **loop cast-on** 1.
On **purl**: **loop cast-on** 1.
LEFT
On **knit**: **twisted-loop cast-on** 1. **P-b** on next row.
On **purl**: **twisted-loop cast-on** 1. **K-b** on next row.

Row below increase   U

Very neat (Fig 2.133). The new stitch must not pull.

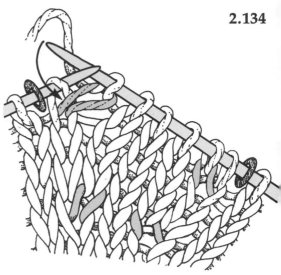

2.134

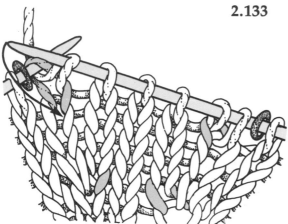

2.133

RIGHT
On **knit**: **k** first into st below, then into st.
On **purl**: **p**1 but do not drop; **p** into st below.
LEFT
On **knit**: **k**1 but do not drop; **k** into st below.
On **purl**: **p** first into st below, then into st.

Lifted increase   U

Also very neat (Fig 2.134). Unless worked loosely, the increases will pull the fabric if placed one on top of another.
RIGHT
On **knit**: **k** the back head of st below next st; **k**1.
On **purl**: **p**1; with left needle pick up head of st below st just taken off needle, from the back; **p-b**.
LEFT
On **knit**: **k**1; with left needle pick up side

loop of st below st just taken off left needle, from the back; **k-b**.
On **purl**: **p** head of st below next st; **p**1.

Bar increase   U

Tightens slightly the stitch over which it is worked (Fig 2.135).
RIGHT
On **knit**: **k** a st first through front and then through back. If using **markers**: sl pwise st before marker; drop marker; return st to left needle; **k** but do not drop; place marker on right needle; **k-b** st.

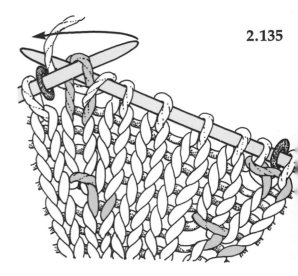

2.135

On **purl**: **p** through front and back.
LEFT
On **knit**: **k** through front and back.
On **purl**: **p** through front and back. If using **markers**: **sl pwise** st before marker; drop marker; return st to left needle; **p** but do not drop; place marker on right needle; **p-b** st.

Knit-and-purl increase S

Blends in well with some patterns (Fig 2.136).

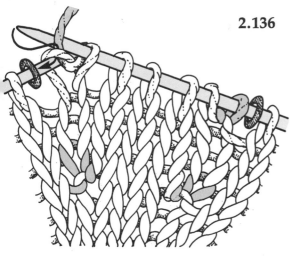

2.136

RIGHT
On **knit**: **p**, then **k**, into 1 st.
On **purl**: **p**, then **k**.
LEFT
On **knit**: **k**, then **p**.
On **purl**: **k**, then **p**.

Loop increase S

Really decorative. The loops could be drawn from a few rows below. Make sure that they do not pull (Fig 2.137).
RIGHT
On **knit**: insert right needle between any 2 sts to the left; **k**; draw a long loop.
On **purl**: '**p**' with left needle between any 2 sts to the right, on row below; **sl** loop onto right needle without twisting.
LEFT
On **knit**: '**k**' with left needle between 2 sts to

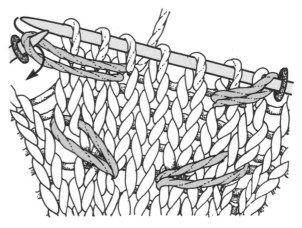

2.137

the right, on row below; **sl** loop onto right needle without twisting.
On **purl**: **p** between 2 sts to the left.
If drawing loops with left needle is awkward, use a **crochet hook**.

Double increases

Two ways of adding two stitches:
FIRST METHOD place 2 **single increases** side by side, perhaps with 1 (or more) **guide stitch(es)** in between. Place **marker(s)** to pinpoint centre line or to define the guide stitch(es).
Fig 2.138 shows a pair of **lifted increases** next to each other, order maintained.

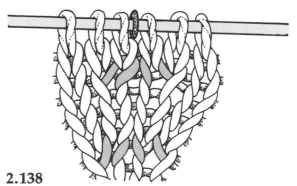

2.138

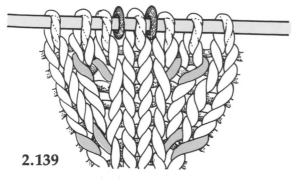

2.139

Fig 2.139 shows them in reverse order, divided by one guide stitch.

SECOND METHOD   use a true **double increase**: similar principles as **single increases** but 2 extra stitches are made each time.

If using **markers**, place one at each side of the **guide stitch**. When increasing only on one side of work, or if the increases do not have a centre stitch, one marker is enough. Markers will need re-positioning each time.

Double eyelet increase   S

A nice, bold hole (Fig 2.140).

On **knit** or **purl**: work a **double over – front to back** and round again. Slip marker between 1st and 2nd wrap.

On next row, work 2nd wrap (the 1st made) **twisted**.

Double cast-on increase   U

A smaller hole (Fig 2.141). Alternate **loop** and **twisted-loop cast-ons** for a subtle criss-cross effect.

On **knit** or **purl**: either **loop** or **twisted-loop cast-on** 2 sts. Place marker between the 2.

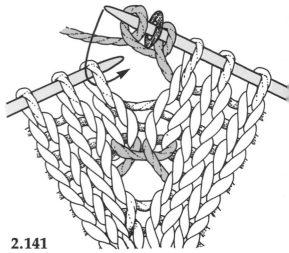

2.141

Over increase   U

No **single increase** counterpart (Fig 2. 142). On **knit**:

a **K1**, but do not drop from left needle.
b **Front-to-back yo.**
c **K** same st again.

2.142

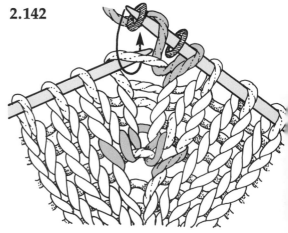

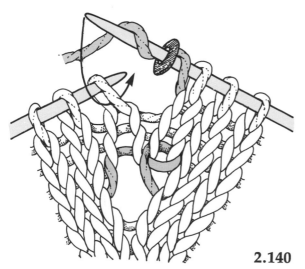

2.140

On **purl**:
a **P**1 but do not drop.
b **Yo** as before.
c **P** again.
DO NOT **twist** the **over** when working next row. Re-position marker(s) next to the over.

Double row-below increase　　U

Decorative (Fig 2.143). Make sure that the stitch worked on the row below does not pull.

2.143

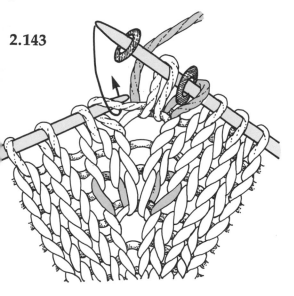

On **knit**:
a **K**1 but do not drop from left needle.
b **K** into st below.
c **K** again original st.
On **purl**:
a **P**1 but do not drop.
b **P** into st below.
c **P** again original st.

Double lifted increase　　U

Work very loosely or it will pull (Fig 2.144).
On **knit**:
a **K** the back head of st below next st.
b **K** next st.
c With left needle pick up side loop of st below st just worked, and **k-b**.
On **purl**:
a **P** head of st below next st.

2.144

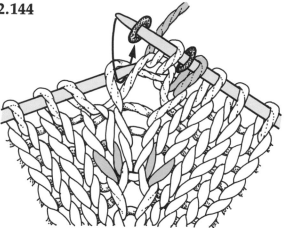

b **P** next st.
c With left needle pick up head of st below st just worked, and **p-b**.
Re-position marker(s) next to the ordinary st.

Double knit-and-purl increase　　S

Figure 2.145.
On **knit**: (**k, p, k**) same st.
On **purl**: (**p, k, p**) same st.
Re-position marker(s) next to the centre st.

2.145

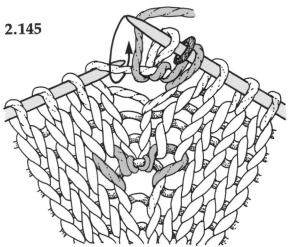

Multiple increases

A development of **double increases**. Most often worked as part of a pattern.

Multiple eyelet increase   S

Real black holes, these! (Fig 2.146).

On **knit** or **purl**: **front-to-back multiple over**, wrapping yarn around needle as many times as sts you want to increase (total of 6 in illustration).

On next row, work alternately 1 wrap through front and next through back. If using marker(s), re-position next to new centre st.

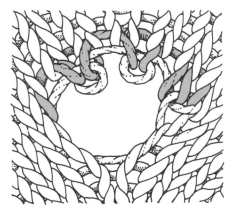

2.146

Multiple over increase   S

Fig 2.147 shows a 6-stitch increase.

On **knit**: (k1, **front-to-back yo**) on same st to obtain 1 st more than you want to increase.

On **purl**: (p1, **front-to-back yo**) on same st to obtain 1 st more than you want to increase.

DO NOT **twist** overs on next row. If using marker(s), re-position next to new centre st.

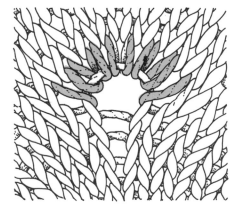

2.147

Multiple row-below increase   S

Fig 2.148 shows a 6-stitch increase.

On **knit**: (k1, **k** unto st below) on same 2 sts to obtain 1st more than you want to increase.

On **purl**: (p1, **p** into st below) on same 2 sts to obtain 1 st more than you want to increase.

If using marker(2), re-position next to new centre st.

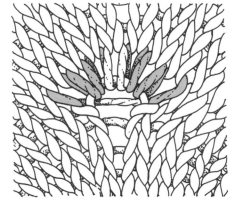

2.148

Multiple knit-and-purl increase   S

Figure 2.149 shows a 6-stitch increase.

On **knit**: (**k, p**) same st to obtain 1 st more than you want to increase.

On **purl**: (**p, k**) same st to obtain 1 st more than you want to increase.

If using marker(s), re-position next to new centre st.

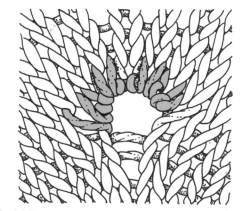

2.149

Paired single decreases

Two stitches are involved.

Work right-hand decreases after the **guide stitch** and left-hand decreases on the two stitches before the guide stitch. If decreasing at the very edge, use a decrease with a right **slant** on the left edge, and vice versa.

Read carefully even if you are an old hand. Advice on pairing decreases has not always been what it should.

Changing the order of **knit, slip** and **twist decreases** from right to left will give more decorative results (Fig 2.126b).

Knit decrease E

The right-slant decrease is often paired with the left-slant of either **slip decrease** or **twist decrease**. Fig 2.150 shows correct pairing.

2.150

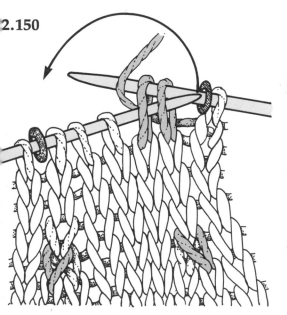

RIGHT (slant to left)

On **knit (ssk – slip, slip, knit)**:

a (slip 1 kwise) twice.

b insert left needle into front of these two sts, from left, and **k2tog.**

On **purl**:

a (slip 1 kwise) twice.

b Return the 2 sts to left needle in this twisted way.

c Insert right needle, from the back, first into 2nd st then into 1st st, and **p-b2 tog.**

LEFT (slant to right)

On **knit (k2 tog)**:

a Insert right needle into front of next 2 sts, from left to right.

b K2 tog.

On **purl (p2 tog)**:

a Insert right needle into front of next 2 sts, from right to left.

b P2 tog.

Slip decrease U

More obvious than **knit decrease** (Fig 2.151).

2.151

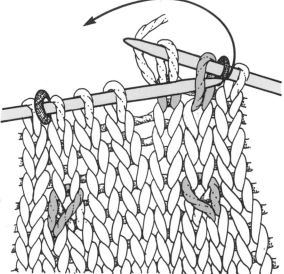

RIGHT (slant to left)

On **knit (slip 1-k 1-psso)**:

a Slip 1 kwise.

b K1.

c With left needle pass **sl st** over st just worked, as in **basic cast-off**.

On **purl**:

a P 1.

b Slip 1 kwise and return to left needle in this twisted way.

c Return **p** st (from **a**) to left needle.

d With right needle pass **twisted** st over **p** st and off needle.

e Sl **p** st **pwise**.

LEFT (slant to right)

On **knit**:

a K 1.

b Sl **k** st back onto left needle, without twisting it.

c With right needle pass 2nd st on left needle over **k** st and off needle.

d Sl **k** st pwise.

On **purl (slip 1 – p1-psso)**:

a Slip 1 **pwise**.

b P 1.

c With left needle pass **sl st** over st just worked and off needle.

Twist decrease $\quad$ S

For projects making use of other **twisted stitches** (Fig 2.152).

2.152

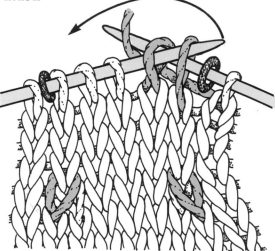

RIGHT (slant to left)

On **knit (k-b2 tog)**:

a Insert right needle into back of next 2 sts.

b K2 tog.

On **purl (p-b2 tog)**:

a Insert right needle, from back, first into 2nd st then into 1st st on left needle.

b P2 tog.

LEFT (slant to right)

On **knit**:

a (Slip 1 **kwise**) twice.

b Return the 2 sts to left needle in this twisted way.

c Insert right needle, from front, first into 2nd st then into 1st st.

d K2 tog.

On **purl**:

a (Slip 1 **kwise**) twice.

b Return the 2 sts to left needle in this twisted way.

c P2 tog.

Loop decrease $\quad$ S

Very decorative (Fig 2.153). Draw long loops to avoid pulling.

2.153

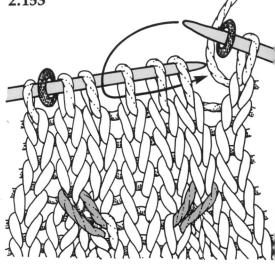

RIGHT (slant to right)

On **knit**:

a Insert right needle, from left, first into 3rd st on left needle, then into 1st st.

b K2 tog.

c Drop 1st st.

d K 2nd st.

e Drop 3rd st.

On **purl**:

a 3 sts before **marker, slip** 1 onto **cable needle** and keep at back.

b P1.

a Sl 1st st back onto left needle without twisting it.

b P2 tog.

LEFT (slant to left)

On **knit:**

a 3 sts before **marker, slip** 1 onto **cable needle** and keep at front.

b K1.

c Sl 1st st **kwise** onto right needle.

d Slip 1 kwise.

e Insert left needle into the 2 sts and **k tog** as in **ssk.**

On **purl:**

a Sl: 1 **kwise,** 1 **pwise,** 1 **kwise.**

b Return the 3 sts to left needle, without twisting them any further.

c P-b tog 3rd and 1st sts.

d Drop 1st st.

e P 2nd st.

f Drop 3rd st.

On next row, catch side of decrease next to centre stitch and pull to make decrease longer at the expense of centre stitch.

Double decreases

(See comments on **double increases**)

Double decreases with a **slant** are shown forming criss-cross patterns. They need not do so: simply work them all with the same slant instead of alternating one of each.

If using **markers,** keep one at each side of the three (or four) centre stitches.

Double knit decrease   E

Just as **knit decrease** but on three stitches (Fig 2.154).

Re-position marker(s).

Double slip decrease   U

Figure 2.155. Similar to **slip decrease,** with the following changes:

SLANT TO LEFT

On **knit (slip 1–k2 tog-psso):**

b K2 tog.

On **purl:**

a P2 tog.

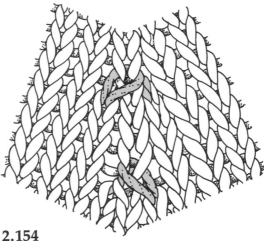

2.154

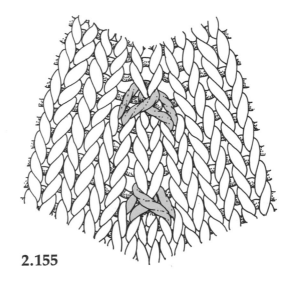

2.155

SLANT TO RIGHT

On **knit:**

a Ssk.

On **purl:**

b P-b2 tog.

Re-position marker(s).

Double twist decrease   S

Work **twist decrease** over 3 sts (Fig 2.156).

Re-position marker(s).

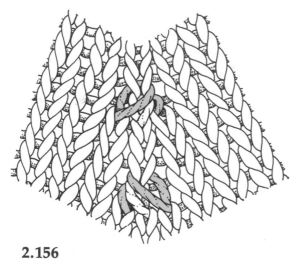

2.156

Double loop decrease   S

Figure 2.157. Similar to **loop decrease**, but worked over 4 sts. First and 4th sts are **k tog** or **p tog.** Second and 3rd sts are (abbreviations from **knit decrease**):

SLANT TO RIGHT

On **knit:**

d Ssk.

On **purl:**

b P-b2 tog.

SLANT TO LEFT

On **knit:**

b K2 tog.

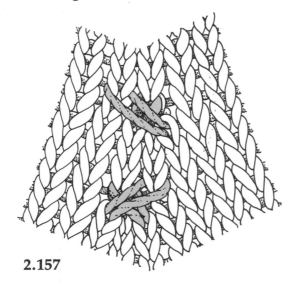

2.157

On **purl:**

a Sl (1 kwise, 2 pwise, 1 kwise).

e P2 tog.

Re-position marker(s) at either side of the 4 stitches.

Straight decrease   S

A clean, vertical line (Fig 2.158). No **single decrease** counterpart.

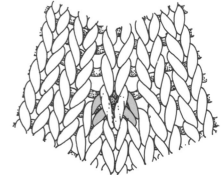

2.158

On **knit (sl2 tog-k1-psso):**

a Insert right needle into front of next 2 sts, from left to right.

b Sl the 2 sts together off left needle.

c K1.

d With left needle pass the 2 sl sts over st just made and off needle.

On **purl (sl-b2 tob – p1 – psso):**

a (Slip 1 kwise) twice.

b Return the 2 sts to left needle in this twisted way.

c Insert right needle, from back, first into 2nd st then into 1st st.

d Sl the 2 sts together off left needle.

e P1.

f With left needle pass the 2 sl sts over st just made and off needle.

Re-position marker(s).

An almost identical version uses a **cable needle:**

On **knit:**

a Sl 1st st onto cable needle and keep at back.

b Slip 1 kwise.

c Return 1st st to left needle.

d K2 tog.

e Pass **sl st** over st just made and off needle.

On **purl**:

a **Slip** 1 onto **cable needle**, and keep at front.

b **Slip** 1 pwise.

c Return 1st st to left needle.

d **P2 tog.**

e Pass **sl st** over st just made and off needle.

Multiple decreases

A development of **double decreases**. Most often worked as part of a pattern.

Avoid leaving holes. If having difficulties drawing yarn through a large number of stitches, try using a **crochet hook**.

Multiple knit decrease   S

Like a **knit decrease** over several stitches – 5 in Fig 2.159.

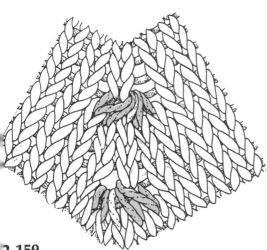

2.159

Easiest to work are **slant to left** on **knit** (ssk-5 in the example), and **slant to right** on **purl** (p5 tog in the example).

In **ssk**, inserting left needle to knit a large number of stitches may be awkward. Try 'casting-off' the stitches, one by one, over the yarn wrapped around tip of right needle as if to knit.

Multiple slip decrease   S

Like a **slip decrease** over several stitches – 5 in Fig 2.160.

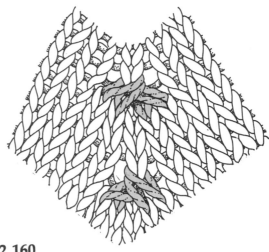

2.160

The easiest to work are **slant to left** on **knit**, and **slant to right** on **purl**.

Half the stitches are slipped, the other half worked together, as in **knit decrease** with opposite slant, and the **sl sts** passed over. If the stitches involved are an odd number, one more is worked than slipped.

Re-position marker(s).

Multiple twist decrease   S

Like a **twist decrease** over several stitches – 5 in Fig 2.161.

The easiest to work are **slant to left** on knit, and **slant to right** on purl.
Re-position marker(s).

APPLICATIONS

Horizontal gathers U

Widely used, for instance to give fullness to the top of a waistband or cuff.

A change of pattern is sometimes enough: from a tight **rib** to a spreading **lace** (Fig 2.162). (See also **choosing a cast-off – gathered edges.**) But the more usual device, often combined with a pattern change, is to work **single increases** or **decreases** at regular intervals along one row. Easier on plain knit or purl rows.

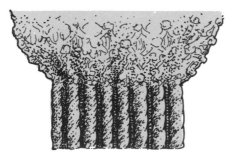

2.162

● To **calculate**, divide the stitches on the needle by the number of shapings. If the result is 7 and you are **increasing**, add a new stitch after every 7 original stitches. If you are **decreasing**, every 7th stitch must be removed. Adjust to fit in with pattern if it makes sense: say, one shaping after 3 stitches and the next after 11 stitches.

In **flat knitting**, work only half the key number of stitches before the first shaping (4 sts in the example). The other half (3 sts) will find their way to the other end of the row. In general, do not shape across **borders**.

Ruching S

Narrow bands of heavy **gathers**.

First, the original stitches are doubled by **increasing** on every stitch. After a few rows, they are **decreased** to the original number.

Extra heavy ruching (Fig 2.163) repeats the increase row to double the stitches again. Decreasing is also done in two rows.

2.163

Vertical darts S

A series of **increases** or **decreases**, one on top of the other, that make the fabric steadily wider or narrower (see **calculating shapings**).

Strictly speaking, darts are placed away from the edges. A raglan sweater only has darts if

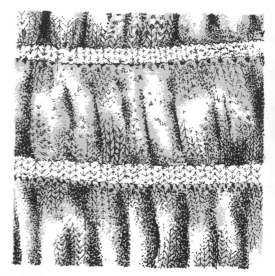

2.164

sleeves and body are worked together in **rounds**.

Use **slanted** shapings and keep **marker** position if one of the sides is vertical (Fig 2.164). Use **double**, central shapings and re-position marker if both sides are diagonal (Fig 2.165). For **single** shapings, see also Fig 2.127.

2.165

If requiring a decorative dart, consider working a central narrow band in contrast pattern.

Mitred corners U

(See also **mitred corners** under **Short rows**, under **Hems and casings** and under **Edgings**)

Mitred corners can be shaped with a **double vertical dart**. A technique often used in neckline bands.

Exact shaping sequence depends on pattern and type of angle required. In **rib** corners, double increases or decreases are usually worked every:

- **row** or **round** for acute angles (V-necks).
- two **rows** or **rounds** for right angles (square necks).
- three or more **rows** or **rounds** for obtuse angles.

Very acute angles may require extra shapings. **Short fabrics** require fewer shapings.

Straight decrease blends in well with **single rib** (Fig 2.166). Symmetrical **knit decreases** separated by two **knit** stitches blend in well with **double rib** (Fig 2.167).

2.166

2.167

Bias knitting S

Increasing at one end and **decreasing** at the other end, on alternate rows, makes the fabric slant whilst maintaining its width. The slant is:

- to the right, if starting with a **decrease** (Fig 2.168).

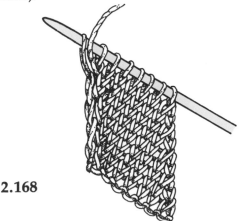

2.168

- to the left, if starting with an **increase**.

All rows, including **cast-on** and **cast-off** edges, show the same slant. Row direction is at right angles to work progress.

Any pattern can be adapted. Choose shapings to fit in with the pattern. Work them right at the edge, or inside a **selvedge** or **border**.

Double or **multiple** shapings, or shaping on every row, will increase the slant.

A tight increase, or an increase into a stitch two rows below, will make the work curve (Fig 2.169).

2.169

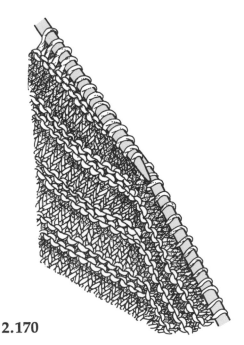

A two-step slant is achieved by adding **short rows** to one side only (Fig 2.170).

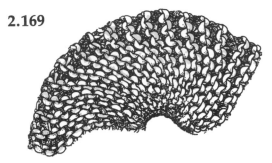

2.170

Diagonal fabrics

Bias knitting works like magic in projects with diagonal bands of pattern: the bands become horizontal (Fig 2.171)! To work a bias square:

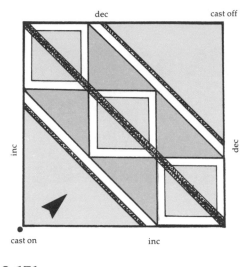

2.171

a **Cast on** 3 sts for 1st corner.

b **Increase** regularly at sides.

c When 2nd and 3rd corners are reached, **decrease** towards last corner.

See also **calculating shapings**. If working a rectangle, calculate narrow and long sides separately. Shape sides at different intervals.

Chevrons

Two **diagonal fabrics**, side by side, moving in opposite directions.

Figures 2.172 and 2.173 show row direction and shapings on a square. Work progress is at right angles to row direction – horizontal stripes will emphasise the effect of the illustrations, but a pattern with vertical lines will appear perpendicular to the rows.

Zigzags

Many **chevrons**, one next to the other. **Welts** and rows in several colours produce a ripple effect (Fig 2.174).

- Edge shapings are **single**. All the others

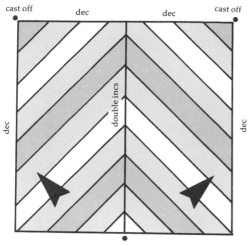

2.172

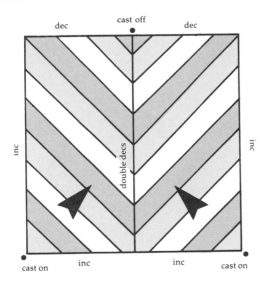

2.173

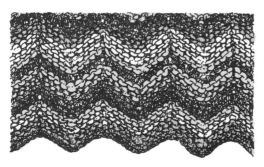

2.174

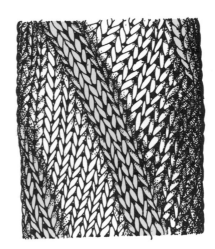

2.175

are **double**, alternating **increases** and **decreases**.

Generally, the bands are narrow, and all the stitches are **cast on** at the same time. **Cast on** and **cast off** loosely at the zigzag points, or they will pull.

If only every other band is on the **bias** (all **slanting** in the same direction), and the rest are straight, the resulting fabric will both ripple and slant at right angles to the bias. In **circular** knitting a **spiral** will form (Fig 2.175).

Curves S

(See also **curves** under **short rows**)

If **darts** are placed in a regular sequence, a curve will form (Fig 2.176). Skirts and yokes are often shaped with many darts. In decorative knitting the scope is very wide.

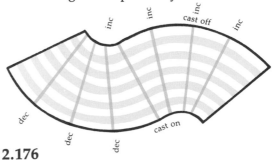

2.176

• **Calculate** the number of **stitches** needed at start and end of the curve, and the number of **rows** involved. Supposing you need 30 stitches more at the start than at the end, you could have 3 darts with 5 **double decreases**, 3 darts with 10 **single decreases**, 5 darts with 3 double decreases, or 5 darts with 6 single decreases. Choice depends on fabric, effect desired and how well each option fits in with the row total (see also **calculating shapings**). The more darts involved in decreasing a given number of stitches, the smoother the curve.

Darts with **increases** are worked out similarly.

Medallions   S

Individual geometric shapes. Many small ones can be sewn together into large patchwork projects.

Medallions worked on two needles are usually shaped every other row. In squares, hexagons etc, this may only be successful in patterns with very **wide** stitches, such as **garter stitch**. It is often safer to work out the rows and stitches involved in one section, and **calculate** the **shapings** accordingly. When sections are divided by **double** shapings, take it as one **single** shaping at each end of each section.

Medallions worked on sets of needles are always best calculated.

Triangles
• Cast on three stitches and **increase** one stitch at one side (Fig 2.177a) or one stitch at both sides (Fig 2.177b). Or, start at the other end and **decrease**. When three stitches remain, work a **double decrease** and pull yarn. Shape at the very edge or a few stitches in. On alternate rows for a tallish triangle, or on every row for a flatter one.

Diamonds
Two triangles, one on top of each other (Fig 2.177c).

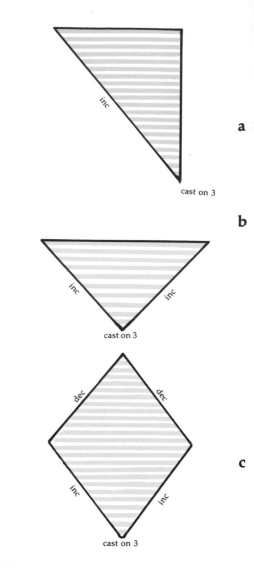

2.177

• **Increase**, work a couple of straight rows and **decrease**.

Squares
Four possibilities (Fig 2.178):
• (a) does not require any shapings.
• (b) is a **diamond** lying on its side. **Calculate** carefully so that the corners are square.
• (c) has **double** shapings along the diagonal. Start with two sides and end in three stitches, or vice versa.

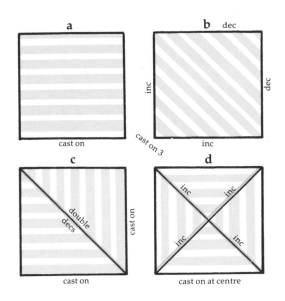

2.178

● (d) is worked in **rounds** on a set of needles; using four needles to hold the work makes sense.

Other polygons

Hexagons and·octagons can be worked in **rows** (Fig 2.179a) or in **rounds**. All the others, theoretically could be worked in rows, but are usually worked only in rounds.

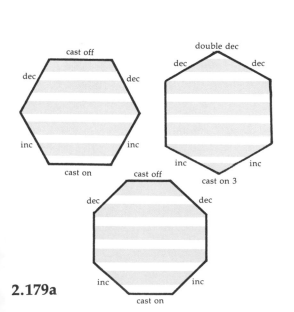

2.179a

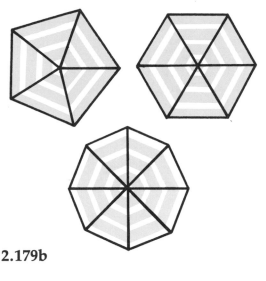

2.179b

● However many sides there are, one line of **double** shapings goes from each outer angle to the centre (Fig 2.179b). If **single** shapings are worked, a swirl forms (Fig 2.180).

To keep good control of progress, each side needs to be on a separate needle. Not very convenient if many sides are involved and the medallion is small.

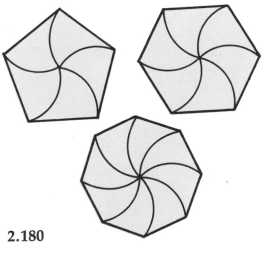

2.180

Circles
(See also **medallions** in **Short rows**)

● They can be worked as many-sided polygons, but other ways are possible, such as having 'shaping circles' rather than 'shaping lines' – many more shapings are worked in the outer circles than in the inner ones (Fig 2.181).

Large medallions can be finished on a circular needle.

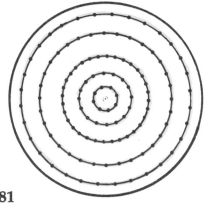

2.181

Embossed knitting S

(See also **Raised patterns** and **cables**.) Often a combination of **increases** and **decreases** with other techniques.

The raising and receding effects of knit and purl stitches can be emphasized with **increases** and **decreases**. The knit blocks will stand out on one side of the fabric and recede on the other side.

Figs 2.182 and 2.183 show the two sides of such a pattern. The diamonds are first **increased** and then **decreased** at both ends, on alternate rows. Stitch total is maintained by staggering the diamonds. The three stitches

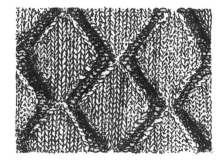

2.182

2.183

between diamonds swing from side to side. Many patterns can be worked on this principle. The secret is to use shapings that leave no holes.

Openwork S

For detailed instructions, consult pattern dictionaries (see **Books**).

Three types of openwork: **eyelets, faggots** and **lace**. Classifying a pattern can be difficult because they often intermingle.

The more holes involved, the quicker the work grows and the less yarn required.

Openwork, especially **lace**, is often **stretched** to make the pattern come to life.

Correct **tension** is absolutely essential.

Eyelets

● A **knit decrease** next to an **eyelet increase** with three or more strands between holes.

Decreasing first gives a marginally rounder eyelet. A pair of **single decreases** each side of a **double increase**, and other combinations, are also possible.

Eyelets can be next to each other on a row, but vertically cannot be closer than every three rows (every four rows, in **flat knitting**, if working them only on the **right side**). Otherwise they become **faggots**.

Often arranged in horizontal, vertical or diagonal lines, when **cords** or **ribbons** can be threaded through to make drawstrings (Fig 2.184). Fancy and geometric designs are also popular (Fig 2.185).

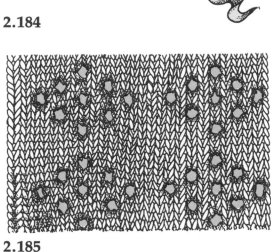

2.184

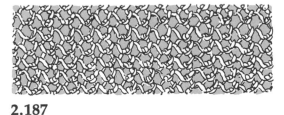

2.187

Lace
Breathtaking knitting (Figs 2.188 and 2.189).

2.188

2.185

Faggots
● Same combination as **eyelet** but only one or two strands between holes.

2.186

Can be worked on every **row** or **round** (one dividing strand), but not next to each other on a row, when they would become eyelets. For arrangements travelling to the right, first **increase**. For those travelling to the left, first **decrease** (Fig 2.186).

All-over faggots, either every row or every two rows, make good mesh patterns (Fig 2.187).

2.189

● **Knit decreases** and **eyelet increases** again, but this time not necessarily next to each other. **Decreases** are often paired and help to delineate designs. The **increases** make the holes. For larger holes, wrap yarn two or three times around the needle, but work it only once on the next row, letting the extra wraps drop (see **elongated stitch**).

Occasionally, the stitch total changes from row to row. Other times the edges are not straight (Fig 2.190).

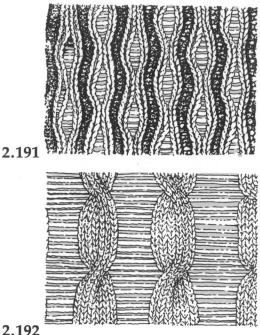

2.191

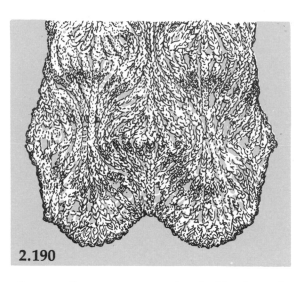

2.190

Lace patterns are very visual. **Charts** and **samples** tell more than pages of text.

Fear of lace knitting can be overcome by simply trying it. Start with patterns where every other row is all knit or all purl.

To check **samples**, measure pattern repeats rather than try to count stitches in 10cm (4in). **Stretch** samples first.

(See also **choosing a cast-on** and **choosing a cast-off**).

Ladders   S

A **ladder** occurs when a stitch is dropped and made to run.

Intentional ladders can be very decorative (Figs 2.191 and 2.192), but they add tremendously to fabric width. Work **samples** first.

Use **needle** and **fabric markers** to keep track of ladder position and length.

2.192

a   Work a **single** or **multiple eyelet increase** at bottom of intended ladder. For a multiple ladder with a flat, ungathered platform, cast off an equal number of stitches on the previous row.

b   Work the extra stitch(es) created by the increase as either knit or purl, taking care not to mix them with the pattern at either side of the ladder.

c   When the top is reached, drop the stitch(es) and make them run down to the increase.

Other fancy work   S

Combined increases and decreases are often used to create 'fancy' textures, some closed, some open.

Any of the techniques explained can be used, plus special ones devised for the occasion. Plus, often, techniques such as **slipped stitches, cross stitches, short rows** etc.

Good pattern dictionaries are full of examples (see **Books**). See also **Raised patterns** and **All sorts**.

Special throws

To **throw** the working yarn is to change its position, often wrapping it around the needle in the process. The most common throws are those used to knit and to purl. Here are some more.

Yarn under   E

The throw is done under the needle, and the stitch count is not affected.

Yarn forward (yf or yfwd)

● Bring yarn from **back** to **front of work**, under needles.

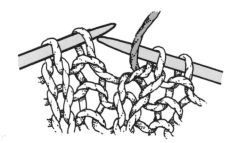

2.193

To be done automatically between a knit stitch and a purl stitch (Fig 2.193). Also used in fancy patterns. In this case, instructions are specific, but between knit and purl stitches instructions assume the knitter knows it must be done.

Yarn back (yb)

● Take yarn from **front** to **back of work**, under needles.

To be done automatically between a purl stitch and a knit stitch (Fig 2.194). Also used in fancy patterns (see **yarn forward** above).

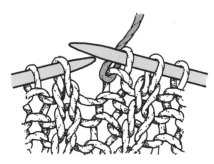

2.194

With yarn in front (wyif)

Often found in patterns with **slip stitches** when the yarn needs to change sides, or just to ensure that it is left on the correct side.
Sl3 **wyif** is another way of saying **yf, sl3, yb**.
If the yarn was already at **front of work**, leave it there.

With yarn at back (wyab)

(See **with yarn in front** above)
Sl3 **wyab** is another way of saying **yb, sl3, yf**.
If the yarn was already at **back of work**, leave it there.

Yarn over (yo)

Also called **over** and **yarn round needle** (**yrn**). Used mainly in **increases** (**eyelet, closed eyelet, double eyelet, over** and **multiple eyelet**) and their applications (**openwork** and **fancy work**).

If worked as it comes on the next row or round (sometimes through front of loop, sometimes through back of loop, but always in the easiest way, without **twisting**), it will leave a hole. Unless instructions say otherwise, patterns with overs must be worked in this manner.

Ways of avoiding the hole include **twisting**, as in **closed eyelet increase**, and **decreasing** by working the over with the stitch next to it as in **Tunisian knitting** and **brioche knitting** (second method).

Notice that, depending on the stitches before and after, some overs are much longer than others.

Front-to-back overs E

The most commonly used.
• Take yarn up front of needle, over the top, and down the back.

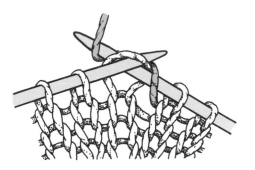

2.195

From **knit** stitch to **knit** stitch: Start by bringing **yarn forward** (Fig 2.195). Sometimes abbreviated in instructions to **yf, k.**
From **purl** stitch to **purl** stitch: End by bringing **yarn forward** (Fig 2.196).

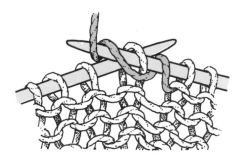

2.196

From **knit** stitch to **purl** stitch (the longest): Start and end by bringing **yarn forward** (Fig 2.197).

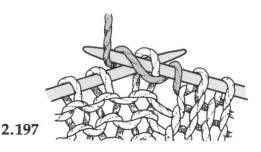

2.197

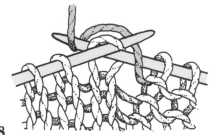

2.198

From **purl** stitch to **knit** stitch (the shortest): No extra yarn winding required (Fig 2.198).

Back-to-front overs U

Used to obtain perfect symmetry in **paired increases**, or identical results in increases worked on either side of work.
Also used to avoid working some stitches of the following row through the other side of the loop in specific situations. In **twisted stocking stitch**, a back-to-front **eyelet increase** will be worked through the back just like all the other stitches. In **garter stitch**, a back-to-front **closed eyelet increase** (sometimes called **garter increase**) will be worked through the front, also like the rest of the stitches.
• Take yarn up back of needle, over the top, and down the front.

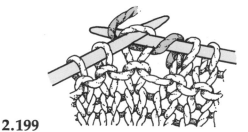

2.199

From **knit** stitch to **knit** stitch: End by taking the **yarn back** (Fig 2.199).

From **purl** stitch to **purl** stitch: Start by taking the **yarn back** (Fig 2.200). Be careful not to tighten up the **over** or the stitch, something easily done because the over ends at the top of the needle. It may be necessary to loosen up the yarn after purling the stitch.

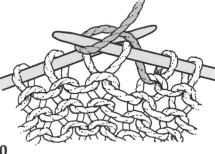

2.200

From **knit** stitch to **purl** stitch (the shortest): Take the yarn up the back to the top of the needle, where it will be ready to purl (Fig 2.201). Loosen up the yarn after purling, or the stitches before and after the over will get distorted.

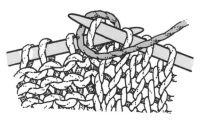

2.201

From **purl** stitch to **knit** stitch (the longest): Start and end by taking the **yarn back** (Fig 2.202).

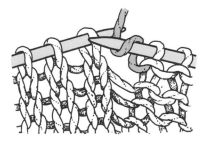

2.202

Double over [(yo) twice]   S

End any of the **overs** described above by wrapping the yarn a full extra turn around the needle. Fig 2.203 shows a **front to back** double over, from **knit** stitch to **knit** stitch.

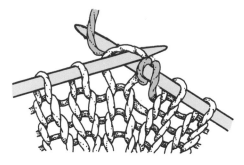

2.203

Used in **double eyelet increase** and in pattern construction, where it can either be used to make two new stitches or to obtain a larger hole. In the first case it is worked twice (once **twisted**, once untwisted). In the second case it is worked only once, and the second wrap is dropped.

Multiple over   S

Work a **double over**, then keep wrapping the yarn around the needle.

Used in **multiple eyelet increase** and in pattern construction.

Selvedge overs   U

Used to **increase** at the start of a row, either for decorative or purely practical reasons.

Before a **knit** stitch, work a **front-to-back over** around the free needle (Fig 2.204).

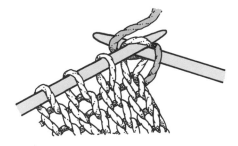

2.204

2.205

Before a **purl** stitch, work a **back-to-front over** around the free needle (Fig 2.205). Be careful not to work too tight. Hold with finger or thumb if necessary.

APPLICATIONS
Elongated stitch   U

Sometimes called **dropped stitch**.

Untwisted elongated stitch
Knit or purl in usual way, but wrap yarn two or more times around needle (Fig 2.206a). On following row, work only the first wrap and drop the others (Fig 2.206b).

a

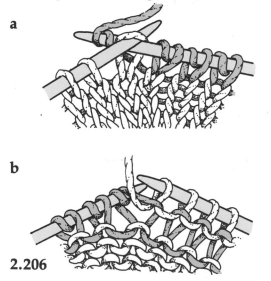

b

2.206

Or, work single or multiple **overs** between ordinary stitches, then drop the overs on next row.

Or, work elongated rows with a much thicker needle (**oddpin knitting**). If this needle is much thicker than the ordinary one, it may be awkward to insert into the smaller stitches. Extra long rows, however, can be worked onto a ruler (Fig 2.207), which becomes the holding needle in the following row.

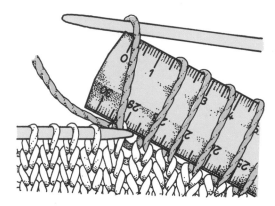

2.207

Use:
● All over for very soft and very loose areas, so stretchy that they will need controlling with adjoining areas of tight knitting.
● On alternate rows for a more controlled effect.

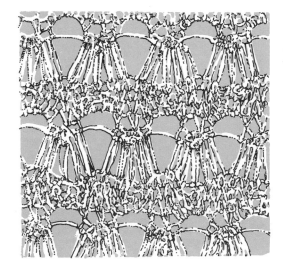

2.208

- In occasional rows, to create loose stripes.
- In occasional rows, later clustered into **shells**. A **multiple increase** has then to be worked to make up for the loss of stitches in the **multiple decrease** that forms the shell (Fig 2.208), unless using the shells to gather the fabric.
- In groups, to create a wavy effect (Fig 2.209).

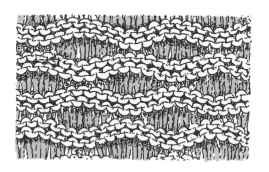

2.209

- In isolation, as part of a solid pattern. Fig 2.210 shows a pattern in which an elongated stitch is **slipped** for two rows, then worked in a different position on the third row.

2.210

Twisted elongated stitch
Also called **veil stitch**.

The yarn is again wrapped twice, but over both needles and as a figure of eight (Fig 2.211). Only one loop is drawn through the original stitch.

Similar uses to **untwisted elongated stitch**.

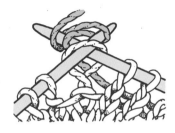

2.211

Twisting the stitches has a tightening effect on the tension. So, all-over fabrics will not be quite so stretchy.

Fur stitch S

Also called **loop knitting** (Fig 2.212).

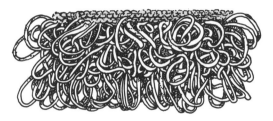

2.212

A number of stitch patterns can be used as a background and made to interplay with the loops, although the loops themselves are always made on knit stitches which are generally worked **twisted** on the next row. Most often, however, the base fabric is **stocking stitch** – **garter stitch** for a **flat** finish.

The loops are usually worked every two (or a multiple of two), rows, and they show on one side only. Working the loops on every row (or on every third, fifth . . .) would make them show on both sides.

For a really dense pile, work a loop on every stitch. For less density, work them on every other stitch (or on every fourth, sixth . . .), and stagger the next loop row.

Fine yarns might be more successful. To increase density, use several strands together on each loop row and/or make several wraps around needle and finger or card. (Multiple

wraps are treated as one single loop and drawn together through the base stitch, if appropriate.)
Further possibilities:

• Work loops in blocks of colour.

• Grade the loop length. Either wrap yarn around more or fewer fingers, or change width of card. Think of the sculptural possibilities of layering short over long (Fig 2.213a) and long over short (Fig 2.213b).

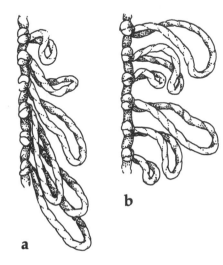

2.213

• Cut the loops for a shaggy finish (Fig 2.214). Starting at the top, draw a needle through the first row of loops, pull and cut close to the needle. Brush up and cut next row. At the end, brush down, spray with water (see **blocking**), comb, pin the edges down and allow to dry.

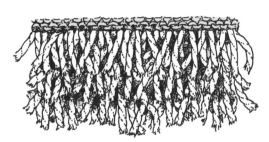

2.214

Loops at front of work

a K1 but do not drop from left needle.

b Yf.

c Wind yarn around left thumb, or around a piece of card.

d Yb.

e K original st again (Fig 2.215) and let it drop.

f Yo from **front to back**.

g Pass last 2 sts on right needle over the **over**, as if **casting off**.

h Withdraw thumb from loop.

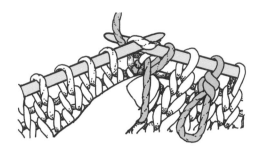

2.215

Loops at back of work

a K1, wrapping yarn around piece of card, or around one or more left fingers, as well as needle. Do not drop st from left needle.

b Place new st on left needle (Fig 2.216).

c K-b together the new st and the original st.

d Withdraw finger(s) from loop.

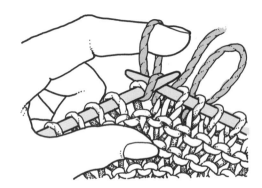

2.216

Loops on a ruler

On a **wrong-side** row:

a **K**1, wrapping yarn first around needle, then around ruler held behind the right needle, then again around needle (Fig 2.217).

b Draw the 2 wraps around right needle, and drop st from left needle.

On next row, **k-b** together the 2 wraps from each loop. Withdraw ruler at the end of the row.

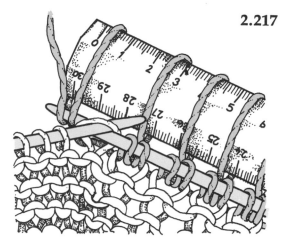

Crossing

In **crossed** work, one stitch (or group of stitches) is worked after the stitch or group that follows. If only two stitches are involved, the result is **cross stitch**. If two groups of stitches are involved, the result is a **cable** and an auxiliary **cable needle** is required.

For a **right cross**, the first stitch or group stays at the **back**. For a **left cross** it stays at the **front**.

Crossing always increases **tension**, making for a denser fabric.

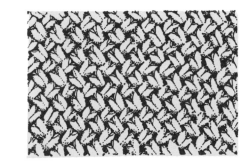

2.218

Cross stitch

Also called **twist stitch, one-over-one stitch, cross-over stitch, travelling stitch** and **wrap-around**.

Used in many stitch patterns, either as miniature **cables**, as backgrounds (Fig 2.218), or in beautiful designs (Fig 2.219). Most pattern dictionaries offer a good selection (see **Books**).

2.219

In fabrics made with many cross stitches, consider working with fairly thick needles and expect some loss of elasticity.

The standard version of the technique includes one or two awkward movements. Several variations exist.

Standard cross stitch

RIGHT CROSS

On **knit**:

a Insert right needle into 2nd st from the front, drawing its front loop across 1st st (Fig 2.220).

b K 2nd st.

c K 1st st.

d Drop the 2 sts from left needle.

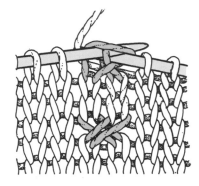

2.220

A less orthodox variation knits the second stitch also from the front but without drawing front of loop across first stitch. Fig 2.221 shows a mock cable obtained by applying this technique to three stitches: k, first, 3rd st; then 2nd st; then 1st st.

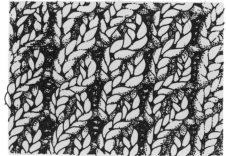

2.221

On **purl**:

a P 2nd st.

b P 1st st.

c Drop the 2 sts from left needle.

Easier than the orthodox knit version.

LEFT CROSS

On **knit**:

a Working round back of 1st st, insert right needle into front loop of 2nd st and **k**.

b K 1st st (Fig 2.222).

c Drop both sts from left needle.

A variation, not so orthodox but easier and practically identical in appearance, works the second stitch through the back loop.

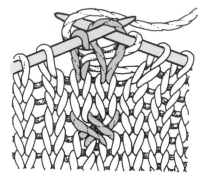

2.222

On **purl**:

a **Sl2 kwise** (1 at a time).

b Insert left needle from right to left into the 2 sts and **sl** them back together. They are now in reverse order.

c P the 2 sts as they are.

Twice-worked cross stitch

This version is somewhat more raised and compact.

RIGHT CROSS

On **knit**:

a **K2 tog**, but do not drop.

b K 1st st again (Fig 2.223).

c Drop the 2 sts from left needle.

On **purl**:

a P 2nd st.

b P 1st and 2nd sts together.

c Drop the 2 sts from left needle.

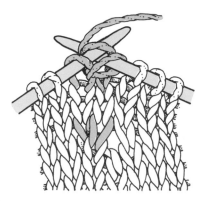

2.223

LEFT CROSS

On **knit**:

a **K-b** 2nd st (Fig 2.224).

b **K** 1st and 2nd sts together, inserting needle into front of 1st st and into back of 2nd.

c Drop the 2 sts from left needle.

A variation, which leaves a **twisted** top stitch, **knits-back** both stitches together.

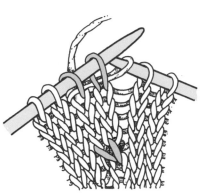

2.224

On **purl**:

a **Sl2 kwise** (1 at a time).

b Insert left needle from right to left into the 2 sts and **sl** them back together. They are now in reverse order.

c **P** the 2 sts together. Do not drop.

d **P** 1st st again.

e Drop the 2 sts from left needle.

Cables U

Cables are most often worked as knit stitches over a purl background (Fig 2.225). They are also possible on a knit background (Fig 2.226), and even in other patterns (Fig 2.227 shows a **purl** and **single rib** cable on a **garter stitch** background).

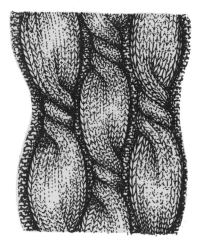

2.225

2.226

Cables have a very marked effect on the width of the fabric, and sometimes a slight effect on its length. The loss in width can be as much as one-third as compared with **stocking stitch**.

There are only two techniques involved. What makes one cable different from another is the width in stitches, the number of rows between crossings, the sequence of

2.227

right and left crossings, and the number of background stitches in between.

In general, cables have an even number of stitches, divided in two equal groups when crossing, and are crossed from the **right side** of the work. Asymmetrical cables, and cables crossed from either side of work, are possible.

Further possibilities, to be complemented with a good pattern dictionary (see **Books**):

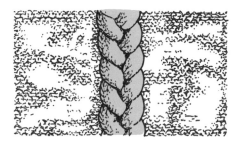

2.228

● Use one colour for the cable and another one for the background (Fig 2.228).

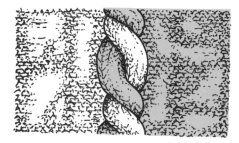

2.229

● Use one colour for the right side and another for the left side (Fig 2.229).

● Make 'braids' travel across the background (by cabling the braid with one adjoining stitch, possibly on every alternate row), then interlace the braids (Fig 2.230).

2.230

● Make cables travel diagonally by using the principle of **increasing** and **decreasing** outlined in **embossed knitting**, or by off-setting the pattern sequence one stitch to right or left on the row after each crossing (Fig 2.231).

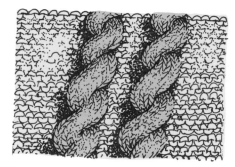

2.231

For best results:

● Use a **cable needle** thinner than the needle(s) you use for knitting.

● To avoid gaps, pull yarn firmly when knitting the first stitch from left needle.

● To avoid a left-edge stitch larger than the rest in knit cables on purl background, see **uneven fabrics**.

● Use **fabric markers** to keep track of the rows between crossings.

Right cross for cables

Also called **back cross**.

On **right-side** or **wrong-side** rows:

a Work to cable position.

b **Sl** half the cable sts (or appropriate number) onto **cable needle**.

c Place **cable needle** at **back of work**.

d Work the cable sts still on left needle (Fig 2.232).

e Work the sts on **cable needle** in their original order.

Left cross for cables

Also called **front cross**.

Work as for **right cross** but keep **cable needle** at **front of work** (Fig 2.233).

2.232

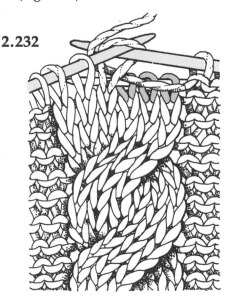

2.233

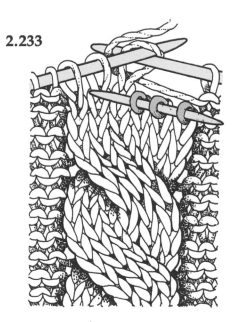

Raised patterns

(See also **embossed knitting, sculptured knitting, clustering** and **pull-up stitch**)

All the techniques in this chapter create motifs that stand above the fabric surface. Try to emphasise this effect when **blocking** (see **frames and moulds** and **improving fabric**), and avoid them in situations where they will get flattened, as at the back of skirts.

The motifs can be worked individually, in rows, in vertical or diagonal or curved lines, in clusters, in geometrical shapes, evenly or randomly spaced in areas or all over the fabric – with a further choice of same or different colour(s) from the background!

Some motifs, such as **bobbles**, can be worked independently and then sewn onto the fabric. This is useful for afterthoughts, but best results are obtained by knitting the motifs in. If not random, either plan them on **ratio graph paper** or follow directions from a patter dictionary (see **Books**).

Almost any pattern can be used as

background. However, when many motifs are involved the result will be considerably thicker and heavier. Allow for extra yarn. **Tension** may be affected too – work **samples**.

Needle and **fabric markers** are often invaluable when determining motif positions.

Tufts or popcorns   S

The smallest of all raised motifs, consisting of a **multiple increase** followed, immediately or almost immediately, by a **multiple decrease**. Worked over one stitch on the **right side**. Always work the next stitch firmly and pull the tuft neatly onto the right side.

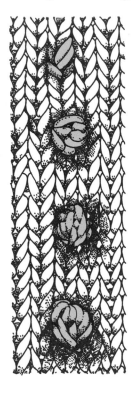

2.234

Fig 2.234 shows a selection of tufts, amongst many that could be invented or found in pattern dictionaries. Exact size of increase is not given – the larger the increase, the larger the tuft.

Flat tuft

Fig 2.234, top. Worked over two rows.
a Work a **multiple over increase**.
b On next row, **p** together all the sts of increase. Use a **crochet hook** if action is awkward.

Crested tuft

Fig 2.234, second from top.
a Work a multiple **knit-and-purl increase**.
b Pass all extra sts over last st made, starting with the one furthest from it.

Cock's comb tuft

Fig 2.234, third from top. This stands out quite vertically.
a **Knitted cast-on** a few sts.
b **K** all sts made and drop original st from left needle.
c Pass all extra sts over last st made, starting with the one next to it.

Thimble tuft

Fig 2.234, bottom.
a **K1**, but do not drop from left needle.
b Place new st on left needle, **k** it and drop it. Repeat **a** and **b** as desired, always working from same original st.
c Drop original st.
d Pass all extra sts over last st, starting with the one next to it.

Bobbles   S

A **tuft** with added rows, worked so that they are independent from the base fabric.

Bobbles can be worked in **stocking stitch** or in **reverse stocking stitch** (Fig 2.235). Their size depends on the size of the original increase and on the number of back-and-forth rows they have. Work next stitch firmly.

Consider working the return rows **from left to right** rather than **turning** (remember to adapt wrong-side rows – **p** for **k** and **k** for **p**).
a Work a **double** or a **multiple increase** (**over** or **knit-and-purl**).
b **Turn. Slip** 1 **pwise**, **p** to end of bobble, for

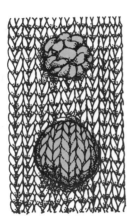

2.235

    a k bobble; **slip** 1 **kwise, k** to end of bob-
ble, for a **p** bobble.

    c **Turn. Slip** 1 **kwise, k** to end of bobble, for
a **k** bobble; **slip** 1 **pwise, p** to end of bobble, for a **p** bobble.

Repeat **b** and **c** as desired. With only 3 sts,
end with a **b** row, then:

d Straight decrease.

With 4 or more stitches, end with a **c** row,
then:

d Decrease as necessary along next row
to leave only 3 sts.

e Straight decrease.

Buds   S

Related to **tufts** and **bobbles** in that they start
with a **multiple increase** and end with a
multiple decrease. Different in that they are
not finished on the same main row.

Again, many variations can be imagined. To
make a bud larger, add more stitches and
more rows. For **rosebud**, also make more
wraps in second row.

Due to fabric curl, knit buds are emphasised
by a purl fabric, but purl buds disappear in a
knit fabric (see **Knit and purl – applications**).

Rosebud
Fig 2.236, top.

a Row 1 (**right side**): Work a **multiple increase** (**over** or **knit-and-purl**) to make,
say, 5 sts out of 1 st.

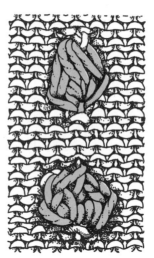

2.236

b Row 2: **p** the 5 sts wrapping yarn twice to
make **elongated sts**.

c Row 3: **sl5 wyab**, dropping extra wraps;
pull yarn tight.

d Row 4: **sl5 wyif**.

e Row 5: **sl3, p2 tog, psso**.

Peony
Fig 2.236, bottom.

a Row 1: like **rosebud**, but make 7 sts.

b Row 2: **p**.

c Row 3: **ssk, k3 tog, k2 tog**.

d Row 4: **p3 tog**.

Hoods   S

(See also **frilled edges**)

Unlike all the previous motifs, hoods stem
from a platform of **cast-on stitches** placed between two stitches of the base fabric.

A shape is worked over the following few
rows on this platform, cunningly **decreasing**
until no stitches remain.

Hoods should be worked on a fabric, such as
stocking stitch, which **curls** in the same way
as the hood. Choice of decreases is equally
important, because of their decorative role.

The most popular shape is the triangle,
which results in:

Bells

Also called **foxgloves** (Fig 2.237).

a Row 1 (right side): **cast on**, say, 8 sts, with one of the methods recommended for **ends of rows**.

b Work 3 rows in **st st,** or chosen pattern, right across work.

c Continue in pattern – **ssk** at start and **k2 tog** at end of every bell on **right-side** row.

d When only 1 st remains, work together with 1 of the adjoining sts.

2.237

Flaps   S

Totally independent motifs, attached to the base fabric on their last row (Fig 2.238). Work any shape you like (see **medallions**), on a **flat fabric,** unless you want a **curly** effect.

2.238

Knit in by placing the needle with the flap next to the main left needle, then working one stitch from each one of these together (Fig 2.239).

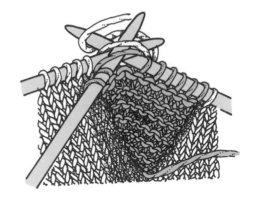

2.239

Tunnels   S

A combination of **short-rows** and **tubular knitting with open sides** (Fig 2.240).

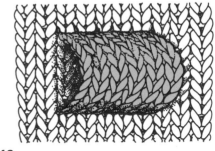

2.240

The motif is made to curl over the base fabric by adding rows to it. In narrow tunnels, consider working the return rows **from left to right**.

Use two balls of yarn, A and B, whether in the same or different colours.

a Row 1 (**right side**): double the number of sts across tunnel with **lifted increases**. Work original sts in main yarn, A, and **increases** in B. Finish row as usual.

b Row 2: work to 1st B st with A. With B,

*p1, **slip** 1 **pwise wyab*** to end of tunnel.

c **Turn**. With B, ***k1, slip** 1 **pwise wyif***, to end of tunnel.

d **Turn**. Repeat the **b** and **c** short rows a few times, possibly giving the tunnel a **selvedge**.

e **Turn**. With A, ***slip** 1 **wyif, p1*** to end of tunnel; end row as usual.

f Row 3: with A, work to tunnel, ***slip** 1 **wyib, k1*** to end of tunnel. End row as usual.

g Row 4: with A, work complete row, taking 1 A st with 1 B st across the tunnel.

All sorts

There are many techniques which are difficult to classify. Some of them are minor. About others one could write whole books and, in fact, some have already been written. This chapter is a collection of some of these techniques, all touched on lightly because of space constraints. There are many others. Some are not included because they are more appropriate to pattern dictionaries (see **Books**), others simply because they are unknown to me, and others because they are being invented as I write – proof that no one can ever know ALL about hand knitting!

Double stitch   U

Double because it is drawn through two stitches – the one in the row being taken off the left needle and the one immediately

2.241

below it. Working through the stitch two rows below makes a **treble stitch** etc.

Double stitches cannot be worked closer than on alternate stitches, otherwise the previous row would unravel.

Mainly used in patterns, especially **brioche**. The resulting fabric tends to be very **wide**, but also very **short**.

a **K** into centre of st below next st (Fig 2.241).

b Drop st above off left needle.

Brioche knitting

FIRST METHOD

Fabrics in which up to every other stitch of every row is a **double stitch**. They are thick, soft, and often deceptive. To the untrained eye, the popular **fisherman's rib** (Fig 2.242), for example, may look like **single rib** worked on thick needles.

The **selvedge** must be **slipped** at the start of every row, or the edges will wave. Make sure that selvedges do not interfere with pattern. All patterns need a preparatory row, usually a **purl** row on the **wrong side**. It takes quite a few rows to see the pattern forming.

SECOND METHOD

Another way of working these patterns, often found in pattern dictionaries, uses **increases** and **decreases** instead of **double stitches**:

a Row 1: an **over** is made next to a **sl st**.

b Row 2: **yo** and **sl st** are worked together.

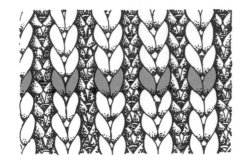

2.242

It is more tedious, but there is a subtle difference. In the first version, the long strand (of the unravelled stitch above) lies UNDER the head of the final stitch. In this second version, the long strand (of the over) lies ABOVE the head of the final stitch. The preparatory row becomes, in this version, a series of **overs, slip stitches** and ordinary stitches.

Dip stitch   U

A loop drawn from a stitch a few rows below to make a long, ornamental stitch over the fabric.

Used in stitch patterns such as **daisies** (Fig 2.243). Depending on the pattern, the long loop is: passed over the next stitch, taken together with a neighbour stitch on the next row, or something else is done to it.

Sometimes the loop will need untwisting, by dropping it and then inserting the needle from the other side, so that it lies flat.

2.243

Always make sure that the loop is long enough. Remember that a similar loop appears at the other side of work, and that neither must pull.

a   Insert right needle into a st a few rows below. This can be directly under, to the right, or to the left of the st last made.

b   'K' and draw a long loop (Fig 2.244).

2.244

Three-into-three stitch   U

● Work three stitches together so that three new stitches result.

Figure 2.245 shows a motif, **cornflower**, worked on the **right side** in this way. The three stitches are first purled, then knitted, then purled again (always together), and finally dropped off left needle.

2.245

Figure 2.246 shows **daisy** or **star stitch**, an all-over fabric worked very similarly, but this time from the **wrong side**. The three stitches are purled, knitted and purled as before (or **p, yo, p** for a less dense fabric). One knit stitch divides each group, and the sequence

2.246

is staggered on the following wrong-side row. The **right-side** rows are knitted. You may need needles thicker than usual.

Clustering S

With the help of a **cable needle**, it is possible to wrap the yarn over and over around a group of stitches. The more times the yarn is wrapped, the more three-dimensional the effect. The tighter it is pulled, the more the stitches will be squeezed.

a After working the stitches to be clustered, transfer them to a **cable needle**. Keep at whichever side of work they feel more comfortable.

b Wrap yarn around sts on **cable needle** as many times as desired (Fig 2.247).

c Return sts to right needle.

d Continue work.

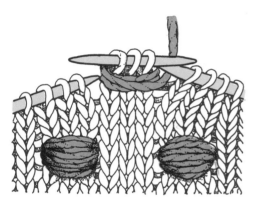

2.247

Smocking

● Working on, say, **double rib, cluster** at regular intervals, staggering the clusters to create a honeycomb (Fig 2.248). On the **right side**, each cluster has a group of knit stitches, one of purl stitches, and another of knit stitches.

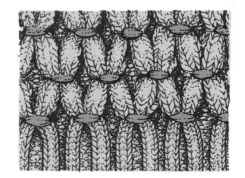

2.248

Pull-up stitch S

Deep textural effects are obtained with this technique.

● Catch the head of a stitch a few rows down and work it with the first stitch on left needle (Figs 2.249 and 2.250).

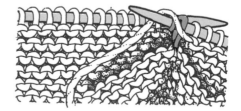

2.249

If a whole row is pulled up, **cording** or **horizontal soft pleats** will result (top of Fig 2.250), depending on how far down that row was. It might be convenient to pick up all the heads of the row below with a fine needle, hold this needle next to the left needle, and work together one stitch from each.

For horizontal waves, pull up a few stitches

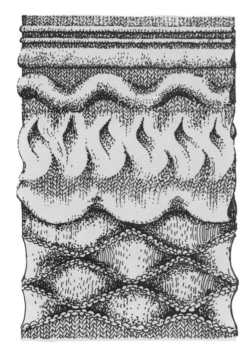

2.250

at regular intervals. Repeat, staggering the arrangement, a few rows further up.

For diagonal effects, pull up consecutive stitches, one at a time, over several rows.

Stocking stitch, pulled up from the **wrong side**, is most often used. Many other patterns, or pattern combinations emphasising the new texture, could be used instead – simple **colour stripes** could become quite dramatic.

Picking from the **right side** is also quite possible. The effect is then reversed (bottom of Fig 2.250), and often some purl stitches, or a couple of rows of **garter stitch**, are introduced to make pulling up easier.

Rug stitch S

Rugs can be knitted as well as knotted on a canvas, but keeping a very even and firm **tension** is essential.

Use strong, unbleached cotton yarn and cut rug wool, or strips of cloth. Unless working with extremely thick wool, the cotton should not be thicker than **double knitting**.

Patterns can be created with wools of different **colour**. Large rugs are worked in strips, later sewn together. The edges are best reinforced with strong tape sewn on the underside.

a **Cast on** and k 1 row in cotton.
b Next row: **k**1; place a strand of wool at right angles and under right needle (make it slightly longer in **front of work**); **k**1; fold the wool under right needle, so that both ends are now at **back of work** (Fig 2.251). Repeat to end of row.
c **K** 1 row.
d Repeat **b**, but start and end with k2 to stagger the wool.

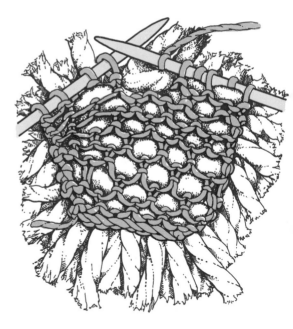

2.251

Twice-knit knitting S

(See **Books**.)

A fascinating way of knitting, with its own special **cast-on** and **cast-off** methods, although casting off is not strictly necessary – the work does not unravel when taken off the needle!

Twice-knit knitting will not snag, and can be cut without fear. It will not stretch, so it can be worked on really large needles.

All this is achieved by working each stitch twice, first with its right neighbour, then with its left neighbour. This has the further effect of making the stitch lie perpendicular to the fabric's surface. As a result, the stitch is always as wide as the yarn, whilst its depth depends more on needle size than on yarn thickness. In other words, forget all you have painstakingly learnt about **stitch size**. Very thick needles are normally used, unless a very, very dense fabric is required.

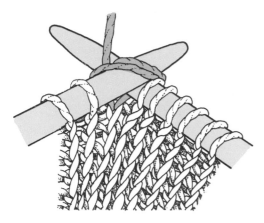

2.252

Figure 2.252 shows what happens to **stocking stitch** when worked this way.

a Work **2 tog.**
b Drop only 1st st.
c Repeat **a** with the st not dropped and the following st.

Repeat **b** and **c** to end of row. The last st is worked once by itself.

Two-strand knitting   s

A type of knitting devised to make thicker, firmer and warmer garments. The two strands can be of the same or of a different colour. They should be carried in the same hand, one around the first finger and one around the second finger (see **holding the yarns** under **Colour knitting**). Changing them so that the new yarn is always on top makes the fabric even firmer and more even.

a Work 1st st with one strand.
b Work 2nd st with the other strand.

Repeat **a** and **b**, even on the **cast-on** row. Moving one yarn to the **right side** whilst working with the other creates a horizontal bar which can be used to form patterns (Fig 2.253).

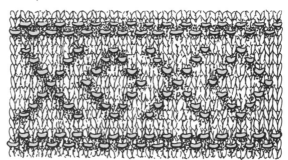

2.253

Filet knitting

There have been attempts to produce knitted versions of the solid-squares-on-empty-squares designs typical of net darning – **filet** being French for net. Unlike crochet, however, knitting is not naturally suited to this type of work and the characteristic sharpness is lost.

A technique best forgotten.

Tunisian knitting   s

Another unusual approach to fabric making. Results are **flat, thick** and not unlike crochet. One of the rows is totally **slipped** whilst the yarn is being wound around the needle. On the next row each stitch is worked together with a neighbouring **over**, through the back of the loops. Watch carefully that the edges do not pull or wave. Unless using thick needles, expect fairly slow progress and to need quite a lot of yarn.

If you have attempted this technique before and failed, try again. The only two references I have found to the **horizontal stitch**, should have been more specific.

Oblique Tunisian stitch

a **Cast on** any number of **sts.**
b Row 1 (**wrong side**): **slip** 1 **kwise, front-to-back over**. Repeat to end. The last **yo** is loose. Keep it in position with left thumb whilst turning work.
c Row 2: **K-b**2 **tog** (a **sl st** and a **yo**) to last st (Fig 2.254). **K-b**1.

2.254

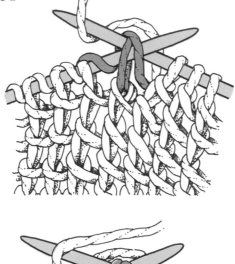

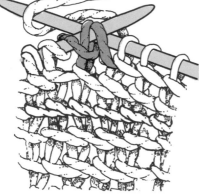

2.255

Horizontal Tunisian stitch

Work as for **oblique stitch** but end Row 1 with a **double over**. In Row 2 the **overs** appear in front of the **slip stitches**, and give a full turn around the needle. This makes in-serting the right needle (Fig 2.255) somewhat more awkward than in **oblique stitch**.

Oddyarn knitting   S

Mixing yarns of different **thickness** and/or **texture** (and perhaps even **colour**) may be a disaster or a revelation, but is certainly worth experimenting with. There are thousands of possibilities, from **raised motifs** or pairs of **garter stitch** rows in thick **bouclé** on a thinner, **high-twist** background, to fine and smooth **lace** insertions on a solid **chenille** background. **Colour knitting** could be a good source of ideas, especially **knitweave** and **multicolour slip stitch**.

Tension needs to be handled with care. Large chunky areas on a solid, medium-weight fabric are likely to require adjustments in the number of stitches as well as a change in needle size. On the other hand, two yarns may be worked in bands so that the fine yarn is so loose that it becomes quite lacy, whilst the thick yarn ensures that shape is retained with, say, **slip stitches** connecting the thick bands. Or, the thick yarn may be knitted in a solid pattern and the fine yarn in a **faggot** or **lace** pattern (Fig 2.256). The holes created by the lace keep the width constant, so there is no need to adjust the stitches.

Careful **blocking** of most of these combinations is essential. Have fun!

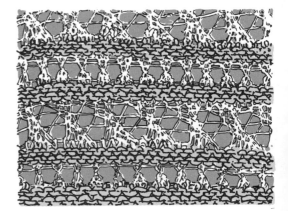

2.256

Colour knitting

Much of what is said in this chapter about colour equally applies to **oddyarn knitting**. Always leave yarn tails long enough for **darning** if you are not **weaving** them **in**. Longer lengths for sewing different areas with matching colour are not necessary if the **ladder stitch seam** is to be used.

Most instructions for colour patterns are perfect examples of a picture being worth a thousand words – crystal clear from a **chart**, laborious to decipher when written **row by row**. In Britain, where knitters rely heavily on written instructions, charts are sometimes omitted. Refuse point-blank to buy **jacquard** or **intarsia** patterns without charts; if the pattern is in a magazine, write and ask for the chart.

The key to successful colour knitting is to keep in mind, at the planning stage, that it has to be knitted. This is not a silly statement. Some designs are thought of in terms of graphics and then forced through the needles. They are 'knitted designs' rather than 'knitting design'. Unusual and exciting effects may be obtained, but often at the high price of awkward work and sub-standard results.

This is not to say that rules should not be broken. Of course they should, or it would be the end of knitting. But only those in full command of the rules (those who know them inside out and back to front) can break them successfully. Otherwise, it is bumpy fabric, knots, distorted stitches, pulling **floats**, uneven fabric, holes . . . Can anyone call that 'exciting'?

No-tangle knitting

Working with fifty, ten, or even two different balls of yarn is, of necessity, more cumbersome than working with one single ball.

Here are a few ideas for not making life more difficult than it need be. Depending on circumstances, one system will work better than others.

ALWAYS:

● Twist yarns only to prevent holes, say for **intarsia**. As explained in **jacquard**, instructions may ask you to twist unnecessarily.

● Turn work so that tangles untwist rather than twist further.

WITH TWO COLOURS ONLY:

● Keep one to your right and one to your left, or both on the same side but well apart and in different bags (Fig 2.257).

WITH SEVERAL COLOURS:

●Thread each colour through a hole, either

2.257

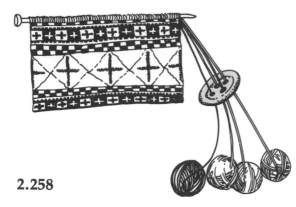

2.258

of a large button or of a punched, stiff piece of card (Fig 2.258).

• Clip balls not in use to the **cast-on** edge with **stitch holders**.

• Keep each ball in its own container – box, jam jar etc (Fig 2.259). Move the containers around if the colour order changes.

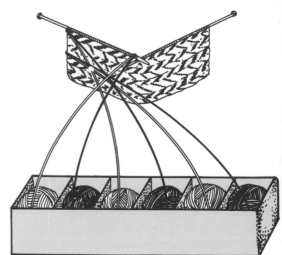

2.260

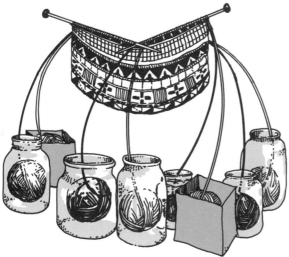

2.259

• Keep the balls in a long container, not wider than the largest ball, and place the working ball(s) always at the right end (Fig 2.260).

• Divide a shoe box into compartments, either by pushing strips of card through slits made at the sides, or by placing several small boxes inside. Make holes on the lid to corres-

pond. Place yarn in compartments and thread through holes (Fig 2.261). Tie the box and turn it every time you turn the work.

• Keep only the working yarns attached to the work. Cut and **join** in new colours as required. This will involve you in much **darning** at a later stage, unless you **weave in** all the ends now.

• Use **bobbins**, unwinding only enough yarn for immediate needs.

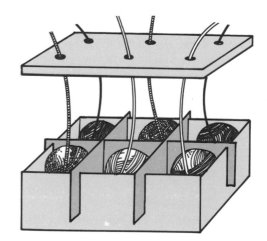

2.261

WITH MANY COLOURS:
- Use **bobbins**, as above.
- Use short lengths of yarn, never ever more than 2m (2yd) long; half that length if you want them really manageable. Leave them dangling. To untangle one particular colour, simply pull. **Weave in** all the ends as you work, unless you have a passion for **darning**.

Choosing colours

Those seriously interested in colour theory should attend a course or study one of the superb texts available (see **Books**).

For those who prefer a less scholarly and more intuitive path, here are a few general pointers:
- Open your eyes and look around. Whenever you see something (room, mountain, picture, garment, floor rug, bird, flower, stone wall, river . . .) that appeals to you, try to identify the different colours. It may be hard to start with, but persevere until you see all the subtle differences. You may well discover many unexpected combinations, and be surprised to see how bright a colour needs to be when only specks of it appear.
- Try knitting a colour scheme that pleases you, either in as many shades as the original, or picking up just a few of them. Choose colours very carefully – darker or lighter than the original might break the balance and ruin the effect.
- Knit several **samples** with the same pattern, but changing the colours around. Some combinations will make the pattern more ob-

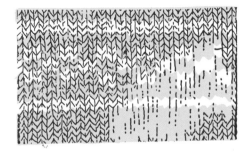

2.263

vious, others will blur it (Figs 2.262 and 2.263). Have the samples around for a few days, and keep looking at them. If they are dull, add small amounts of a bright colour for accent. If they are too harsh, try again in more muted shades or introduce a neutral colour. If you still like a sample after a few days, start knitting.
- If working stripes, wrap the yarns around cards or around your fingers in different combinations before doing any samples.
- Do not be prejudiced. Colours interact with each other. By itself, you may not like one of them, but knitted with others you may love the final effect – or vice versa.
- If colour knitting is 'your thing', stock up balls of yarn in as many shades and hues as you can find. Keep them together by colour: reds, blues, greens, yellows, browns. Start a file with oddments, fabric scraps, photographs, magazine cuttings, postcards etc. Look at them often and observe how you react to different colours and different arrangements.
- Consider using more than one **dye lot** of the same colour to increase subtlety.

Changing colours

This has always been a tricky business because, as the last two illustrations show, it can have a deep effect on the overall look. But now it need not be any more.

New York photographer Matthew J. Ferro has come to the rescue of those who like a certain design but want to knit it in different colours – either because they do not like the

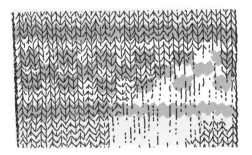

2.262

original ones, or because they cannot find them. His brilliant contribution is a simple, clear table, inspired by the work of Ansel Adams (a master photographer who refined a system for ranking colours in terms of the monochromatic spectrum). Research involved photographing in black-and-white, and comparing, 118 yarn colours.

This is the table:

If you want to change a colour scheme, start by gathering all the recommended colours. You can do this at the woolshop. If exact colours are not available, try to match intensity rather than precise colour if you cannot match them both. If even this is not possible, work from a colour photograph. Then:

a Analyse the first original colour. Decide which colour group it belongs to (navy, blue, brown etc), then whether its shade is

COLOUR VALUE GUIDE FOR YARN SUBSTITUTION

Colour Group	Darkest Value	Medium Value	Lightest Value
Black	1*	1*	1*
Navy (all shades)	1*	1*	1*
Rusts, Burgundies	2	3	4
Reds, Magentas	2	4*	***
Violets, Purples	2	4	6
Blues	2	4	6
Greens	2	4	6
Browns	2	4	6
Pinks, Roses, Mauves, Plums, Peaches	3	5	7
Greys**	3	5	7
Beiges	5	6*	6*
Oranges	5	6	6
Off-whites	7*	7*	7*
Yellows	7*	7*	8
White	8*	8*	8*

*Yarns of this colour and shade have predominantly one value.
**Black and white heathers (charcoal) range in value from 2 to 3.
***See the 'Pinks, Roses, Mauves, Plums, Peaches' colour group.

Reprinted from **Vogue Knitting** magazine by permission of the Butterick Co Inc. Chart copyright Matthew J. Ferro.

dark, medium or light. Look up the corresponding value in the table and write it down. You can use an intermediate value when a yarn falls between dark and medium, or between medium and light.

b Eliminate all the colour groups outside the value of the original colour.

c Choose a new colour from the remaining colour groups, substituting bright for bright, pastel for pastel etc.

Repeat **a**, **b** and **c** for each colour, always working in the same lighting.

d Look at all the new colours together. Introduce changes if necessary, but keep to the correct values. If any of the colours needs to go one point up or down, try to make all the other colours do the same.

Multicolour yarns   U

Perfect for a lazy day. Take, for instance, an **ombré** or a **twist** yarn, and from **cast-on** to **cast-off** you will never have more than one strand. Or, work together several fine strands in slightly different or highly contrasting shades. You will still have several balls to contend with, but because they are worked at the same time, tangles become far less important or likely.

Yarns with great colour, and perhaps texture, interest, are usually best worked in simple patterns; but the obvious **stocking stitch** often makes them flat and dull. Sometimes, merely using the **reverse** side, perhaps worked sideways, is enough to improve the look. Best effects, however, are often obtained with patterns that break the straight row arrangement, such as **slip stitch**, **double stitch**, **dip stitch**, **faggot** or **chevron** patterns.

An additional problem with **ombré** yarns regularly spaced at short intervals is the zebra, or colour-blob, effect they produce (Fig 2.264). To keep the effect regular, do not break the colour sequence when **joining** in new yarn, and start at the same point in the sequence when working identical pieces.

2.264

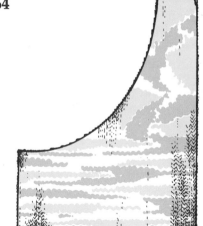

Shapings, or dividing the work for, say, a neckline, will always have an effect. If you want to mask the zebra, use two balls of yarn and change from one to the other every two rows.

Stripes   U

Horizontal stripes are the easiest way of working with two or more colours. Simply **join in** a new colour at the start of a row.

Vertical stripes are worked in **jacquard** if they are narrow and in **intarsia** if they are wide. They can also be worked horizontally and used sideways.

With very wide stripes it is best to cut the yarn at the end of each stripe. Otherwise, the yarn can be carried up the work to avoid **darning** or **weaving in**. Wrap the working

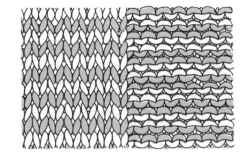

2.265

yarn around the other yarn(s) every 2–3cm (1in). Make sure the yarns do not pull.

Stripes in **stocking stitch** make a clean line on the knit side and a broken line on the purl side (Fig 2.265 – see also **the knitted stitch**). In **garter stitch** one side is clear-cut and the other not. In other words, on the purl side of the change-in-colour row the colours overlap. If you want a clean stripe in your **ribbings**, make the first row of the new colour a knit row (purl row if worked on the **wrong side**). Expect some loss of elasticity.

Odd-row stripes

In **flat knitting** it is easier to work stripes with an even number of rows. Odd-numbered or single-row stripes, however, only need a little planning or a little cunning.

Carry some colours up the right edge and some up the left edge. Arrange the stripes so that the colour you want next is already at the appropriate edge (Fig 2.266). You will need at least three balls of yarn.

Or, work with **double-pointed** or **circular** needles, if not all the time at least for the last row of the odd-row stripe. At the end of this row go back to the beginning of it, without turning the work, and join in the new colour. This method may involve you in more **darning** or **weaving** than the first one.

Helix stripes

A truly ingenious way of avoiding steps at the start of the rounds, and having to carry yarns at back of work, when knitting one-row stripes in **circular knitting**.

a Divide the work into as many, roughly equal, groups of stitches as colours you want to use. Either put each group on its own **double-pointed needle**, or use **needle markers** if working with a **circular needle**.

b Work 1st group in 1st colour, 2nd group in 2nd colour, etc. Fig 2.267 shows an example with 3 colours.

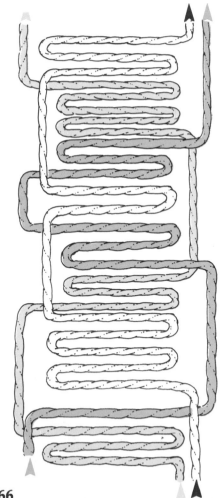

2.266

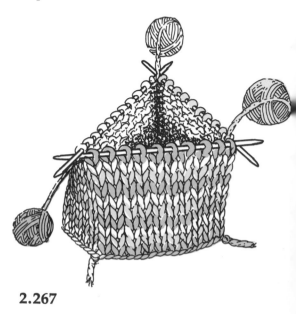

2.267

c Work next round similarly, but using the colours as they come – 1st group with last colour from previous round, 2nd group with 1st colour, etc (Fig 2.268).

Repeat **c.**

If working in this way right from the start, cast on each group in a different colour.

2.268

Interlocking stripes

Use **slip-stitch** techniques to make the old colour blend into the new one whilst never working the two at the same time. In Fig 2.269:

- the top stripe starts with a *k1, slip 1* row.
- the centre stripe **slips** every 6th st on 1st row and every 12th st on 2nd row.
- the lower stripe **slips** 3 sts out of 4 on 1st row, and the centre st of the group of 3 on 2nd row.

Many other combinations can be used.

Pattern stripes

A far cry from conventional stripes. Many patterns have rows that are not straight; a colour change often produces interesting results.

2.270

Zigzags are possibly the best-known example (Fig 2.174). **Sculptured knitting** is dramatic (Fig 2.116). Other good examples would be **daisy stitch** worked in two-row stripes (Fig 2.270) and **reverse st st bobbles** worked in the first of two rows of **garter stitch** on a **st st** background (Fig 2.271).

2.269

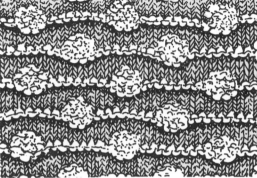

2.271

Intarsia U

Also called **geometric, tartan, collage** or **patchwork knitting.**

A technique used for working totally independent blocks of colour, as in large geometrical arrangements and 'picture knitting' (Fig 2.272).

2.272

Each colour block has its own ball of yarn. Depending on how large the blocks are, use a complete ball, a **bobbin**, or an unwound length of yarn. When changing from one colour to the next, twist one yarn around the other to join the two blocks (Fig 2.273). Expect the twist to show on the purl side (Fig 2.274).

On vertical lines, twist the yarns on every row. On diagonal lines, twist only on the rows, if any, on which the yarn changes at the same point that it did on the previous row.

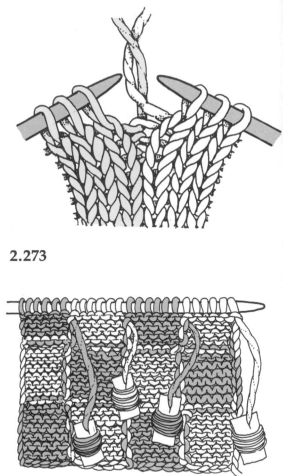

2.273

2.274

After changing colours, check that the last stitch of the previous block is the correct size and shape.

In **circular knitting** the yarn is at the wrong end of the block on the next round and needs to be cut and joined in – an awkward job, leaving many tails to be **darned** or **woven in**.

Stocking stitch is the most popular pattern for intarsia. Other patterns can be used, but you may have to experiment to either stop the twisting of the colours from showing on the right side, or to use this to advantage.

Unless improvising, **charts** are essential. Do not accept row-by-row instructions only.

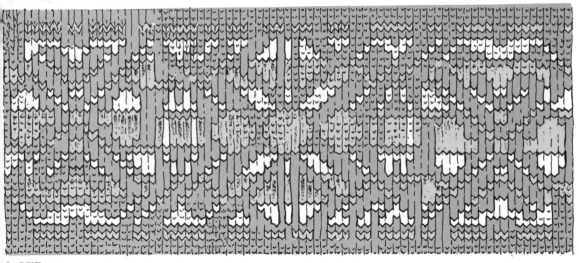

2.275

Jacquard U

Also called **Fair Isle, stranded, two-colour,** and **double knitting**.

Unlike **intarsia**, jacquard has two-colour or multicolour motifs rather than blocks of solid colour (Fig 2.275). Two or more yarns are carried from end to end of each row, although only one is worked (usually in **stocking stitch**) at any one time.

Innumerable patterns have been published. You can also devise your own or adapt from other sources, such as tapestry or embroidery charts.

Fair Isle is only a type of jacquard, with its own rules and characteristic patterns. It is confusing to use the name of this Scottish island to describe jacquard in general. It is confusing and wrong to say that if a pattern uses only two colours in a row it is Fair Isle, and if it uses three or more it is jacquard. Many non-Fair Isle patterns use two colours only.

In jacquard:
- Unless improvising, **charts** are essential. Do not accept row-by-row instructions only.
- The fabric is thick and warm – the **floats** (extra strands carried at the back) form an additional layer.
- More yarn is required.

- Very thick yarns may result in an uncomfortable and heavy fabric.
- More than two colours in a row add thickness, warmth, yarn weight and technical difficulty.
- On the **right side** the pattern is clear; on the **wrong side** only the floats of the non-working colour(s) show.
- Floats, **stranded** or **woven in**, must be loose enough for the intervening stitches to stretch, yet not so loose that they sag. Easier to control when not too long.
- Long stranded floats have the extra disadvantage of being easily caught in fingers, buttons etc.
- Pulled floats are the most common cause of a tight **tension**; try loosening the floats before changing to thicker needles.
- Jacquard may give you a different **stitch size** from self-coloured work in the same stitch pattern – work **samples**. It may also give you a less elastic fabric.

Circular knitting is the most sensible way of working jacquard. If you knit all the time, you see the pattern forming before your eyes and mistakes are easily avoided or spotted. Much traditional knitting is done this way, although Taquile Island Indians (see **yarn around neck**) produce stunning work (Fig 2.276) whilst purling all the time! A fabric

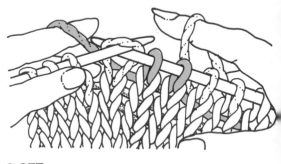

2.276

requiring openings, such as neckline or armholes, can still be worked in rounds by the clever use of **bridges.**

Floats can be **stranded** or **woven in**. Stranding is easiest, but keep to the rules below. Weaving in (below also) can show on the right side; this adds subtlety to some projects, and ruins others.

Isolated motifs can be worked in either technique but using individual **bobbins**, or short lengths, of the contrast colour(s) for each motif. This avoids carrying yarn unnecessarily across wide areas of background. Very small and isolated motifs, or non-horizontal fine lines, might be best **embroidered** in **Swiss darning**.

Holding the yarns
(See also **Holding the work**, and **Stranding** and **Weaving in** below).

FIRST METHOD
Keep the working colour in one hand, and drop it to pick up the next colour. This is a slow method, especially when the instructions say twist the yarns around each other at each colour change. This, essential in **intarsia**, is totally unnecessary in jacquard, except sometimes to prevent a hole in the first colour change of the row or round.

SECOND METHOD
Often recommended: keep one colour in each hand (Fig 2.277). As we have only two hands, working with three or more colours means problems. The technique then needs to be combined with the first or with the third methods. In either case, it may persuade you of the wisdom of having only two colours at any one time.

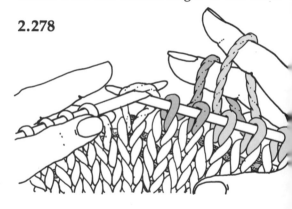

2.277

One problem with this method is that you may need to learn a second, unfamiliar way of knitting. This takes time. To start with, carry the colour with fewer stitches in the less-practised hand. Another problem is loss of rhythm. A group of stitches requires the right needle to move and the left needle to be still, whilst the next group requires the opposite.

THIRD METHOD
A good method: keep one colour over the index finger in the usual hand, and the other colour over the middle finger of the same

2.278

hand (Fig 2.278). Try a third colour over the ring finger, if you dare. This method also needs getting used to, but the change is not nearly as drastic as with the second method, and there is no loss of rhythm.

Stranding

The **floats** are left loose and untwisted: one colour is always on top and the other below (Fig 2.279).

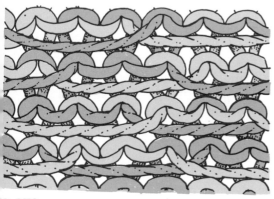

2.279

If holding the two yarns in one hand, keep the index finger above needles, whilst working with the middle finger, and the middle finger below needles when working with the index finger. If holding one yarn in each hand, keep the right colour to the right of needle tips whilst working with the left colour, and the left colour below needles whilst working with the right colour.

DO NOT pull the floats. Spread the last group of stitches to their full width before bringing in the new colour. Otherwise, the floats will tighten up the **tension** and you will not obtain the expected width (Fig 4.1). Keep **measuring** overall width to make sure that the work is not pulling.

AVOID long floats. If longer than 2–3cm (about 1in), floats are difficult to work even. They also snag more easily when in use. Consider introducing odd contrast-colour stitches, or small complementary motifs, to break long stretches of colour. If long floats are essential to maintain a balanced pattern, **weave** them

in. If this advice reaches you too late, see **neatening floats** for a rescue operation.

Weaving in
Also called **knitting in**.
The **floats** are caught by the working yarn, either on alternate stitches (Fig 2.280), or every 2–3cm (about 1in). To work the other stitches, keep the float out of the way.

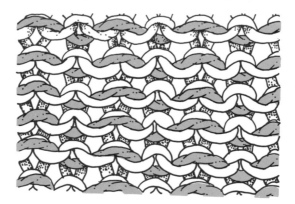

2.280

DO NOT pull the floats. Keep **measuring** overall width to make sure that they are not tightening the **tension**.

ONE YARN IN EACH HAND

To weave-in left yarn (kept above needles when not weaving it in):

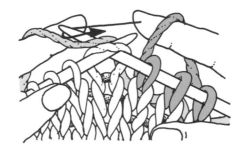

2.281

a Either on **k** (Fig 2.281) or **p** (Fig 2.282), bring the float up.
b Insert right needle into st and under float.
c **K** or **p** st as usual, under float.

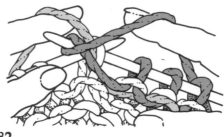

2.282

To **weave-in right yarn** (kept to the right of needle tips when not weaving it in, and more awkward than left yarn):

a Insert right needle into st.

b Wind float around needle. On **k**, wind float as if to **k** (Fig 2.283). On **p**, wind float first under and then over needle (Fig 2.284).

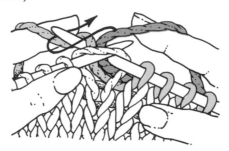

2.283

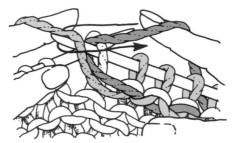

2.284

c Wind working yarn around needle as usual.

d Return float to its previous position.

e Draw st through.

BOTH YARNS IN RIGHT HAND

To **weave-in index-finger yarn** (kept above needles when not weaving it in):

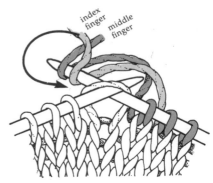

2.285

a On **k** (Fig 2.285) or **p**, insert right needle into st.

b Wind float and working yarn around needle as usual.

c Return float to its previous position.

d Draw st through.

Work next stitch keeping float above needles.

To **weave-in middle-finger yarn** (kept below needles when not weaving it in, and more awkward than index-finger yarn):

a On **k** (Fig 2.286) or **p**, insert right needle into stitch.

b Take float over both needles and hold with left thumb and/or index finger.

c Wind working yarn around needle as usual.

d Return float to its previous position.

e Draw st through.

Work next stitch keeping float below needles.

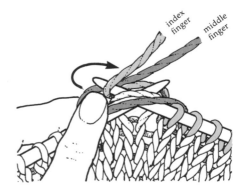

2.286

To weave-in index-finger yarn (kept above needles when not weaving it in):

a On **k** (Fig 2.287) or **p**, insert right needle into st.

b Take right needle over float and work st as usual, drawing it from over the float.

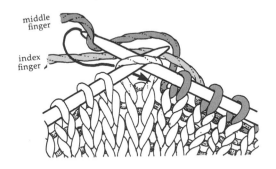

2.287

To weave-in middle-finger yarn (kept below needles when not weaving it in, and slightly more awkward than index-finger yarn):

a On **k** (Fig 2.288) or **p**, insert right needle into st.

b Pass right needle under float and work st as usual, drawing it from under the float.

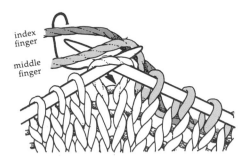

2.288

Jacquard variations S

Although **stocking stitch** is, by far, the most popular base fabric for jacquard, other patterns can also be used.

Knit-and-purl jacquard

Purling some of the stitches adds texture and breaks the horizontal line between colours (Fig 2.289). The occasional **slip stitch** adds even more subtlety and intricacy.

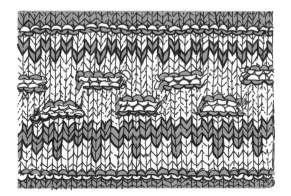

2.289

Garter-stitch jacquard

Two rows instead of one are worked for each stitch, always in **garter stitch**. The result is thicker and sharper because there are no Vs as in **stocking stitch**, and squarer because of the nature of garter stitch (Fig 2.290).

To avoid **floats** showing on the **right side**, on alternate rows each yarn has to be taken to the **wrong side** when not in use, and brought back when required for working.

2.290

Double-sided jacquard

Clever use of the **double-pointed needle** version of **tubular knitting** can produce reversible fabrics with two-colour patterns on both sides (see **Books**). The patterns may be identical, totally different, mirror images or colour-reversed as in Figs 2.291 and 2.292.

A fascinating way of knitting, which gives a very thick and firm fabric.

2.293

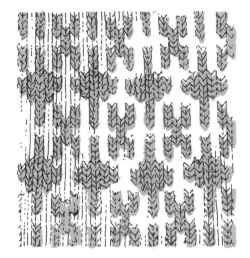

2.291

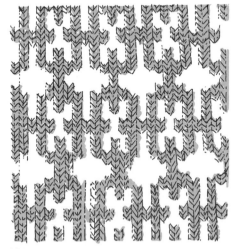

2.292

Fluted jacquard

● Work vertical stripes and pull **floats** as hard as you can (Fig 2.293). Use thick needles and strong, well-twisted yarn that will not break easily. Many stitches are needed.

Try interchanging the colours, in some sort of checkerboard, and/or changing float position.

Great for creating **gathers** without altering the number of stitches.

Knitweave   S

● Weave into the fabric a second yarn, much thicker than the working yarn if you want to, without working any stitches with it.

Knitweave may be done as if **weaving in** for **jacquard**, staggered as in Fig 2.294, or non-staggered as in Fig 2.280; the woven yarn stays all the time on the **purl** side, which is now the **right side**. Or it can be used to form designs similar to those in **jacquard** (Fig 2.295). The woven yarn is brought to the **right side** (the usual **knit** side) when the **chart** shows a contrast stitch, whilst the background yarn works the actual stitches.

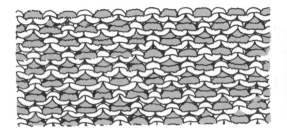

2.294

2.295

All-over arrangements may also be worked by taking the yarn from right to wrong side of work, and can be made to look rather like woven fabric or like bands of **running-stitch embroidery** (Fig 2.296) – weaving in is faster than embroidering once you have the knack.

2.296

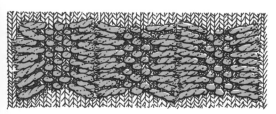

2.297

Blocks of long floats alternating with very short floats may be cut to produce a fringed fabric (Fig 2.297). Keep fabric stretched whilst cutting. Beware of **slippery yarns** that could easily be pulled free.

Multicolour slip stitch U

(See also **slip-stitch knitting**)
A huge variety of textures, better explored with a good pattern dictionary (see **Books**). The amount of **slipped stitches** in any one row makes the patterns slow to grow, but this is made up for by there being no need for more than one yarn at a time. Figs 2.298 and 2.299 show a couple of examples.

2.298

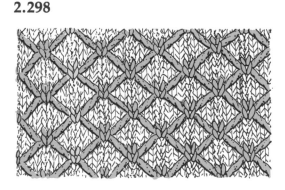

2.299

Slip-stitch patterns are excellent for **oddyarn knitting**. Another advantage is that the **wrong side** can sometimes be used in its own right, especially in patterns worked with

double-pointed needles where rows can start at either end. The result is a reversible fabric.

Mosaic knitting

A type of geometrical **multicolour slip stitch** worked from **charts** in **garter stitch, stocking stitch**, or a combination of knit and purl stitches.

• Each line of the **chart** is worked in two rows. The second row repeats, in the same colour, the sequence of worked and slipped stitches. The two rows of the following line are worked with the second colour. The third line is worked with the first colour, and so on.

Each line of the chart must start with the working colour for that line.
Fig 2.300 shows a characteristic pattern, out of thousands possible.

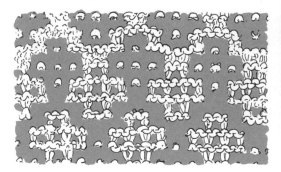

2.300

Beads and things

Beads, sequins, and all sorts of little **objects** (bells, shells, miniature toys, coins, seed-pods, mirrors, feathers, curtain rings, costume jewellery, stones . . .) can be incorporated into a knitted fabric.
To simplify, objects can be divided into:
• **beads**, including sequins and things with a small hole (which may need to be especially drilled).
• **rings** and things with a ring-like hole.
• **blind objects** (anything without a hole).
Objects will always make a project heavier. Too many heavy objects may even make it unworkable after a while. Even a small area of decoration may make the fabric sag. Always match the weight of the object to the strength of the yarn and the weave of the fabric.
Avoid objects that may stain the fabric, and make sure that they can be subjected to the same cleaning processes. **Wash** or **dry-clean samples** if necessary.

Do not use fragile objects in projects where they could be easily broken.

Beads

(See also **embroidered edgings**)
If the fabric is allowed to show, it is **beaded knitting**. If the beads are so touching each other that the fabric is pushed behind the beads, it is **close-bead knitting**. The beads, in most cases, show only on the **right side**. In any case, the **tension** should be tight enough to keep the beads on the side they are meant to be.
Normally use beads with holes just large enough for the yarn to go through. Huge holes are only advisable for special effects, say to allow the bead to dangle freely at the end of a long loop. If the hole is too small for the yarn, or if the yarn has no strength, consider working two strands together: a

strong, but fine, strand to carry the bead, and a thick strand to give texture. Both strands must blend in well together.

Bead threading

The beads should be threaded onto the yarn before starting to work. If they are to form a pattern, work from a **chart** and thread the beads in strict order, starting with the one to be used last. In **flat knitting**, check carefully where the bead rows end. Some may end at the right edge and some at the left edge of the chart.

In general, the bead hole will be too small for a **sewing needle** large enough to carry the yarn. To thread the beads (Fig 2.301):

2.301

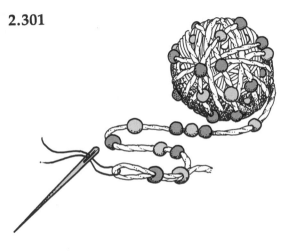

a Thread the two ends of a short piece of sewing cotton into a dressmaker's sewing needle.

b Pass end of yarn through cotton loop.

c Thread beads, push down the yarn, and rewind ball.

When many beads are used, a **marker** between beads of different rows is a help. The marker must be removable (knotted yarn, paper clip, coil ring) and smaller than the beads.

For massive amounts of beads, consider threading a few rows at a time. There will be more tails to be **darned** or **woven in**, but work will be more manageable.

If the beads have a right and wrong side, work **samples** to see which side should be facing you when threading them.

In general, it is best not to have beads at the **selvedges**. Leave one or two stitches on each side if working **flat**.

Beaded knitting S

Beads, of one or more colours and shapes, are knitted into the fabric. The fabric remains visible. The shape of the bead, the way it is threaded, the position and direction of the hole, and the technique of insertion, will determine how the bead hangs. For projects with large numbers of beads, it is advisable to try **samples** with different beads, different inserting techniques and even different knitting patterns.

Possibilities are endless:

● Working in **garter stitch**, place one bead after each stitch on all **wrong-side** rows (Fig 2.302). This gives the closest possible arrangement in beaded knitting.

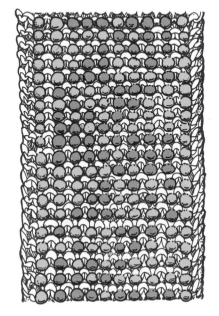

2.302

• Place beads at random, or in isolated motifs, over any unobtrusive pattern. **Stocking stitch** is often used, although other patterns lend themselves better to the purpose – like **moss stitch** in Fig 2.303.

2.303

• Arrange beads in regular patterns such as lines, squares, diamonds or chevrons.
• Use the beads to highlight an edge (Fig 2.304).

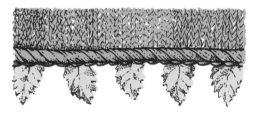

2.304

• Use the beads to highlight a knitting pattern of more or less complexity, such as **faggot** meshes (Fig 2.305), **fur stitch** (Fig 2.306) or **eyelets** (Fig 2.307).

2.305

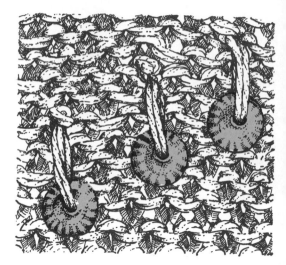

2.306

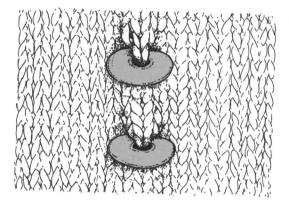

2.307

Beads on purl stitches

Fig 2.308 (see also **the knitted stitch**)
Because the yarn makes a loop between every two purl stitches, it is easy to insert a bead by simply bringing it up next to the fabric after working a stitch. This applies to **reverse stocking stitch, garter stitch** and any pattern with at least two consecutive purl stitches on the **right side**. The beads can be inserted either when purling from the right side or when knitting from the wrong side. The bead stays perfectly horizontal but, because of its position between stitches:
• A single bead cannot be centred on an odd

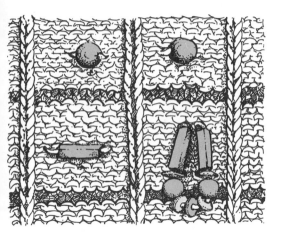

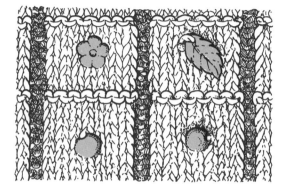

2.308

number of stitches (top left-hand corner of illustration);

● The number of stitches required to insert a line of beads is always 'number of beads plus one';

● Unless very small, a bead will push the fabric to the sides; many beads could distort the fabric.

To have a central bead on an uneven number of stitches, plus an undisturbed fabric, **slip purlwise** one stitch after bringing the bead next to the fabric (top right-hand corner).

If the bead is very wide, slip several stitches (bottom left-hand corner).

Bead loops need a little trick to prevent a hole forming (bottom right-hand corner):

a **P-b1**, but do not drop.
b Bring the beads next to the st.
c **P tog** 1st st and st next to it.

Beads on knit stitches

Fig 2.309.

Inserting beads on knit stitches comes less naturally. If it does not interfere with the design, consider purling the stitch before and the stitch after the bead. Any of the first three purl situations above could then be used; for **loops**, see below.

To avoid purl stitches (bottom right-hand corner of illustration), on a right or wrong side row:

a Take yarn to knit side.

2.309

b Bring bead up and **slip** 1 **pwise**.
c Take yarn back to purl side.

The fabric is slightly distorted – the yarn lifts the side stitches when taken from one side to the other.

For a nearly vertical bead (bottom left-hand corner), use the **close-bead knitting** method of working a **twisted stitch** and pushing the bead right through it when drawing the new loop. The bead is now part of the stitch, and its position on the fabric is therefore higher than with the first method.

Some beads with a hole at the top (top right-hand corner), can be slanted if, on a knit row, the stitch before the bead is purled and the bead brought up before returning the yarn to a knit position. For a symmetrical slant, knit the stitch after the bead on a purl row. If the bead has a wrong side, try a **sample** to see whether it should be threaded front-to-back or back-to-front.

When the hole of the bead is a little wire ring, or similar device, protruding from the back, the bead can be inserted between any two stitches. The protruding hole goes through the fabric and is secured between two purl stitches on the wrong side, whilst the bead itself stays on the right side (top left-hand corner). **Bead loops** can also be inserted in this way.

Beads on other stitches

Yarn over stitches, such as the **faggot** mesh of Fig 2.305, are particularly suited to inserting beads. Simply bring the beads up next to the fabric and make the **over**. On the next row, make sure that the beads remain on the right side.

An altogether different technique is used in Fig 2.310:

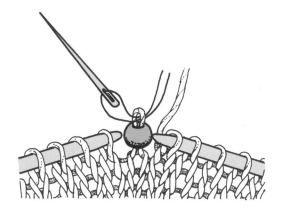

2.310

a Pass a **crochet hook** through the bead. If the bead is too small, use a dressmaker's sewing needle and a length of cotton.

b Drop a stitch from knitting needle and catch either with hook or with sewing needle.

c Draw the stitch through the bead and replace on knitting needle.

A small bead threaded on a solid fabric will create only a little distortion. A large bead such as the one in Fig 2.307 is best used in **openwork**.

Close-bead knitting   s

The beads are so placed as to hardly let the fabric show. Every stitch of every row has a bead, and every stitch is **twisted** to ensure that the bead goes right across the stitch and hides it. The base fabric is **twisted stocking stitch**.

Compare Fig 2.311 with the **beaded knitting** on a **garter stitch** base of Fig 2.302. Both have the same pattern, but it shows better in the former because the beads are closer together.

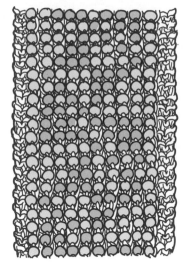

2.311

The overall size of Fig 2.311 is smaller, despite having one stitch more than Fig 2.302. Finally, the fabric of Fig 2.302 was **flat**, whilst that of Fig 2.311 required drastic **blocking**. Apart from the natural fabric curl, it also **slanted** badly due to the **twisting**.

The slanting cannot be dismissed, or totally corrected, but it can be used to advantage. Choose patterns that will not be spoiled by it, and consider mixing **twisted** with **plaited stocking stitch** which slants in the opposite direction. If straight side edges are required, you may need to **increase** at one end and **decrease** at the other.

In **circular knitting** the slant will create a spiral effect which, used properly, might enhance a project. Another advantage of circular knitting is that it avoids the awkward purl rows.

Match carefully stitch and bead sizes. Small beads will not hide the fabric and will tend to go through it onto the wrong side. Very large beads will be awkward to work and may give uneven **tension**.

Both on **knit** (Fig 2.312) or **purl** (Fig 2.313):

a Insert needle into back of loop. When purling, the right needle should be placed above bead of previous row.

b Bring bead up, but not so close as in **beaded knitting**.

2.312

2.313

c Wind yarn in the usual way; the bead should now be behind the right needle, from where it will more easily go through the st.

d Draw yarn and bead through st.

Rings   S

In the same way as a **bead** can be slipped around a stitch (Fig 2.307), a ring can be slipped around one or more stitches. Fig 2.314 shows a ring used to emphasise the clustering effect of a **cable**.

Very deep rings may require holes in the fabric if serious distortion is not wanted. **Openwork** would be an obvious answer. In solid fabrics, consider **eyelets**. Or break the yarn and work three independent areas for the depth of the ring, before inserting it (see **vertical slits**). After insertion, continue work in the usual way.

On **right side** or **wrong side**:

a **Sl** sts to be inserted through ring from left needle onto a **cable needle**.

b Pass one end of **cable needle** through

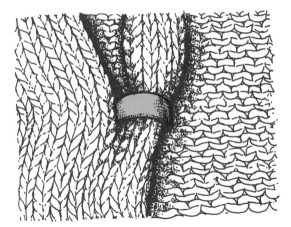

2.314

ring, and carefully slide sts to other end of cable needle, so that this 2nd end can also pass through ring.

c **Sl** the sts back to left needle, without twisting them.

d Work the sts in the ring.

Blind objects   S

Objects that cannot be hung have to be enclosed, usually in a **tubular pocket**.

Use ordinary **tubular stocking stitch** when you want to **stuff** the pocket but do not want to show what is inside it. Otherwise, wrap the yarn two or three times around the needle to make **elongated stitches** (Fig 2.315).

On **right side** or **wrong side**:

a Work a **single increase** on every st of the pocket area.

2.315

b Work in **tubular stocking stitch** for a few rows over the pocket area, and in the usual way over the rest of the fabric.

c **Sl** the front tubular layer onto the right needle, and the back tubular layer onto a **cable needle**, to open the pocket.

d Drop the object inside the pocket.

e Return the sts to left needle, without twisting them or changing their order.

f Work 2**tog** across top of pocket.

Bead markers   U

Fig 2.316

Used to make easy work of counting rows, and as a reminder of, say, changes in pattern or shapings to be worked at regular intervals. Invaluable for blind knitters and for those with poor eyesight, but also very useful if you have no vision problems.

Use lightweight beads in more than one colour or shape – depending on whether you can see or not. In **circular knitting**, position at the start of the rounds; if using a circular needle you will not need the usual **needle marker**. In **flat knitting**, position between first and second stitches at one of the edges or at any convenient place.

a Take a piece of yarn, preferably **slippery**, about twice the expected length to be knitted. Tie one end to the **cast-on** tail. If using a **provisional cast-on**, simply leave a long enough tail.

b On the slippery yarn, thread a bead for every 2 rows you are to work. Use a contrast bead when you have to change pattern, work a shaping etc. If not sure about total number of rows, thread more beads than you think you will need.

c Thread an extra bead or small button and tie at the free end. Leave beads dangling at **back of work**.

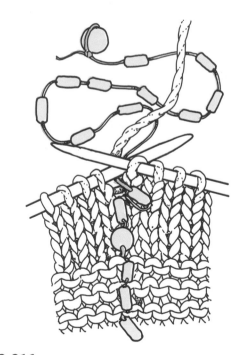

2.316

d Work one row or round. When you reach the beads, take them to **front of work** under the needles – the slippery yarn should not be caught when making the next stitch.

e Work another row or round. Now, take the beads to **back of work** but leave one bead at the **front**.

Repeat **d** and **e**. If you had too many beads before a change of pattern, leave the extra on the **wrong side**.

When the work is finished and you are sure that you will not need the beads any longer, cut the tied end of the slippery yarn and pull the other end (or vice versa if using the tail of a provisional cast-on you do not want to unpick yet). The beads will drop – to stop them going all over the place, place the knitting over a box or bowl.

Edges and selvedges

(See also **Edgings, left edge too long** and **stretched edges**)

Knitting should have firm edges – not tight, or they will break; not sloppy, or they will wave and look horrid. Watch **yarn tension** when changing rows. If you cannot obtain firm edges with **slippery yarns**, try the **double chain selvedge**.

The right selvedge for the right job makes life easier, and gives more rewarding results when it comes to finishing a project. Plan selvedges ahead, because later you will not be able to change them. If following a commercial pattern, check what selvedges (if any) it recommends. Alter, or add, if not satisfied.

Do not 'always slip the first stitch' or 'always knit the first and last stitch', just because you are in the habit of doing so. You could be using a sound practice in exactly the wrong place.

Seam edges

Before **casting on** read **planning for seams** and choose a **seam** or **join** – these will recommend a selvedge and advise if any extra stitches need to be cast on to accommodate it.

In seams to be turned back, if the selvedge is taken in by the seam, **cast off** the selvedge stitch(es) then **cast on** again at the point where the seam will change from one side of work to the other.

Edges for picking up stitches

You will probably need a **chain selvedge**, but check **Picking up stitches** first.

Free edges

(See also **loop buttonholes**)

These should be especially tidy. In general, avoid **joining in yarn**.

Most **flat** patterns, including **garter stitch**, benefit from a **slipped garter selvedge**. **Moss stitch** and a few others, however, may look best without a selvedge if they have been worked to a fairly tight **tension**. Try **samples**. If the pattern has deep rows and the slipped garter selvedge pulls too much, use a **garter selvedge** instead. If planning a **crochet edging**, use **chain selvedge**.

Use these same selvedges on **curly** fabrics if you want to maintain the curl. Otherwise, work a border in a **flat** pattern (see **knitted-in border** below, **separate borders** and **picked-up borders**).

For a hint of decoration, use:

double slipped garter
picot
double picot

For stronger decoration, use:

picot-point
cast-on
fringe
tubular
pattern

Shaped edges

The selvedge of a strongly shaped edge must be worked loosely or it will pull. The selvedge is now on the diagonal rather than on the vertical, and its usual row depth is not enough. **Knitted-in borders** will require additional **short rows** (see **row adjustments**). In shaped **free edges**, always work any **increases** or **decreases** inside the selvedge or border.

In edges for **seams** or for **Picking up stitches**, be flexible. Shaping inside the selvedge (perhaps even two or three stitches from it) gives a clearer, straight line for sewing or picking up. It might even add interest to a plain design. But, at times, it is best to shape on the selvedge to avoid interrupting the pattern with increases or decreases, or to add much-needed length to a strongly shaped edge.

Knitted-in borders

(See also **tubular borders** below, **picked-up borders** and **separate borders**)

● Work a certain number of stitches by the edge of the fabric in a different pattern than the rest. A **needle marker** might be useful.

A border in a **flat** pattern, apart from being decorative, keeps the edge of a **curly** fabric flat. This is far from saying that it makes the entire fabric flat. Take the typical cardigan in **stocking stitch** with a **rib** border. It stays flat because the body is inside and corrects the curling-in tendency. But make it up so that the purl side shows and, unless it is carefully buttoned up, the curling-out tendency is so strong that the whole border folds back.

A knitted-in border:

● may need **row adjustments**;

● can be worked as a continuation of a horizontal border (Fig 2.317);

● if worked consciously tighter than the rest, may save you from working a separate border on finer needles (see **ribbings**);

● may require a selvedge (see **free edges**);

● if in **rib**, will look better with knit rather than purl stitch(es) next to the selvedge.

In borders knitted separately, the **seam** edge is likely to need a different selvedge from the free edge (see **Seams and joins**). If the border is to fit a curve, use a tightening selvedge for the inner curve (say, **slipped garter** or even **double chain**) and a non-tightening selvedge for the outer curve (say **no-selvedge**, or **garter** if the pattern rows are not very deep).

A different type of border consists of using the natural curliness of some fabrics to make a **roll**. Fig 2.318 shows a **reverse st st roll** at the edge of a **st st** fabric. The **roll cord** in Fig 3.116 shows another possibility.

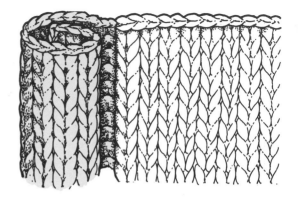

2.318

No-selvedge selvedge E

Use for **ladder stitch seams** and whenever it is essential not to disrupt pattern structure. In **free edges** is usually best avoided, although there are exceptions. Try **samples**. Fig 2.319 shows a **stocking stitch** fabric with no special selvedges.

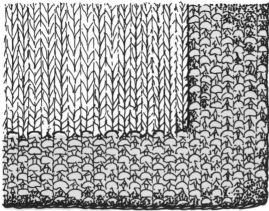

2.317

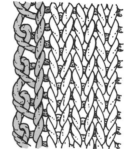 

2.319

• Simply work the whole row in pattern, from end to end, taking care not to loosen the **tension** when turning rows. In complex patterns where it is best to work with complete pattern repeats, and where taking the last stitch into a seam would spoil the arrangement of repeats, make a **stocking stitch** selvedge:

Right-side rows: **k** 1st and last sts.

Wrong-side rows: **p** 1st and last sts.

If this makes the edges of a particular pattern pull or wave, loosen or tighten **yarn tension** on the selvedge stitches.

Chain selvedge U

Fig 2.320. (See also **chain-garter** and **double-chain selvedges**).

Good for some **seams** such as **backstitch**, and excellent for **Picking up stitches** and **crochet edgings**. Some people like it on **free edges**, but I often feel that it looks unfinished.

There are several ways of obtaining the same result:

• **Right-side** rows: **sl** 1st st **kwise**, **k** last stitch.

• **Wrong-side** rows: **sl** 1st st **pwise**, **p** last st.

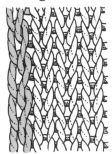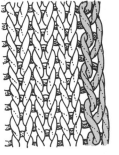

2.320

Or:

• Last stitch: **sl kwise** on all rows.
• First stitch: **k-b** on **right-side** rows, **p** on **wrong-side** rows.

Or:

• **Right-side** rows: **sl kwise** 1st and last sts.
• **Wrong-side** rows: **p** 1st and last sts.

Slipping knitwise rather than purlwise, and vice versa, gives a twisted chain.

For a variation in **garter stitch**:

• All rows: **sl** 1st st **pwise, wyif; yb** and **k** to end.

Garter selvedge U

The first of a family of three selvedges that prevent curling of the edge stitch(es) and form a neat row of 'pips' – hence their name **beaded selvedges** in French and Italian. Each pip equals two rows.

Good for patterns with **medium** stitches, such as **stocking stitch** (Fig 2.321).

• All rows: **k** 1st and last sts.

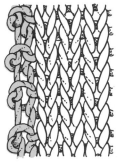

2.321

Slipped garter selvedge U

Figure 2.322.

A firmer edge than **garter selvedge**. Good for patterns with **wide** stitches or when extra tightness is required.

• All rows: **Sl kwise** 1st st, **k** last st.

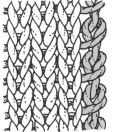

2.322

Double slipped garter selvedge U

Figure 2.323.

A slightly more decorative version than **slipped garter**, often used in **free edges**.

All rows:

- **Sl** 1st st **kwise**, through back of loop.
- **K** 2nd st.
- **K** last 2 sts.

A variation slips the first stitch also **knitwise** but in the usual way.

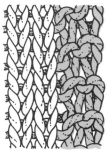

2.323

Chain-garter selvedge S

Figure 2.324.

Same uses as **chain selvedge**, but the **garter** stitches add firmness and a hint of decoration.

- **Right-side** rows: sl 1st st **kwise**, **wyab**; p 2nd st; p last but one st; **sl** last st **kwise**, **wyab**.
- **Wrong-side** rows: **p** 1st 2 and last 2 sts.

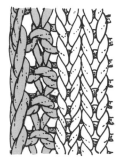
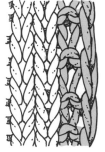

2.324

Double-chain selvedge S

Fig 2.325. (See also **chain selvedge**)

To control sloppy edges when working with **slippery yarns**, when all else fails. Or, when a tightening effect, plus a chain, is required.

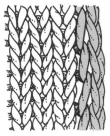

2.325

- **Row 2**: work to last st, pick up horizontal strand between last 2 sts and place on right needle; **sl** last st **kwise**.
- All following **right-side** rows: **k-b tog** 1st st and lifted loop; end as for Row 2.
- All following **wrong-side** rows: **p tog** 1st st and lifted loop; end as for Row 2.

Picot selvedge S

Slightly decorative (Fig 2.326). Good for **free edges** in **openwork** patterns, for some **seams**, and for projects that make use of **picot cords**. Pin the loops away from the fabric when **blocking**.

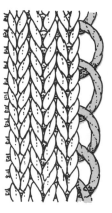

2.326

- **Right-side** rows: **selvedge over, k** 1st 2 sts together; **ssk** last 2 sts.
- **Wrong-side** rows: **selvedge over, p** 1st 2 and last 2 sts.

Double picot selvedge   S

Bolder than **picot selvedge** (Fig 2.327).
- **Right-side** rows: **selvedge over, slip decrease** over first two stitches (**slip 1 kwise – k1 – psso**); **k** last two stitches.
- **Wrong-side** rows: **selvedge over, purl** first two stitches together; **purl** last two stitches.

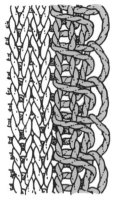

2.327

Picot-point selvedge   S

A good match to **picot-point cast-on** (see **edging cast-on**) **picot-point cast-off** and **picot-point fringe** (Fig 2.328).

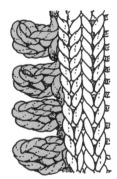

2.328

- All rows: work a **picot point** on 1st st; for perfect symmetry, **p** instead of **k** the **wrong-side** row picots.

Cast-on selvedges   S

To reflect a **decorative cast-on** and/or a **cast-on cast-off**.
- Carry one or more strands of yarn at each edge to 'cast-on' a stitch on alternate rows, probably between the two edge stitches. **Decrease** the new stitch either by **casting off** or by working with the adjacent stitch.
Experiment with different cast-on/pattern combinations.

Fringe selvedge   S

Sheer fun (Fig 2.329 – see also **fringes**).
- **Cast on** as many edge stitches as you want, by a **loop** method. Work all the way in **stocking stitch** or any knit-and-purl pattern. Drop the edge stitches before casting off and ladder them.
For a straight fringe, thread a knitting needle or cord through the loops and **block** tensioned, rather like in Fig 3.23.
The laddered fringe is surprisingly long. Try **samples**.

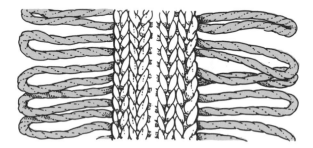

2.329

Tubular selvedges   S

(See also **tubular cords** and **loop buttonholes**)
One type is the **slip-cord** shown in **edging**

cast-on (Fig 2.48). Allow three to five stitches per cord.
- Right edge: **sl** cord sts **pwise** on **wrong-side** rows and **k** them on **right-side** rows, pulling the yarn fairly tightly for 1st st.
- Left edge: **sl** cord sts **pwise** on **right-side** rows, **p** them on **wrong-side** rows.

Unless the pattern stitches are very **wide**, the **slip-cord** will need **row adjustments**, even on edges without shapings.

Tubular border
(See also **knitted-in borders** above, **picked-up borders** and **separate borders**)

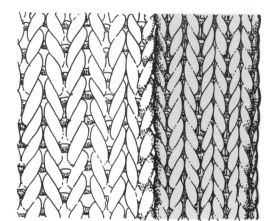

2.330

Another tubular selvedge is achieved by working the last few stitches in **tubular stocking stitch**. This makes a very neat border or **hem** (Fig 2.330), but will require many **row adjustments**.

Pattern selvedges   S

For high decoration, consider using motifs normally placed away from the edges.
Cables, leaves (Fig 2.331) and other patterns with a **stocking stitch** base make good edges.

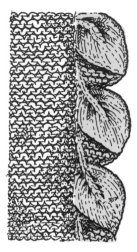

2.331

Picking up stitches

'Pick up stitches' is such a universally accepted term that anything different may create confusion. Yet, it is a misleading expression that encourages the bad practice of catching the edge loops of a knitted fabric with a needle. **Pick up and knit** and **knit up** describe much better the action of taking a ball of yarn and making a row of entirely new loops (see **from right to left** and **from left to right** below for a detailed description).

Catching the edge loops is bad practice because it:
- distorts the original fabric;
- leaves holes;
- badly reduces elasticity and may lead to the join pulling, and even breaking;

● does not hide the edge.

To enclose the edge is a high priority, both to avoid holes and to hide yarn joins and any other causes of unevenness. Catching the loops might keep the work flatter, but let me stress that the key word in knitting is not 'flat', it is 'neat'.

For good results:

● Plan ahead so that any edge or **selvedge** to be knitted up is of the most appropriate type (see below).

● Aim for sharpness. Keep straight lines straight, curves smooth and angles pointed.

● Use a knitting needle or crochet hook one or two sizes finer than used so far, even if you revert to the original size on the first row.

● Secure the new yarn by tying it to the work before knitting up the first stitch, or by knitting up the second stitch with the short end as well as the long end of yarn; on the first row, work only the long end – the short one will unravel when you drop the stitch.

● Do not split the yarn when inserting the needle or hook.

● Do not leave holes; if inserting the needle or hook into a certain stitch makes a hole, insert it into a different stitch, or make it go first through an adjoining strand.

● If about to knit in a contrast colour, consider knitting up with the original colour and changing to the new one on the first row.

● If knitting up a stretched edge, thread a contrast, **slippery yarn** along the edge and pull to correct length. Remove the contrast yarn after a few rows.

Distributing stitches

To **calculate** the number of stitches to be picked up is like calculating any other number of stitches: measure the edge, find out the **tension** of the fabric to be added, and multiply the number of stitches in 1cm (1in) by the total length.

Or, you can make things even easier. Divide the edge into 2.5, 5 or 10cm (1, 2 or 4in) lengths, using **fabric markers** (Fig 2.332) and knit up between markers however many stitches the new pattern has in that distance.

You can also try another approach. Divide:

$$\frac{\text{sts in 10cm (4in) in new pattern}}{\text{rows in 10cm (4in) in edge}}$$

for a **vertical edge**, or:

$$\frac{\text{sts in 10cm (4in) in new pattern}}{\text{sts in 10cm (4in) in edge}}$$

for a **horizontal edge**. Then find the figure closest to the result in the following table, and knit up accordingly:

Result	No of sts to knit up	Out of every rows/sts
1.05	20	21
1.07	14	15
1.10	10	11
1.12	8	9
1.14	7	8
1.16	6	7
1.20	5	6
1.25	4	5
1.33	3	4
1.50	2	3
2.00	1	2

Do not follow any simpler rules of thumb. A quick look through pattern books shows that 20 stitches in **stocking stitch**, the knitting yardstick, might need anything from 23 to 32 rows to make a square! Yarns, recommended **tension** (tight or loose) and knitters obviously have an effect. See **stitch shape**.

In **diagonal** edges you will need to knit up more often than if you were working on the same number of stitches **horizontally**, or the

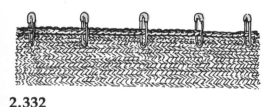

2.332

same number of rows **vertically**. A diagonal line will always be longer.

If you want the new piece of work to gather the original fabric, or vice versa, start by knitting up roughly as for flat fabric. In the first row, **decrease** or **increase** as the case may be. If working with sets of **double-pointed needles**, decide beforehand which are the best points for changing needles. Knit up accordingly, even if some needles end up with more stitches than others.

From right to left

The most common direction for knitting up. The right side is facing. In **flat knitting**, therefore, the first row will be a **wrong-side** row – consider the knitted-up stitches a foundation row, rather like a **cast-on**.

Knit up as explained, whatever stitch pattern follows. If all, or some, of the knitted-up stitches are **twisted**, work them through the back of the loop on the first row.

The last of the three methods explained here is the fastest, once you get the hang of it.

Knitting-needle method

Fig 2.333.

a Insert right needle into fabric.
b Wind yarn around needle as if to **k**.
c Draw through a loop.

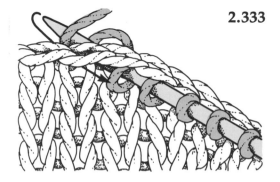

2.333

First crochet method

Possibly a good method for **left-handed** knitters (Fig 2.334).

a Insert hook into fabric.
b Draw through a loop.
c Place loop onto knitting needle.

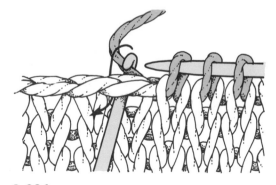

2.334

Second crochet method

Fig 2.335.

a Keep inserting hook into fabric and drawing loops, until hook is full.
b **Sl** the sts from back of hook, onto a knitting needle.

Sometimes hooks have large central areas that do not allow stitches to slip through, but the usual flat, thin area is rarely any problem in medium to thick hooks.

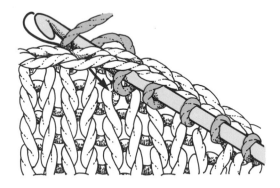

2.335

From left to right

When picking up from left to right, the yarn is ready to start a **right-side** row. Occasionally, this is an advantage.

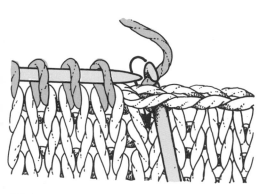

.336

● Left-handed knitters can use the **knitting-needle** and **second crochet methods** in reverse. Right-handed knitters should use the **first crochet method** in reverse (Fig 2.336).

Changing circumstances

Horizontal edges

For greatest elasticity, use a **provisional cast-on** or **provisional cast-off**. Unravel and catch the free loops with a knitting needle (Fig 2.337). Make sure that the needle points towards the end you want to start knitting. If you need more or less stitches than there are, **increase** or **decrease** regularly on the first row. When picking up from a provisional cast-on, you will very likely find there is one loop less than there were stitches.

For a slightly decorative effect, use **chain**

cast-on, or **loop cast-on** and pick up without unravelling. These are two of the exceptional instances where, if the cast-on was loose enough, you could catch the loops directly with a needle, without yarn.

For a bolder effect, use a **decorative** cast-on or cast-off and knit up from whichever place is most convenient, without affecting the original edge. With obvious exceptions such as **picot cord cast-on,** do not knit up the new stitches from under one single thread.

When a non-decorative edge cannot be unpicked (see **curves** below for a possible situation), knit up into the row below the edge (Fig 2.338). For extra stitches, knit up between original stitches as well as into them.

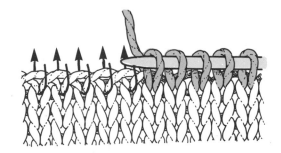

2.338

Vertical edges

Best done from a **chain, chain-garter** or **double-chain selvedge**.

Each chain spans two rows. Knit up from under each complete chain (Fig 2.339). For extra stitches, knit up also, as required, from

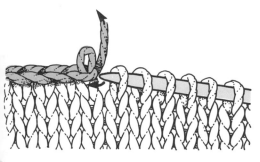

2.337

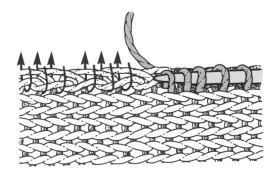

2.339

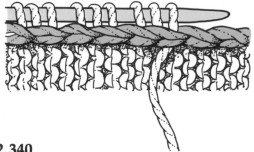

2.340

the tight point where two chains overlap. On the **wrong side** the chain should look quite untouched (Fig 2.340).

With any other edge, knit up at least two strands in from the end of the fabric. Make sure that all the stitches you knit up from are on a straight line.

Angles

For a sharp angle, knit up a stitch from the very corner.

Diagonal edges

(see also **shaped edges** under **Edges and selvedges**)

Try to work from a **chain, chain-garter** or **double-chain selvedge**. If the selvedge is not interrupted with shapings, proceed as for **vertical edges**.

If the selvedge is interrupted by shapings, knit up at least two strands in from the edge

2.341

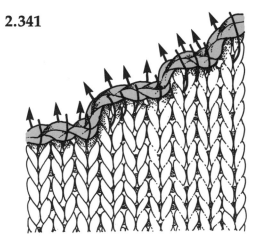

on the interruptions. Take care to keep a straight line.

When the shapings are groups of **cast-on** or **cast-off** stitches, work as for **horizontal edges**. In between groups, knit up at least two strands in from the edge. For a smooth line, do not hesitate to knit up further from the edge if there is a step that breaks continuity (Fig 2.341).

Curves

When the edge is a combination of **horizontal**, **vertical** and **diagonal**, follow the rules explained for each one. It might then seem a good thing to leave in waiting, rather than to **cast off,** the horizontal areas. Many patterns actually recommend that. But there are good reasons against this seemingly brilliant idea:

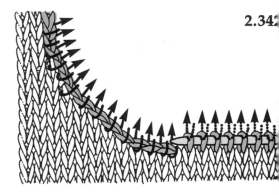

2.342

• the waiting stitches are larger than the ones being knitted up on a finer needle;

• knitting up inside the edge gives a slight 'lift' to the new stitches because a double layer is formed – the horizontal stitches remain flat and look less crisp;

• there might be a difference in level between the edge and the stitches in waiting – Fig 2.342 is not the fruit of my malicious mind but a faithful copy of an illustration on how to pick up stitches 'correctly'; I have only added a few extra arrows to emphasise the point.

Centre of work

Knit up in any direction you want, using one of the **crochet-hook** techniques explained

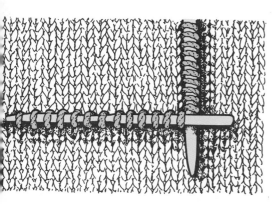

2.343

above. Keep the yarn under the work, in your left hand, and the hook on top (Fig 2.343). Run a coloured thread through the fabric if you have problems in keeping a straight line.

On **purl** and some other fabrics it is possible to knit up without going through the fabric, for instance for a **pocket** lining. Draw the new loops through the stitch heads (Fig 2.344). This is an exception to the rule of knitting up at least through two strands. The large arrow shows the direction in which work will continue, when the needle or hook is inserted as shown by the small arrows.

2.344

From cloth

This is best done on a straight edge.

- Draw a thread, right by the edge of the fabric. This will be easier in loosely woven fabrics.
- Cut along pulled thread. The edge is now absolutely straight.
- Draw a 2nd thread, a little way in – enough to fold edge into a small hem.

d Tack the hem.

e Start a row of **double crochet** over hem by inserting hook DOWN into right edge of 2nd pulled thread.

f Catch yarn and draw a loop through fabric.

g Catch yarn and draw a new loop through loop on hook.

h Insert hook DOWN through fabric, to the left of first st, catch yarn and draw a new loop through fabric.

i Catch yarn and draw a new loop through the 2 loops on hook (Fig 2.345).

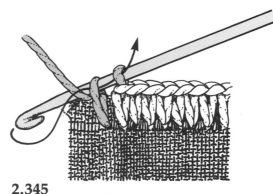

2.345

Repeat **h** and **i** along hem. To space sts evenly, try counting threads. The cloth is now ready for picking up stitches as in **vertical edges** with a **chain selvedge**.

Experiment with crocheting and/or knitting up from either side of work. Try catching only one side of the chain when knitting up if you wish.

APPLICATIONS

Picked-up borders   U

(See also **knitted-in borders, tubular borders** and **separate borders**)

A border is generally worked in a **flat** fabric, but sometimes a **curly** fabric such as **stocking stitch** is used, and is either left to curl into a **roll** of its own accord, or is folded in two and sewn into place.

Ribbed borders are often folded to hide the chain of **basic cast-off**. Although this may not be a bad thing if it is a design feature, in general the resulting thick edge is not very attractive. **Tubular cast-off** solves the problem in a much better way, and avoids wasting time working an unnecessary layer.
Because borders are meant to control the fabric edge, they should always be on the tight side. But be careful they do not pull.

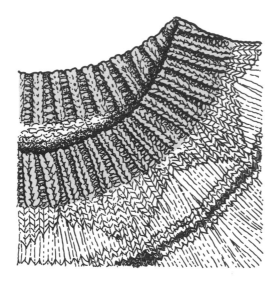

2.346

Curves, such as necklines, are often given a ribbed border because of its great elasticity. The knitted-up end is kept fairly stretched, and the cast-off end is left to gather in (Fig 2.346). Closed curves are infinitely best worked in **rounds**. Beginners who cannot find a **circular needle** short enough, and are worried about sets of **double-pointed needles**, can work **flat** by leaving one seam undone (see **planning for seams**).
Curves in **moss stitch** or **garter stitch** need **decreases** to take a good shape. In **garter stitch** these will be practically unnoticeable.

● **Pick up** sts from the edge, work for required depth of border, and **cast off**.

Entrelacs

A clever combination of **stocking stitch** squares that look like basketweave because of the way the fabric curls. The impression can be easily reinforced with colour (Fig

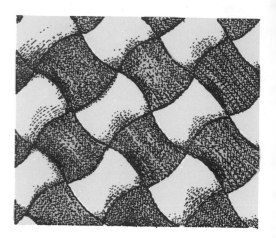

2.347

2.347). Each square has twice as many rows as it has stitches. An even number of stitches is normally used.
a **Cast on** all the squares required.
b Work base triangles with **short rows**. Start with 2 sts, add 1 st every 2 rows. Work one triangle after another.
c Work 1st row of squares, again one at

2.348

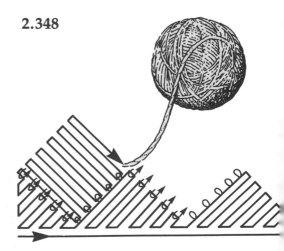

time. **Pick up** sts from the side of 1st triangle. On every other row you will be next to sts left in waiting from following triangle; **decrease** by working 1 of them together with last st in your present row (Fig 2.348).

d Repeat rows of squares as many times as required. In **flat knitting**, one row will be k and the other **p**. Arrange decreases to match.

e At the top, work another row of triangles, this time in reverse – shorter and shorter rows.

For straight sides, work triangles at the start and end of rows; **decrease** one stitch on alternate rows, at the very edge.

Slits and buttonholes

(See also **Fastenings**)

Slits are straight-line cuts in the knitted fabric. They can be **horizontal, vertical** or **diagonal**. ey can also be **closed** or **open**, **knitted-in** or **cut**.

Buttonholes are small **closed slits** with the practical purpose of fastening a **button**. They can equally be **knitted-in** or **cut**, and travel in any direction. Additionally, they can be **spot**-like and **loop**-like.

Buttonholes are often placed in **borders** (**knitted-in, picked-up** or **separate**).

For best results:

● Choose a method that will not require oversewing or reinforcing. If, however, an added finish is needed or desired, see **reinforced buttonholes**.

● Leave at least three stitches between the edge and the start of a buttonhole or closed slit.

● In **ribs,** start and end **horizontal** slits or buttonholes in purl and keep **vertical** ones also in purl. In other patterns, work wherever the texture makes a 'low' rather than a 'high'.

● **Knit-in** for speed and neatness. **Cut** to avoid planning ahead.

● If working with **slippery yarns**, a strand or two of matching sewing thread will add stability. Use only on the slit or buttonhole area. Join in one row in advance.

● A **button** will not stay right in the centre of a horizontal buttonhole – movement will pull it to the outer end. If buttons are to be on a certain line, place buttonholes slightly away from fabric edge.

● Avoid tiny buttonholes for even tinier buttons in thick yarn. They look out of scale.

● Remember that knitting is elastic. A button may easily go through a smaller hole than you think. Try **samples**.

● Place men's buttonholes on left side, and women's on right side if you want to follow convention.

● Choose buttons first if you can (see **buying** and **making buttons**). To make a buttonhole that fits is easy – just try a couple of small samples. To find a button to fit a hole might be impossible.

Spacing buttonholes

Do not place first and last buttonholes too close to the edge. When many small buttonholes are very close to each other, in fine yarn, the first could be just 1cm (½in) away from the edge. But, in the much more common case of a jacket front, in medium to thick yarn, less than 2–3cm (about 1in) is likely to look out of balance.

Do not worry about the lower edge pulling open below the buttonhole. If you **cast on** all the necessary stitches at the correct **tension**, the edge will stay where it should.

Having placed the two end buttonholes, space the rest evenly between. You will need one more space than there are buttonholes left to place. And you will need to know the exact number of rows or stitches between end buttonholes – a tape measurement would be far from accurate. The row/stitch total, and/or the position of the end buttonholes, may need adjusting.

Spacing 'evenly' is an open statement. Fig 2.349 shows several possibilities; experiment to find others. Two or three buttonholes closer together than the rest at the bottom of

a jacket front (as in **b**) help to control **rib** waistbands.

Ignore rules of thumb when spacing. A thick or loose jacket needs fewer buttons than a thin or tight one. Garments in your wardrobe will be of more help to you than any rules.

Above all, remember that the buttonhole-button arrangement is of vital importance, whether you want to play it low key, or make a feature of it. Use it creatively.

Spot buttonholes   U

Traditionally used in baby clothes and whenever a very small button is required. Start work on **right side**, unless samples suggest otherwise.

In heavy yarns, the size of button that can go through such a buttonhole is almost always too small to look good, unless many are used in close arrangement. One may, however, be used for an out-of-sight fastening.

Ordinary eyelet
The simplest of all. Work an isolated **eyelet** (Fig 2.184). Either make a **front-to-back over** and **k2 tog,** or **ssk** and make an **over.**

Reinforced eyelet
Stronger and neater (Fig 2.350).
Row 1:
a Work to buttonhole position.
b **Front-to-back over.** Continue work.
Row 2:
c **Sl over.**
d **Front-to-back over.** Continue work.
Row 3:
e **Sl kwise** st before overs.

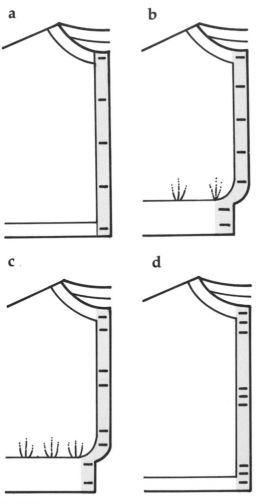

2.349

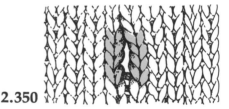

2.350

f K overs tog. Do not drop from left needle.

g Pass **sl st** over st just made, as in **basic cast-off**.

h K3 tog – overs and next st.

Large eyelet

Makes a bigger hole, but seems to have toothache (Fig 2.351). Also called **three-row buttonhole**.

Row 1:

a Work to buttonhole position.

b Front-to-back double over.

c K-b2 tog. Continue work.

Row 2:

d P 1st over and drop 2nd. Continue work.

Row 3:

e Work to over purled on previous row.

f K into hole below over, and drop next st from needle.

2.351

Horizontal buttonholes

The most common type (see also **cut slits** for afterthoughts).

Start work on **right side** unless samples suggest otherwise. For immaculate results, use **tubular buttonhole** in **single rib** and related fabrics, and **cast-off buttonhole** in other patterns. Beginners should try **standard** or **increase buttonholes**.

For **circular knitting**, use **increase** or **one-row buttonholes**.

Standard buttonhole has one weak point – its sides, especially the left one. It is sometimes suggested that **increasing** on the edge stitch and **casting on** one stitch less than required will solve the problem. Depending

on the increase, the result is a stray strand across the left corner. Considering that some popular cast-ons leave a stray strand across the other corner, it is no wonder that embroidering the outline is so often recommended!

There are no weak sides in **reinforced buttonhole** or **one-row buttonhole**. The second is the strongest, but has less give and may require more stitches.

To **reinforce** the outline may be necessary if a weakish method has been used, perhaps when learning to knit – weak methods tend to be easier.

Standard buttonhole

Simplest procedure (Fig 2.352):

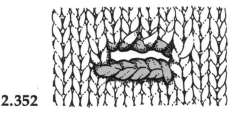

2.352

a Cast off required number of sts in one row.

b Cast on same number of sts in next row.

Use **basic cast-off** and work two stitches past the buttonhole position before passing the first stitch on top of the next. Pass the last cast-off stitch over the stitch that forms the buttonhole left edge. Pull edge-stitch tight; it tends to loosen up.

For firm fabrics use **buttonhole cast-on, double-twist loop cast-on** or **cable cast-on**. For lace and loose fabrics use **loop, twisted loop, alternate loop** or **chain cast-ons**.

Loop cast-ons are both the easiest and the weakest; they may need **reinforcing**.

Cable and **chain cast-ons** leave a ghastly strand across the right corner, unless the last cast-on stitch is transferred to left needle **with yarn in front**.

Buttonhole cast-on is excellent and does not require turning the work, but needs a little practice.

E

Reinforced buttonhole U

A stronger version of **standard buttonhole**. The instructions may look lengthy but are not difficult (Fig 2.353).

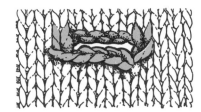

2.353

Row 1:

a Work to buttonhole position.

b **Right lifted increase: k** first the back head of the st below next st, then **k** the st.

c *k1, pass previous st over*. Repeat as in **basic cast-off** for all the buttonhole sts but 1.

d **Right lifted increase** as before, then pass previous st over the 2 sts of the increase. Continue work.

Row 2:

e Work to 2 sts before buttonhole.

f **P2 tog.**

g **Cast on** total buttonhole sts plus 2 (see cast-on methods under **standard buttonhole**).

h **P2 tog.** Continue work.

Row 3:

i Work to st before buttonhole.

j **Ssk** side st and last cast-on st.

k Work to 1st cast-on st.

l **K2 tog** – 1st cast-on st and side st.

Increase buttonhole U

An effective but not very well known technique (Fig 2.354).

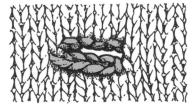

2.354

It is impossible to give exact number of **overs** required; **samples** are essential. Try two overs for a 4–6 stitch buttonhole and one over for a 2–3 stitch buttonhole. For a 2 stitch buttonhole a loose stitch on the previous row might even be enough.

Row 1:

a **Cast off** required number of sts (see **standard buttonhole** comments).

b **Yo** one or more times. Continue work.

Row 2:

c Work to over(s).

d Drop over(s) and pull 1st st on left needle.

e **P** long st alternately through **front** and **back** of loop to obtain number of cast-off sts plus 1.

f Continue work.

To reinforce right edge, follow **a** to **c** in **reinforced buttonhole**, but **cast off** all buttonhole sts in **c**. On next row, **p2 tog** after working the **increase**.

To adapt to **circular knitting**, work over(s) before the stitch that frames the buttonhole right edge. **K**, instead of **p**, the resulting long stitch.

One-row buttonhole U

Very strong and neat (Fig 2.355). May need more stitches than other methods because it has less elasticity. Very unobtrusive in **garter stitch** and in **reverse stocking stitch** when worked from the knit side.

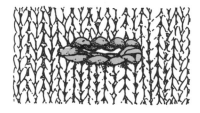

2.355

a Work to buttonhole position.

b **Slip** 1 **pwise wyif.**

c **Yb**, and leave it there; it will not be used for **d** and **e**.

d *Slip 1 **pwise**, pass previous st over as in **basic cast-off***. Repeat for all buttonhole sts.

e **Sl** last cast-off st back to left needle. Turn work.

f **Yb.**

g **Cable cast-on** all buttonhole sts.

h **Cable cast-on** another st, but **yf** before placing it on left needle. Turn work.

i **Slip** 1 **kwise** and pass extra cast-on st over it.

Cast-off buttonhole U

Matching top and bottom edges. Fig 2.356 shows the results in **backstitch cast-off**.

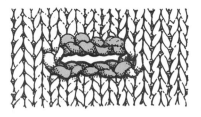

2.356

If working in fancy pattern, knit or purl one stitch at either side on the buttonhole row, plus all the stitches between these two on the row before and the row after. Knit-and-purl combinations do not count as fancy patterns.

a **K** buttonhole sts in contrast yarn, preferably **slippery**. Leave a long loop of main yarn at back, for later finishing – at least 30–40cm (12–16in). Cut contrast yarn. Finish work. **Block.**

b Remove contrast yarn and place free loops on spare needles or **holders**.

c Cut main-yarn loop and **crochet, backstitch** or **stem-stitch cast-off** all around edge, working into the loops and edge sts.

d **Darn** and trim ends.

(See **cut slits** for variation)

Tubular buttonhole S

Ideal for **single rib** (Fig 2.357), with knitters who can use the **tubular cast-off**.

a Work buttonhole sts in **single rib** with a short length of contrast yarn, preferably **slippery**. Leave a long loop of main yarn for later sewing – at least 30–40cm (12–16in). Cut contrast yarn. Finish work.

b Remove contrast yarn and place lower sts

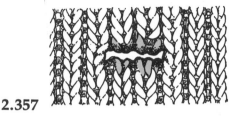

2.357

on a needle and upper loops on a **holder**.

c Cut the yarn loop in half and **tubular cast-off** lower sts. Anchor yarn to the side, **darn** and trim.

d Again with a sewing needle, thread 2nd yarn end through upper loops and anchor to side with a vertical st.

e Repeat **d** 2 or 3 times more, alternating direction. **Darn** and trim.

Horizontal slits U

A **closed horizontal slit** is simply a large version of a **horizontal buttonhole**.

An **open horizontal slit** is placed at the edge of the fabric, so that it has three sides instead of the usual four. **Casting off**, therefore, starts at the beginning of the row.

Broadly speaking, any buttonhole technique can be used, although **increase buttonhole** might be awkward on a large number of stitches. **Tubular buttonhole** will need adapting if the top edge is to be elastic. Instead of working with a contrast yarn, try this:

a Leave lower sts on a **holder**.

b End row and work next row to slit position. Leave work in waiting.

c **Tubular cast-on** the sts required with new yarn and new needles, leaving yarn tail long enough to **tubular cast-off** lower sts and anchor sides. Stop before **tubular st st** rows. Cut yarn.

d Return to main work and join in cast-on sts. On next couple of rows, work **tubular st st** across new sts if desired.

e To finish, anchor 1st side, **cast off** lower sts, anchor 2nd side. **Darn** and trim.

If the fabric is not **flat** the slit will curl, either in or out. If this is not desired, work a **flat border** around the four sides of **closed slits** (Fig 2.358), or around the three sides of **open slits**. In open slits the border could be continued along the free edge. **Needle markers** will be useful between border and main pattern.

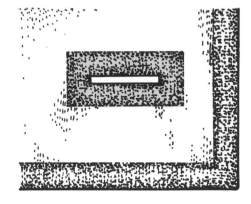

2.358

Overlapping slits
The top edge starts behind lower edge, making a second layer. Borders are restricted to the overlap.
Closed slits are the basis for **horizontal slit pockets**.
FIRST METHOD:

a Having reached start of overlap, continue working complete rows, but use **border** pattern across slit area. **Increase** or **decrease** on 1st row and/or introduce **row adjustments** if necessary. Consider working tighter across border sts, especially in **ribs**. **Needle markers** might be useful.

b At top of overlap, **cast off** slit sts or leave on **holder** for **tubular** or other special **cast off**. End row. Leave work in waiting.

c With new yarn and needles, **cast on** slit sts plus 2. Leave long end for sewing one side.

d Work in **border** pattern for same number of rows as before. Cut yarn – leave end long enough to sew other side (and to cast off lower edge if necessary).

e Return to main work, joining 2nd border on 1st row. Work sts at either side of slit together with edge sts of 2nd border, to add strength.

f To finish, sew sides of overlap with a **slip stitch** and **cast off** lower edge if required. **Darn**, and trim yarn.

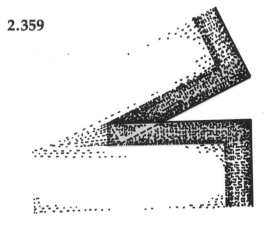

2.359

Fig 2.359 shows an unseamed, **open, overlapping slit**.

SECOND METHOD (Fig 2.360):

a **K** slit sts in contrast yarn, preferably **slippery**. Return sts to left needle and work again, this time with ordinary yarn. Cut contrast yarn. Finish work.

b Remove contrast yarn and place free loops on needles or **holders**.

c On each of the two edges, in same or contrast colour, do one of the following:

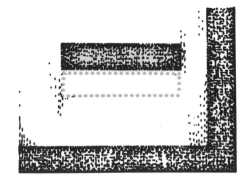

2.360

- work a border;
- use a **decorative cast-off**;
- work a few rows in a **curly** pattern and let curl into a **roll**;
- add an **edging**, with or without **casting off** first;
- **increase** heavily and work a few rows to form a frill;
- add a **hem**.

d **Seam** ends, if necessary; **darn** and trim yarn.

Similar results are obtained in afterthought slits by working steps **a** to **c** of the second method for **cut slits** instead of **a** and **b** above.

Vertical buttonholes   U

Use when the fastening will have a vertical pull, or to obtain **horizontal buttonholes** when working vertical rows (see also **cut slits**).

The two sides are worked separately. Either work at the same time with two balls of yarn, or work first one side and then the other, cutting the yarn as required. Stitches left in waiting can be kept on **holders** or on the working needles.

Leave yarn tails long enough for **darning**.

Although it is possible to work either without a special **selvedge**, or with a **garter** or **slipped garter selvedge**, and although it is usual to keep the number of stitches unaltered, for neatest results work as follows (Fig 2.361):

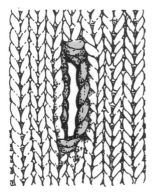

2.361

a Work right side with a **chain selvedge** (first method).

b Before starting left side, make a **right lifted increase** on 1st st.

c Work left side also with a **chain selvedge** (second method) – the selvedge is the increased st.

d On 1st row across at top of buttonhole, work together the 2 selvedge sts. End work.

e To finish, make a couple of horizontal sts at top and bottom ends with a **sewing needle,** to add strength. **Darn** up and down the back of the selvedge chains. Trim yarn.

Both sides of the buttonhole must end with either a **right-side** or a **wrong-side** row.

Vertical slits   U

A **closed vertical slit** is a large version of a **vertical buttonhole**.

An **open slit** is placed at the **cast-on** or **cast-off** end of the fabric, so that it has three sides instead of four.

To prevent **curly** fabrics rolling, work a **knitted-in border**. In **closed slits** the border starts before, and ends after, the actual slit. The result will be similar to Fig 2.358 on its side. A decorative selvedge (see **free edges**) could also be used just along the slit. Try **samples** to see whether there are any problems. In **open slits**, the border can be continued along the cast-on or cast-off edge.

If the two sides are not worked at the same time, keep the stitches in waiting on **holders**.

Overlapping slits

Either the right or the left side gets wider and makes a second layer behind the other side. Borders, or decorative selvedges, are restricted to the overlap.

Closed slits are the basis for **vertical slit pockets**. An **open slit** at start of work is often used for sweater side vents or buttoned cuffs. At the end of work it can be used for buttoned necklines.

FIRST METHOD:

a Work upper layer, with **border** if there is one. (Use a **needle marker**.)

b Before starting under layer, **cast on** sts for overlap, leaving yarn tail long enough to sew side of overlap. Or, for neatness and strength, **pick up** overlap sts as in Fig 2.344 if pattern is such that sts will not show on **right side**.

c Work under layer.

d At top of slit, **cast off** all overlap sts but 1 on the last under-layer row; on 1st row across, work together the edge upper-layer st with the remaining overlap st. Or, for best results, DO NOT **cast off**; on the 1st row across, work together 1 st from each over-lap layer, as in **cast-on edge hems**.

e To finish, sew under layer with a **slip stitch** if necessary. **Darn** and trim yarn.

An **overlapping open slit** at a cast-on or a cast-off edge would look like Fig 2.359 on its side.

SECOND METHOD:

This gives a result similar to Fig 2.360 on its side:

a Work as for **vertical buttonhole**. Finish work.

b On each of the two edges, do one of following:
  • work a **picked-up border**;
  • work an **edging** (perhaps a **cast-off edging**);
  • **pick up stitches**, work a **curly** pattern and let curl into a **roll** – this effect could also be achieved by the first method;
  • **pick up stitches** and add a **hem**;
  • **pick up stitches, increase** heavily and work a few rows – the result will be a frill.

Diagonal buttonholes s

Work as for **vertical buttonhole** but **increase** regularly on one side, before **selvedge**, and **decrease** similarly on the other side.

Fig 2.362 shows the use of **closed eyelet in-**

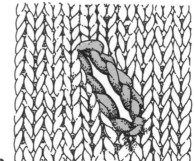

2.362

crease and **knit decrease (k2 tog)** on alternate rows.

Use:

• in **bias knitting** to obtain horizontal or vertical buttonholes;

• when the fastening has a diagonal pull;

• for **corners** demanding total symmetry.

Diagonal slits s

Less common, but with similar applications to **vertical slits**.

In theory, it is possible to work them like large versions of **diagonal buttonholes**. In practice, shaping is usually done with **short rows**. Keep the non-working stitches on **holders**.

Non-overlapping slits

They will almost certainly need a small **edging**.

a Work the **decrease** side first, with a **diagonal cast-off** – the **dart** method is more common.

b With the 2nd ball of yarn, **cast on** total number of sts spanned by slit.

c Work 2nd side, incorporating on alternate rows a few of the **cast on** sts – the two sides must follow same sequence.

d Continue work across. Finish work.

e Work an **edging** around slit.

Overlapping slits

Work exactly as just described from **a** to **c**. Then,

d Work one of the finishes described in the **second method** for **overlapping vertical slits**.

Borders can be worked in three shapes (Fig 2.363):

- straight;
- with vertical edges – **increase** at right edge and **decrease** at left edge;
- with horizontal edges – **decrease** at right edge and **increase** at left edge.

Reverse border shapings if working slits symmetrical to those illustrated.

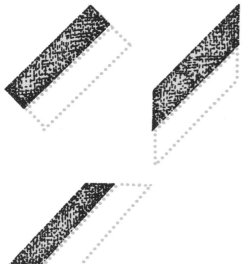

2.363

Cut slits   S

Use when you do not want to decide slit or buttonhole position beforehand, or when it is too late to knit them in. Always try on **samples** first. **Block** work before cutting.

FIRST METHOD:

For **horizontal** or **vertical** slits or buttonholes:

a Mark precise position with contrast thread.

b Work one line of **close stitching** at each side of mark (see **cut and sew**).

c Cut fabric by mark.

d **Reinforce.**

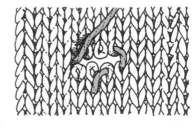

2.364

SECOND METHOD:

On **horizontal** slits or buttonholes only, it is better to:

a Decide exact position and tack around it – one row below and one row above.

b Cut centre st.

c Unravel cut yarn to free loops (Fig 2.364). Place free loops on needles or **holders**.

d **Crochet, backstitch** or **stem-stitch cast-off** all around to close loops and strengthen sides. Secure free ends as much as possible at same time.

e **Darn** and trim ends. If cut ends are very short, anchor with matching thread.

f Unpick tacking.

Final results look like **cast-off buttonhole** (Fig 2.356).

Bridges

(See also **cut and sew**)

Used in **circular knitting** to prepare the work for **vertical slits**, especially **open** ones. Invaluable for working **jacquard** and whenever seeing right side of work all the time is an advantage; make a bridge for each opening (jacket front, armhole, sleeve top, neckline, or decorative).

FIRST METHOD Fig 2.365:

a **Cast on** a few sts (8 to 14 depending on yarn) at start of slit, to form bridge base. Use one of the **end of rows** methods.

b **K** the bridge sts for length of slit. If working with two colours, **k1** in each colour.

c At top of slit, **cast off** bridge.

d To finish, work one or two rows of **close stitching** at either side of centre line. Cut through centre and stitch back – consider **binding** for neatness.

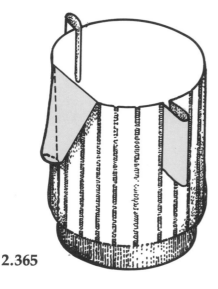

2.365

SECOND METHOD:

a Make, say, 15 to 20 **overs** to bridge the slit on every round, with all yarns being used on that round.

b On each round, drop overs from previous round.

c To finish, cut long loops in half. **Darn** and trim – consider **binding**.

If the slit is to become a free end, you may want to allow a couple of extra stitches in pattern, to be turned in after cutting, especially with the second method.

Shapings can be worked at either side of the bridge.

Loop buttonholes   U

Generally used on the edge of the fabric. Many possibilities:

• For the thinnest loop, **crochet** a **chain** (Fig 2.51). Attach to **wrong side** with the ends of yarn coming out of first and last chain (Fig 2.366). A row of loops could be made out of one single chain.

• For contrast, make the loop with a piece of leather thonging. Closely **overcast** the two ends, jointly or separately, with matching cotton, on the **wrong side**. Other materials and other structures (see **Cords**) could be used.

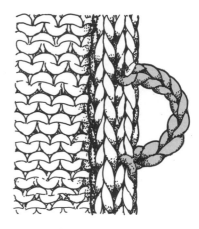

2.366

• If you prefer sewing, anchor matching yarn to the selvedge, leaving a shortish end. Anchor again a few stitches away, and then again on first stitch, each time forming a loop. **Buttonhole stitch** over the two loops and the yarn end (Fig 2.367).

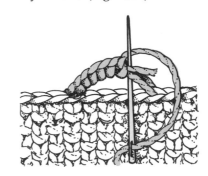

2.367

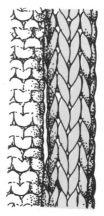

2.368

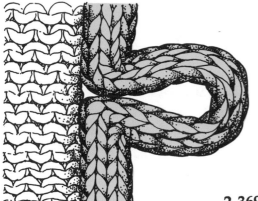

2.369

● It is sometimes possible to disconnect an **edging**, a **border**, or a **selvedge** such as **slip-cord tubular selvedge** (Fig 2.368), for a few stitches or rows, thereby creating an instant buttonhole. In some cases, the edge or edging can even be made to form a proper loop (Fig 2.369) by simply adding extra rows to it.

Pockets

These can be practical or purely decorative. The innumerable variations fall neatly into four categories:
● **patch pockets** attached to the **right side**;
● **slit pockets** attached to the **wrong side**;
● **loose pockets** hanging from a **slit**;
● **tubular pockets** forming part of the fabric.
Flaps can be added to any of these, to hide the opening. Crisp, unfussy flaps are difficult to achieve. Avoid unless you are an experienced designer or are following very good instructions. **Block** carefully.
For the best pockets:
● **Pick up** stitches and **graft**, in preference to **casting on** or **off** and **slip-stitch seaming**, to increase elasticity, strength and neatness.
● Before starting a **border** or **edging** that will need sewing on the right side, decide how it is going to be sewn and what **selvedges**, if any, will look best.
● Keep straight lines straight, angles sharp and curves smooth.
● If not sure about size and/or exact pocket position, use **patch pockets** or **cut pockets** (see **horizontal slit** and **loose pockets**).

These can be decided when the work is finished.
● In general, work linings in the same yarn as the rest. Use also the same pattern, unless highly textured, and try to align with a change of pattern on the main fabric.
● Unless using different patterns, check lining depth by counting rows rather than measuring.
● With very thick yarns, work linings in a finer, matching yarn. Adjust stitches and rows as required.
● If working linings in different patterns and/or yarns, the area closest to the opening must be like the rest of the work. Allow at least 3cm (1¼in); more for large pockets.
● Cloth is difficult to add successfully, but can be considered for **patch pockets** and for linings of **loose pockets**.

Patch pockets

Two types: **applied** and **picked up**. Use **picked-up pockets** only when you want a colour change, a drastic pattern change or a fun shape. Square picked-up pockets look very much like **slit pockets**, which are easier.

Applied pockets U

(See **choosing seams**)

• Work an independent shape and sew it onto the **right side**, leaving an opening (Fig 2.370). Shapes could include **medallions, coils** and pieces of **fluted jacquard**.

2.370

Pockets in **flat** patterns are easiest to apply. Thin fabrics are tricky because the seam is difficult to hide. The edge may have to be turned in – even all-round hems have been recommended. These are bulky methods, based on dressmaking, and not always successful in knitting.

For easy sewing and a much-improved pocket, work one of the ideas suggested under **overlapping vertical slits** (second

method) all around the edge. Some may ask for **picking up stitches** and **circular knitting**. An edging, however small, gives a good, uniform finish and a firm base for sewing.

Picked-up pockets S

The shape most commonly seen is the square, perhaps with a diagonal opening. There is no need to be so conventional (Fig 2.371).

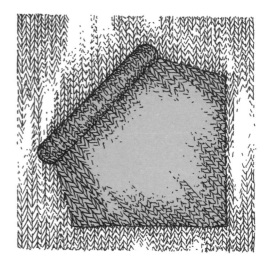

2.371

a **Pick up sts from centre of work**, following outline of pocket, except for opening. One st per st and/or row is required.

b Start work from one row of picked up sts, or from one corner st as in illustration.

c At start and end of each row, work 1 of the picked-up sts still on needles together with the edge st. **Increase** or **decrease** if necessary.

d If pocket ends with a straight row, finish as suggested for **overlapping horizontal slits**. If it needs shaping with **short rows**, finish as for **diagonal slits**.

Or, pick up only sts for the first row, then **knit on** the edges.

Slit pockets

Worked exactly like **overlapping slits** (horizontal, **vertical** or **diagonal**) but with a lining instead of the hidden overlap layer.

Horizontal pockets

U

The most common pocket of all (Fig 2.372).

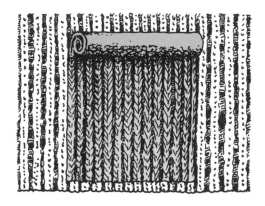

2.372

Work as for **overlapping horizontal slits** but with a long upper overlap layer that will become the lining. Instead of **c** and **d** in first method:
• work an independent lining or, preferably,
• work a lining from stitches picked up as in Fig 2.344, or
• work a lining from stitches picked up both at the bottom and at the sides.
OR work as for second method except for finishing the top edge. Then:
• work one of the three linings above and **graft** to top edge, or
• work the lining from the top-edge stitches down. **Graft** or **free-loop backstitch** last row; or **cast off** and sew.
OR leave the stitches for border or edging on a **holder** (**cast off** instead if more appropriate for edging), work lining, join lining in, finish work, then finish edge.
OR decide pocket position after work is finished, and work as for the second method explained but from a **cut slit**.

Vertical pockets

U

Work in isolation, with the opening to the left (Fig 2.373) or to the right, or make a large pocket with two openings, one on each side.

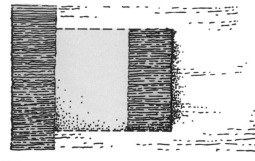

2.373

Work as for **overlapping vertical slits** (first method) but, in **b**, cast on (or preferably pick up) extra stitches to make a lining rather than an overlap. You could also pick up stitches for the side of the lining, and work together one of them with the edge stitch of each row.
OR work as for second method for the upper layer, and as for first method for the under layer.
OR work as for **vertical buttonholes**. Finish the upper layer as for second method of **overlapping slits**, then **pick up** stitches from the under layer and work the lining across. **Graft** or **free-loop backstitch** last row; or, **cast off** and sew.

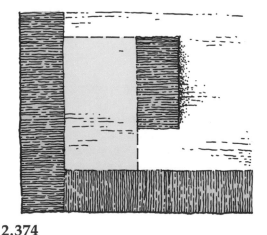

2.374

For a deeper pocket (Fig 2.374), work lining independently to give the extra depth, then join in under layer.

Diagonal pockets S

If the diagonal is not very steep, the lining is worked as in **horizontal pockets** (Fig 2.375).

2.375

If the diagonal is very steep, the lining is worked as in **vertical pockets** (Fig 2.376).

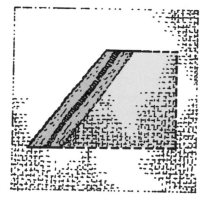

2.376

In both cases, start by working the upper layer (Fig 2.377):

a Put any sts not required for the pocket's upper layer on **holder 1**.

b Depending on finish you want to give to the pocket edge, work a **diagonal cast-off** or a **dart**, until you reach top of pocket.

c If a dart has been used, put the dart sts on **holder 2**.

d Put any sts left on **holder 3**.

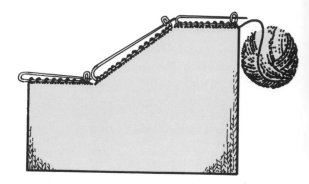

2.377

For a **horizontal-type lining**:

e Either **cast on** or, preferably, **pick up** sts and work until you reach **holder 1**.

f Join in sts from **holder 1**, and continue work until you reach **holder 3**.

g Join in sts from **holder 3** and finish work.

For a **vertical-type lining**:

e Either **cast on** or, preferably, **pick up** sts. Work independently for a little while only if you want a lining like the one in Fig 2.374.

f Join in sts from **holder 1**, and work until you reach **holder 3**.

g Work together 1 st from **holder 3** with the corresponding st from lining, as in **cast-on edge hems**, and finish work. Or, **cast off** lining, then join in sts from **holder 3**.

In either case:

h Finish sts on **holder 2** with any of the suggestions given in the second method for **overlapping vertical slits**. Borders can have any of the three shapes described in **overlapping diagonal slits**.

Loose pockets U

Like **horizontal slit pockets**, only a slit and an edging or border shows on the **right side**. But on the **wrong side**, instead of a one-layer lining attached to the fabric, they have a two-layer lining dangling from the slit. Therefore, they are bulkier.

Having reached the top of the pocket:

a Leave any sts at either side on **holders**.

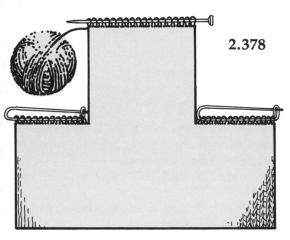

2.378

- put lower-edge sts on a needle, work lining and **graft** to upper-edge sts; or,
- place upper- and lower-edge sts on a set of **double-pointed needles**, work a **circular** lining and **graft** the front sts to the back sts to close it at the bottom.

Finish as in **d** above.

Tubular pockets   S

Of more use in decorative work (to enclose **blind objects** (Fig 2.315) or **stuffing**) than in garment making.

a At the start of the pocket, **increase** as necessary to double the number of sts required to obtain pocket width.

b Work in **tubular knitting** across this area, keeping rest of work in pattern. Make any necessary **row adjustments**.

c At top of pocket, **sl pwise** the back-layer sts onto right needle and the front-layer sts onto a **holder**.

d Sl back-layer sts back to left needle without twisting and continue work, adjusting number of stitches if necessary. Finish work.

e Finish front-layer sts as suggested for **overlapping horizontal slits** (second method).

If a **closed pocket** is desired, work **a** and **b**, then continue as explained in **blind objects**.

b Continue on pocket sts for twice the required depth (Fig 2.378), to form pocket lining.

c Fold lining in two and join in sts on holders. Finish work.

d **Pick up** sts from pocket edge if necessary. Work border or edging as suggested in **overlapping horizontal slits** (second method).

Depending on the intended edge finish, you could mark the fold-line as for **hems**. The fold-line at the bottom of the lining could also be marked.

Alternatively, work steps **a** and **b** of **overlapping horizontal slits** (second method), or work a **cut slit**. Then, either:

Pleats

Permanent pleats in knitting do not quite have the look of those in cloth. The fabric is heavier and more elastic. Also, the crease is basically achieved with technical tricks rather than with massive steaming under mechanical pressure. The resulting pleat may be sharp, but will not have the knife-edge sharpness found in cloth.

The base fabric will also have an effect. If it is not **flat,** both the creases and the lower free end will tend to curl.

On the other hand, fabric curl can be used to advantage. Choose the right pattern, and you will have a **fluted,** or **mock-pleated** effect without any extra effort. In fact, it would be a gross mistake to try to flatten these patterns – for one thing, you would never win. Broad **ribbings**, both regular and irregular, produce fluting. So do other, more sophisticated knit-and-purl combinations (Fig 2.379) to be found in pattern dictionaries (see **Books**).

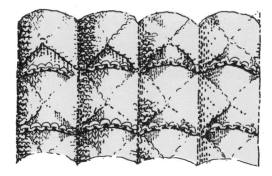

2.379

Accept knitted pleats for what they are. Trying to achieve an effect that does not come naturally will involve you in much pressing (with consequent flattening of texture) and much bother – from working across and constantly changing three different pairs of needles, to sharpening each crease with tiny stitches in matching thread.

Block very carefully and spray well on both sides.

Use **needle** and/or **fabric markers** to highlight **fold-line** positions.

Vertical pleats

There is only one basic pleat (Fig 2.380), made out of three layers: **face, turn-back** and **underside** . These must all have the same number of stitches.

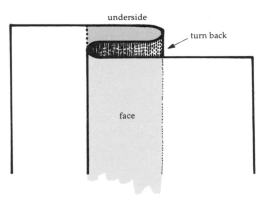

2.380

Permanent pleats

Mark the **front fold-line** on the last stitch of the face and the **back fold-line** on the last stitch of the turn-back. Use the same technique in both cases, or one fold-line will be longer than the other. Either:

● Make a **slip chain** – on right side for front fold-line and on wrong side for back fold-line. On **right-side** rows: **slip 1 pwise – wyab** for front fold-line and **wyif** for back fold-line.

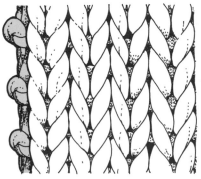

2.381

On **wrong-side** rows: **p** each of the 2 sts in turn (Fig 2.381). Or,

• Work just one **garter stitch** on each fold-line: **p** on all rows (Fig 2.382).

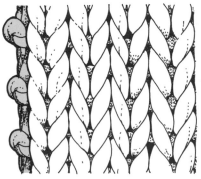

2.382

The slip chain pulls more, and may distort the side stitches when **blocked** to full length. The garter-stitch fold-line works more naturally with purl than with knit fabrics, which need more **blocking**; it makes a 'bumpy' rather than a smooth edge, but somewhat corrects, rather than increases, fabric curl.

To **close** the pleat:

a **Slip face** sts **pwise** onto a **double-pointed needle**.

b Repeat with **turn-back** sts and a 2nd needle.

c Fold **pleat**.

d Work together 1 st from each of the 3 **pleat** layers (Fig 2.383). **Cast off** at same time if desired.

2.383

Variations

Soft pleats: Like **permanent pleats**, but without marking the fold-lines – simply work as if there was no pleat, then **close** at the top. Do not crease whilst **blocking**.

Knife pleats: The **permanent pleat** as explained. Many can be put next to each other, either pointing to the left (Fig 2.384a) or to the right (Fig 2.384b).

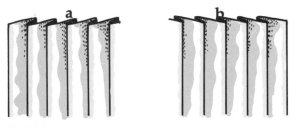

2.384

Box pleats: One right and one left **knife pleat**, pointing away from each other (Fig 2.385).

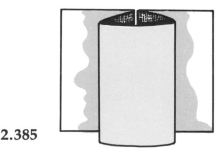

2.385

Inverted pleats: One left and one right **knife pleat**, pointing towards each other (Fig 2.386).

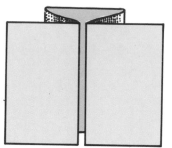

2.386

Accordion pleats: A series of **knife pleats**, in which the **turn-back** of one pleat becomes the **face** of the next pleat (Fig 2.387). To **block**, spray before folding concertina fashion. If the top is to be closed, all the layers have to be worked together; a **crochet hook** may help to work the stitches through the many needles.

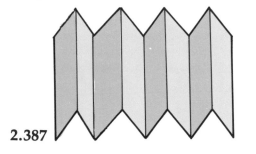

2.387

Sunray pleats: Like **accordion pleats**, but wide at the bottom and narrow at the top (Fig 2.388). **Decrease** at regular intervals at either side of the **back fold-line**.

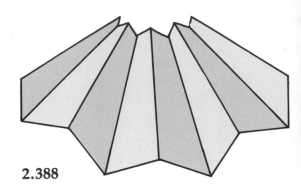

2.388

Horizontal pleats

(See **pull-up stitch**)

These are really **tucks**, rather than pleats, because the back fold-line needs to be secured all along its length. Otherwise, the pleat would unfold.

Fig 2.250 shows, at the top, the smallest of all tucks – **cordings**; soft pleats follow. For **permanent pleats**, mark the front fold-line as for **horizontal hems** (Fig 2.389).

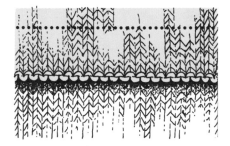

2.389

Hems and Casings

Are hems necessary in knitting? The answer to that is very rarely, certainly far less than their use would make us think.

Cut cloth needs a hem because it frays. So does much of **cut-and-sew** knitting. But shaped knitting does not fray. So, why add bulk and waste time working on something not to be seen? To prevent fabric curl? Hems do not always cure that problem – why not use a **flat** fabric, all over or on a **border**? To add weight to the lower edge? – then why not use a more interesting, less apologetic technique?

Knitting has its own rules. Let's get rid of dressmaking preconceptions, avoid hems on curved edges altogether, and use hems only where there is a function for them:

- as casings for **drawstrings** or **elastic**, for rods to hang wall-hangings from etc;
- in designs that make positive use of the double-layer edge as an integral feature.

General rules

Hems and casings can be vertical or horizontal, knitted in or picked up. They can have a crisp fold-line or a rounded fold-line. They can be worked in the main colour or in a contrast colour, in the main yarn or in a finer yarn, in the main stitch pattern or in a different one. Casings can also be placed in the centre of work as well as at the edge.

For best results:

- Choose, in preference, hems that do not require sewing.
- Make sure that the fold-line is straight in sewn hems. Pin or tack before sewing.
- Sew on a straight line – always on the same row or along the same stitch. Tack a contrast thread to mark sewing line if necessary.
- Sew loosely, so that the seam can stretch without pulling the main layer; not so loosely that the hem sags, though.
- Make sure that the sewing does not show on the right side.
- If the two layers are in the same pattern and yarn, do not measure with a tape; count rows (or stitches) instead.
- If the two layers are in different patterns and/or yarn, remember that each may need a different number of stitches and/or rows. Check both **tensions**.
- Use only **tubular hem** for **ribbings**.
- In methods where the fold-line can be marked, do so for crisper results if you are sure that you will not want to alter it later.

Horizontal hems S

The most popular type. When the fabric is to remain flat, it needs to be the same width as the main layer of fabric. At most, it may have one stitch less at each end, to make sure that the edges do not stick out.

However, when the fabric is to form a closed or open tube (as in skirts and jackets) the hem becomes a ring. Almost without exception, the ring is on the **wrong side**; that is, inside the tube (Fig 2.390). Accounting for fabric thickness the ring must, therefore, be smaller than the tube.

A popular way of making the ring smaller is

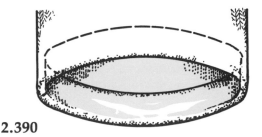

2.390

to work the hem in finer needles – one to three sizes finer than for the main layer. This also tightens the **tension** and makes a stiffer hem.

If the extra stiffness is not desired, try the less common method of having 10 per cent less stitches in the hem. **Increase** or **decrease** (depending on whether the hem is made at the start or end of work) one row away from the fold-line.

Avoid **cast-on** and **cast-off** edges (except, obviously, in **picked-up** and **tubular hems**) because they add unnecessary thickness and may pull or wave. The methods described below give much better results.

If you want to **mark the fold-line**, work one of the following:

• a contrast row – such as a purl row on a knit fabric (Fig 2.391) or vice versa;

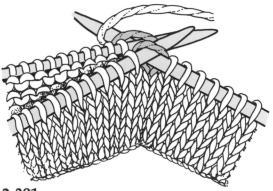

2.391

• a row on a thinner needle;
• a row where every other stitch is **slipped**;
• a row of **eyelets** next to each other, for a picot effect (Fig 2.396).

Or, for an even crisper fold-line, work a **picked-up hem**.

Other ways of emphasising the edge, in special circumstances, are to work an **edging**, or to **pick up** stitches and work a **decorative cast-off**.

On the other hand, for a soft, rounded fold-line, do nothing or work a **tubular hem**.

Cast-on edge hems
(See also **picked-up hems** and **tubular hems**)

Two methods. The first gives the strongest and neatest results.

FIRST METHOD:
a **Provisional cast-on** sts required for hem.
b With hem yarn and pattern, work for desired depth – with fewer sts until the last row but one, or on finer needles, if appropriate.
c **Mark fold-line**, if appropriate. Change to main yarn and needles, if required. If not marking fold-line, place a **fabric marker**.
d Continue in main pattern, to obtain exactly the same depth of work from fold-line.
e **Unravel** provisional cast-on and place free loops on a spare needle, pointing in same direction as last needle worked.
f Fold and work together 1 st from each needle (Fig 2.391). If hem has fewer sts than main layer, work some evenly spaced, main-layer sts by themselves. If hem has more sts, work **2 tog** with a main-layer st at regular intervals.
g Continue main layer.

SECOND METHOD:
Work **a** to **d** as before but leave a long strand of hem yarn when joining it in for later sewing. Then:
e Place a **fabric marker** on last row. Finish work.
f **Unravel** provisional cast-on and place free loops on a spare needle.
g **Free-loop slip stitch** sts on needle to the corresponding sts on row with **marker** (Fig 2.392). If hem does not lie quite flat,

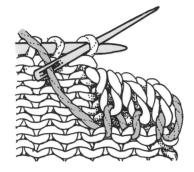

2.392

work on next row. If hem has fewer sts than main layer, skip row sts as required. If hem has more sts, sew **2 tog** to a row st as required. For an even neater hem, see **grafting to rows**.

Cast-off edge hems

Like the second version of **cast-on edge hems**, but at the other end of work.
a Work main layer up to fold-line.
b **Mark fold-line** if appropriate, then change to hem yarn and needles if required. If not marking fold-line, place a **fabric marker**.
c Continue in hem pattern. If requiring a hem with fewer sts, **decrease** after one row.
d When desired depth of hem is reached, do not cast off. Fold work, and **free-loop slip stitch** last row to main layer, as just explained for **cast-on edge hems**. Or see **grafting to rows**.

Picked-up horizontal hems

For a crisper and/or more decorative fold-line.
Use either on cast-on or cast-off edges.
a **Cast-on** or **cast-off** with a **decorative method**. Or, work a **provisional cast-on**, finish work, unpick cast-on yarn, and **decorative cast-off** the free loops.
b **Pick up** sts from the **wrong side** of the cast-on or cast-off, possibly as in Fig 2.344.
c Work for required hem depth.
d **Free-loop slip stitch** last row to main layer (see **g** in 2nd version of **cast-on edge hems**), or see **grafting to rows**.

Tubular horizontal hems

Ideal for **single rib** (Fig 2.393). Useful for other fabrics when only very small hems are required. If no stitches are added it is likely to gather the work.
Work a **tubular cast-on** or a **tubular cast-off**, but with a few more rows in **tubular stocking stitch** than the usual two or four. Total number of tubular rows must be an even number, and they must be worked with **open sides**.

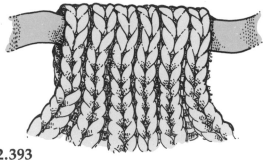

2.393

It can be seen now that **stocking-stitch tubular cast-on** is nothing more than a very small, ordinary hem. The only difference is that, instead of working together one stitch from each needle, as in Fig 2.391, when casting on one stitch is knitted and the other purled, as in Fig 2.44.

Vertical hems   S

(See also introductory comments to **horizontal hems** above, and **vertical pleats**)
In general, vertical hems tend to be used flat. If, however, the fabric is to form a tube (as in skirts knitted across), the difference in length is solved with **row adjustments**.
To **mark the fold-line**, either:
• work a **slip chain**: slip 1 **pwise wyab** on right-side row; **p** on wrong-side row (Fig 2.381); or,
• work 1 single **garter stitch** (Fig 2.382).
Or, for a crisper fold-line, work a **picked-up hem** (see below).
Edgings and **decorative cast-offs** worked on **picked-up** stitches can also be used to emphasise the edge.

Ordinary vertical hem

a **Cast on** sts required for main area of work, plus additional hem sts.
b Work to end, **marking** fold-line and **adjusting rows**, if required.
c To finish, fold and sew **selvedge** to main layer of fabric with a **slip stitch**, or ladder edge st as in **fringe selvedge** and work a **lifted ladder join**.

Picked-up vertical hems

Work as for **horizontal picked-up hems**, except:

a Work a decorative **free-end selvedge** or, work a **chain selvedge, pick up** sts from it, and work a **decorative cast-off**.

Tubular vertical hems

Work as for **tubular borders**.

Turning corners   S

Much ingenuity has gone into devising ways of making a hem turn an inner or an outer round corner, but the results always look contrived. Not surprisingly, since the fabric is being forced into doing something it does not do of its own accord.

Considering that knitting does not require hems, anyway, it would seem sensible to spend less time finishing round corners poorly, and more time designing them correctly – without recourse to a hem to tidy up the edge.

The only hem that makes any sense in a round corner is a **tubular horizontal hem** at the end of a **single-rib** area defining an inner corner. This is because of the gathering effect of this hem. An example would be a **drawstring** casing at the end of a round neckline or yoke.

Square corners

These are turned much more satisfactorily, and in a number of ways.

An ordinary corner combines a **horizontal hem** with a **vertical hem** (Fig 2.394):

a **Cast on** as required for horizontal hem, except for the width of the vertical hem.

b Work in the usual way, **increasing** regularly at the edge so that full horizontal-hem width is obtained when the fold-line is reached.

c Continue **increasing**, so that full vertical-hem width is obtained when the horizontal-hem sewing line is reached. Continue straight. Finish work.

2.394

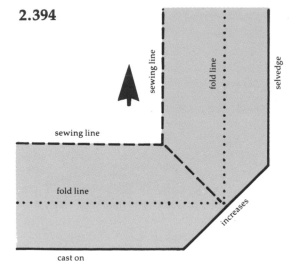

d Fold and sew hems as usual. Join the hem mitre with hidden stitching.

Work in reverse, **decreasing** instead of increasing, on a **cast-off** edge.

Mitred corners

If worked with a **double horizontal dart** – see **mitred corners** under **Short rows** – (Fig 2.395):

a Work as for **vertical hems** until start of corner.

b Work 1st **dart** in the usual way until number of sts left to be worked is the same as number of hem sts.

c Continue dart, but work a symmetrical dart on the hem at the same time.

2.395

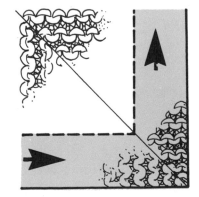

d When no sts are left, work darts in reverse. Finish work.

e Fold and sew hem edge.

For a corner worked with **decreases** – see **mitred corners** under **Increases and decreases** – (Fig 2.396):

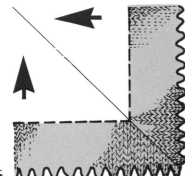

2.396

a **Cast on** as required for the two sides of the sewing line.

b Work hem, **increasing** regularly at the mitre to obtain full width when fold-line is reached.

c After fold-line, work in the usual way. Finish work.

d Fold, **unravel** cast-on and **free-loop slip stitch** (Fig 2.392) the hem (or see **grafting to rows**).

Work in reverse for an **increased** corner on a **cast-off** edge.

All the above methods are for outer corners. Inner corners are worked similarly, but the sewing line is longer than the fold-line, and the hem should be shaped accordingly (Fig 2.397).

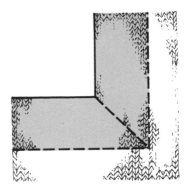

Mid-way casings S

These happen somewhere in the centre of work.

They can be worked in **tubular knitting**, adjusting the stitches before and after the casing.

They can also be worked as two layers:

a **Increase** on every st, or as required, to continue the main layer and obtain a 2nd layer to form the casing.

b On next row, work main-layer sts only; **sl** the others **pwise** onto a **holder**.

c Continue on main layer for depth of casing. Leave sts in waiting.

d Work sts on **holder** for same depth.

e Join the 2 layers by working together 1 st from each layer (Fig 2.391).

f Continue work.

For afterthought casings:

a **Pick up** sts from the **wrong side** (Fig 2.344). .

b Work casing for desired depth.

c **Free-loop slip stitch** (Fig 2.392) or see **grafting to rows**.

PART THREE
FINAL TOUCHES

Making up

Making up is often approached in a negative frame of mind. Some dread it as a boring chore. Others feel apprehensive that the results may not come up to expectations.

We reap what we sow. If you keep thinking that making up is awful, when the moment comes you will find it unbearable. If you buy a yarn that you are not very sure of, choose or design a project that is not perfect, do not bother with **tension samples**, do not double-check the size you need, do not keep checking and measuring the work, and want to finish making up in half an hour, it will be a miracle if you get good results!

In Britain, the bad press making up has is partly due to the ghastly **home**made (as opposed to competent **hand**made) look of so much knitting. If what surrounds you is poor quality, you obviously assume no better can be achieved. Nothing is further from the truth. Good results can be obtained at no great cost, so long as you ignore the crude techniques that often pass as 'professional'.

Be positive

Making up is the art of giving life to an assortment of knitted pieces. When you start, they are dull, crumpled and disconnected. When you finish, they are smooth, assembled and a proper reflection of your craftsmanship.

To be the force behind this transformation can be very exciting, and creative. Try a positive attitude, and see the difference.

Three approaches

All knitting, but knitwear in particular, can be viewed from three angles. You can either consider it as:

- a fabric to be dealt with exactly as cloth;

- a continuous fabric that grows in many directions and avoids seams at all costs;
- a fabric which will be joined by some seams but which is not like cloth.

The first is the **tailoring** approach. It makes great use of **pressing, binding, lining** and other dressmaking techniques. Taken to the extreme, a large rectangle is knitted, then **cut** to shape.

The second is the **circular knitting** approach. Favourite techniques are leaving stitches on **holders, picking up stitches, provisional cast-on** and **cast-off**, and **grafting**. It is popular with knitters who do not like (or think they would not like) sewing and with knitting purists but, as explained in **Rows and rounds**, it is not all roses.

The third approach uses **seams** in moderation, taking advantage of their structural possibilities, and **planning seams** ahead so that they either 'disappear' or become part of the design. Work is mainly **flat** and may well use some of the techniques favoured by the second approach. **Shaping** plays an important role. Pressing, lining and binding are totally out. **Cold-water spray blocking** is in.

Making-up order

Your general approach to knitting, as just outlined, will dictate to a certain extent the order in which to proceed with the finishing process, and to a much greater extent which steps are relevant and which are not.

The following list is a very general guide, to be adapted as required.

a **Fitting**, especially of knitwear. Tack pieces in position with contrast yarn, or join with safety pins. Try on, **wrong-side** out. Allow for the fabric not having been blocked.

b **Darning** of all yarn tails not needed for sewing.

c **Blocking**, including **improving fabric**.

d **Cutting**.

e Cutting of **lining**.

f **Grafting** or **seaming** of joins. Tubes are easier to join when they are open. In knitwear, it is easier to join the shoulder seam, then fit the sleeve, then join the side and sleeve seams (Fig 3.1), than to fit the sleeve after the side and sleeve seams have been joined (Fig 3.2).

3.1

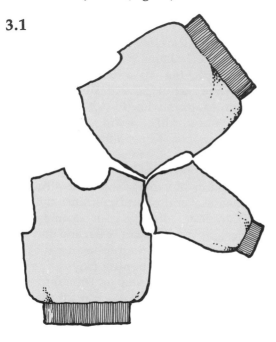

g **Blocking** or **pressing** of joins.

h **Embroidery**.

i **Edgings, borders** etc.

j Fixing of **fastenings** and **elastic**.

k **Brushing, fulling, painting** etc.

l **Lining**.

m Cords, **belts** and **wiggle-woggles**.

3.2

Commonsense will tell you what adaptations are necessary, on lines such as:

● Fabrics that are to be stretched will only fit properly after blocking. But the yarn will then be 'set', and will need **re-conditioning** if something has to be **unravelled**.

● Yarn tails of fabrics to be stretched are best **darned** after **blocking**, to avoid pulling.

● Some seams may be easier to block before joining other seams.

● Some edgings or embroidery may be best worked before joining all or some of the seams.

● **Zips** may be easier to insert before seaming, when the two sides can be laid flat.

Darning

(See also **Making up** and **joining in yarn**)

Except for long tails that can be used for sewing, all yarn ends should be **darned** (or **weaved**) in such a way that the fabric loses no elasticity. Fabrics to be stretched, therefore, should have their tails darned after **blocking**. It is also important to pull the fabric gently before changing direction and/or trimming, to ensure that the darning 'gives'. If unsure, leave trimming for after blocking. It is also essential that the darning does NOT show on the **right side**. Keep checking. Sometimes, following knobs or ridges, or darning each tail over its own colour, may be an advantage. In **openwork** patterns, stick to the solid areas.

For best results:

• Check that the direction you are taking the yarn in is not leaving a hole or a flaw on the right side; two ends, at mid-row or at the edge, generally need crossing.

• Leave yarn tails not shorter than 15cm (6in).

• Darn up and down for anchorage. With **slippery yarns** consider darning the yarn a third time (Fig 3.3).

3.3

• Unpick any knots or double stitches made when **joining in yarn**.

• Avoid darning along edges that will be stretched and released whilst in use (necklines, waistbands etc). If darning is unavoidable, work at right angles to the edge.

• Avoid darning in free edges.

• Avoid unnecessary darning. In **colour** knitting, consider carrying the colours up the side of the work, or use **woven yarn joins**.

The illustrations show darning with a **sewing needle**. A **crochet hook**, or a latch hook such as used in machine knitting or rug making, can also be used.

Types of darning

Basic darning can take three directions: horizontal, vertical and diagonal. Additionally, there are tricks for **neatening** loose **loops**, and long **jacquard floats**. Finally, there is **knotting**.

Free edges
Neaten loops if required. Use either **horizontal** or **vertical darning**, whichever shows least. In general, **garter stitch** requires horizontal, and **ribbing** vertical darning.
Try working **vertical darning** one or two stitches in from the edge.

Seam edges
Neaten loops if required. Use **vertical darning** right on the edge if the **selvedge** is taken in by the seam. Use **diagonal** if not; **knotting** when the amount of ends is overwhelming.

Middle of row
Diagonal darning, unless texture or colour suggest otherwise. **Neaten floats** if required.

Neatening loops

Long loops, such as the ones that sometimes form at the end of **basic cast-off** or at one end

3.4

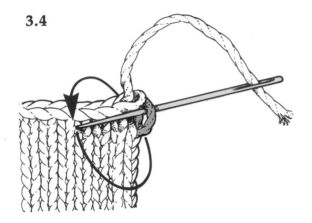

of **yarn-over tubular cast-on**, should be controlled either whilst darning or whilst **seaming**. Choice depends on whether or not there is a tail to be darned next to the loop.

In both cases (Fig 3.4):

a Insert a sewing needle through the loop.

b Give the needle a complete turn, so as to twist the loop.

c Catch a strand at back of work – whichever will make the loop look tidiest.

d Darn or sew in the usual way.

Missing loops or half-loops can be corrected by imitating knitting with the sewing needle. The general idea is to add, or hide, as required to make the fabric look perfect.

Horizontal darning

Figure 3.5. With **wrong side** facing:

a Follow a row of 5 or 6 sts taking advantage of fabric texture. Either insert needle al-

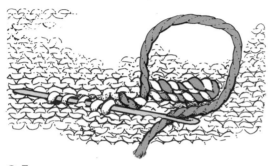

3.5

ways from the top (or from the bottom), as in illustration, or alternate once from the top and once from the bottom. Choice depends on pattern.

b Repeat in opposite direction, either over same row or over next one.

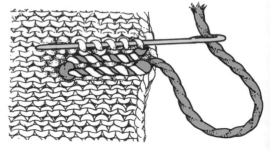

3.6

If there is a second end, repeat away from the first one over the same row(s). At free or seam ends, repeat on a parallel row (Fig 3.6). Remember that, if there are two ends, they will probably need crossing to avoid holes.

Vertical darning

Figure 3.7. With **wrong side** facing:

a Follow a st line for 5 or 6 rows. Either insert needle always from the same side (as in illustration), or alternate once from

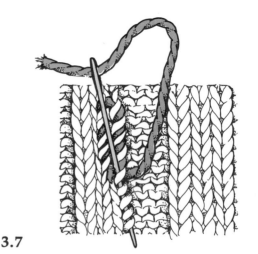

3.7

the right and once from the left, depending on pattern.

b Repeat in the opposite direction, either over the same st line or the next one.

If there is a second end, repeat away from the first one over the same stitch line, as in illustration. Or work parallel to the first end, over an adjoining stitch line.

In free edges, try to work one or two stitches in from the edge. In seam edges, work right at the edge (Fig 3.8).

If there are two ends, remember they may need crossing to avoid holes.

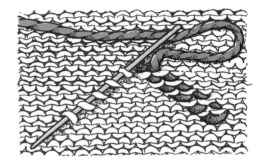

3.9

Knotting

Use only at edges, such as seams, that will remain hidden from view. Fig 3.10.

a Tie ends in pairs, using **square knots** (Fig 1.62). Ordinary, 'granny' knots, tend to come undone.

b Trim to leave a neat fringe, not too short.

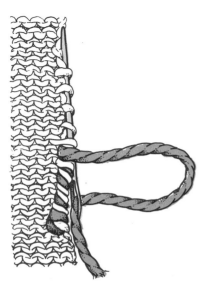

3.8

Diagonal darning

Figure 3.9. More elastic than the other two. With **wrong side** facing:

a Follow a line of 5 or 6 sts, each 1 row and 1 st further away from the 1st. Take advantage of fabric texture, and follow the line that leaves a better surface on the right side – usually going down and left (right) if you are darning the right (left) tail.

b Repeat in the opposite direction, either over the same sts or the ones next to them.

If there is a second end, repeat following a different diagonal, possibly forming a V with the first one.

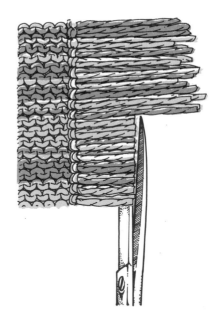

3.10

Coarse yarns, and yarns that 'plump up' when washed (such as Shetland) should not cause trouble. Fine yarns, and especially **slippery yarns**, may be best secured with a **running stitch** or **backstitch** in matching thread. If worried about the fringe, cover with **binding**.

Neatening floats

If you have read the advice given on **jac-quard knitting** too late, and have a mass of lengthy **floats**, you can do one of two things: add a **lining** or secure the floats.

Lining is best left for wall-hangings and other decorative projects, and for **tailored** knitwear. Never line knitwear if you want it to preserve the elastic moulding qualities of the fabric.

To secure the floats (Fig 3.11):
● Work a vertical **running stitch**, catching the back of the st on every 2nd row. If worried about the stitching showing on the right side, insert needle through yarn instead of lifting the whole stitch-head. Repeat at about 2.5cm (1in) intervals.

An alternative is to work lines of **slip-stitch crochet** at similar intervals.

If the original yarn is thick, use finer yarn matching the main colour.

3.11

Blocking

Also called **dressing**. (See also **Making up**)

To block is to give a permanent 'set' to knitting. By means of steam or water, the yarn is made to take the shape of the waves that form each row or round. If you want to re-use yarn that has been blocked, you will have to **re-condition** it to make it straight again.

There are two steps to blocking: **dampening** and **shaping**. Dampening can take a number of forms. In some the shaping is done **right side** up, in others **wrong side** up. In some, shaping is done before, and in others after dampening. Finally, some forms allow for very precise shaping and much **fabric improvement**, others do not.

Unless circumstances clearly suggest otherwise (for instance, if you want to **starch** cotton lace), I strongly recommend **cold-water spray** for all fabrics, even **flat** ones which are sometimes left unblocked – setting the yarn into permanent waves improves their per-

formance. Other methods have been included to cater for special circumstances and other personal preferences.

Used items can be re-blocked after **washing** (see **Aftercare**). Proceed as explained in **washing** below.

Dampening

Unless otherwise specified, KEEP KNITTING HORIZONTAL whilst drying or cooling.

Cold-water spray
Fig 3.12
a **Shape** each knitted piece **right side** up.
b Spray with an ordinary, fine-mist plant sprayer. Some fibres need more water than others. **Wool** may only require a light spray. **Man-made fibres** or **silk** may require much more, but no fibre is likely to

3.12

need as much wetting as if you were to wash it. Use **tension samples** to check degree of dampness.

c Allow to dry, away from direct sun or heat, but in a warm atmosphere if possible.

This is a foolproof method, that minimises shrinkage risk because wetting is done after shaping. There is total control of dampness and of texture. No pressure is applied, and so raised textures can be made to raise even further. Uneven stitches can often be successfully corrected.

With very limp fabrics, consider spraying a little starch after a first spray with water. Try first on sample (see also **starching** below).

Identical pieces can be blocked in pairs, if they have a smooth texture. Shape the first one and spray **wrong side** up. Place the second one on top, **right side** up, re-pin and spray.

Damp towel

a **Shape** knitting **right side** up.
b Lay a damp towel, or cloth, over the knitting.
c Leave overnight, remove towel and allow to dry.

Thick knitting may need a second damp towel underneath.

It is more cumbersome than **cold-water spray**, and texture cannot be raised as much, especially if following the old-fashioned ad-vice of placing heavy books on top, or sandwiching the lot between newspapers and placing under a rug to be trodden on!

Washing

(See also **Aftercare**)

Washing for blocking should only be necessary on those rare occasions when the yarn changes character after washing. **Tension** should then be checked on a washed sample, before any work is done.

If washing is done after assembling, much control is lost. Even washing before assembling can cause some loss of control, because the fabric starts to 'set' before it is shaped.

● **Shape, right side** up, and allow to dry.

Starching

This is often used for cotton lace. Limp yarns and heavy decorative work may also benefit from starching.

If using a spray, proceed as for **cold-water spray**, perhaps spraying the **wrong side** before shaping. Instead of starch, wall hangings and other decorative items can be treated with the laminating spray used for making window blinds. This also helps to protect them from dirt. Apply on both sides, but try on **samples** first.

If wet starching:

a Make a solution of starch powder, 'instant' starch powder, gum arabic or white sugar. Use sugar only on items that will not get wet later – they could become sticky.
b Dip knitting into starch.
c Squeeze out excess starch and stretch knitting in all directions.
d **Shape, right side** up, and allow to dry.

Steaming

The old-fashioned method is to hold the knitting on top of a pan of boiling water (Fig 3.13), or a non-automatic kettle. When the steam has penetrated, **shape** and allow to dry. Shape the knitting quickly, before it gets too dry or too cold.

Apart from the risk of subjecting the wrong fibre to heat, you can burn your fingers.

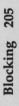

3.13

For a modern alternative: (Fig 3.14):

a **Shape** knitting **wrong side** up on top of very thick, absorbent padding.

b Go over the knitting with a steam iron set at the lowest steam temperature, and constantly kept 2–3cm (about 1in) above the surface.

c Cool and dry before unpinning.

3.14

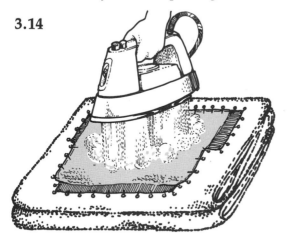

If the fibre can take the steam (try first on a **sample**), results are good. However, having to shape wrong side up, in case the iron accidentally touches the fabric, is a drawback. The arm that holds the iron can get very tired.

Pressing

A surprisingly popular method, given all its drawbacks. There is little control of texture because pinning must be done **wrong side** up. Resting the iron may cause over-flattening. Accidentally using too high a setting or touching the fabric may cause shining or scorching of **natural** fibres, and may totally ruin **man-made** ones.

Proceed as explained for **ironing**, but on individual pieces.

Shaping

The following techniques are all suitable for **cold-water spray**, but some are not suitable for some of the other methods. As a rule, shaping **wrong side** up and relying on an iron are both restrictive. Dampening before shaping may restrict if you are trying to raise the texture or stretch fibres that are shorter when wet, but may be an advantage if added weight if desired.

In general:

• Work on a pinnable surface, such as a bed, carpet, or large foam cushion. Dressmaker's cutting boards, notice boards, polystyrene, flattened packing cartons etc can also be used, but pinning is harder. Beds are good because you can sit on them, which is much more comfortable than kneeling on the floor. Use ironing boards only for small items.

• If shaping **wrong side** up, cover the area with thick, smooth padding.

• Cover pinning surface with clean cloth. A checked cloth helps in keeping straight lines, but avoid small checks because they are confusing.

• If **pressing** or using a **damp towel,** use small, non-rust dressmaker's pins, and push them down to their heads. Otherwise, use long glass-headed pins and half-push them only.

• **Improve fabric** texture as much as you can. Some improvements can only be done after **pinning** or **stretching**, others are done before or during pinning or stretching.

Specific circumstances will suggest what comes first.

- Respect the fabric's natural tendencies. Although you may obviously want to eliminate excessive curling, do not expect a **curly** fabric to become perfectly **flat**, and do not try to eliminate **fluting** or **welting** effects. If that is what the fabric wants to do, use it to advantage.

Pinning

With tape measure in hand, spread the knitting until it reaches the intended main length and width. With **natural fibres** you may be able to adjust minor discrepancies by slightly shrinking or stretching the knitting, but do not rely on it. For best results, the knitting must be totally devoid of wrinkles, without being stretched. If you **measured** it often and correctly whilst you were working, you will have no trouble.

Pin all strategic points (Fig 3.15). Then pin between these points at close intervals – how close depends on how flat the fabric is. The edges must be quite smooth (Fig 3.16). If each pin draws out a point, you are either stretching too much or not using enough pins.

Ribbings should be **dampened** without the slightest tensioning, unless the design specifically requires them to remain open. If the adjoining fabric is so gathered that it cannot be blocked without stretching the ribbing:

a Stretch the ribbing and cover with dry towel, plastic sheet or foil.
b Spray or steam the rest. Allow to dry.
c Release the ribbing.
d Cover what has already been blocked and spray the ribbing. Allow to dry.

If dealing with gathering **borders**, or other areas, that have no give and cannot be stretched, block around a cushion (Fig 3.17), or prevent the situation arising. Instead of working the border, and gathering heavily just above it, knit first the wider area starting with a **provisional cast-on**. Block, unpick the cast-on and work the border in the opposite

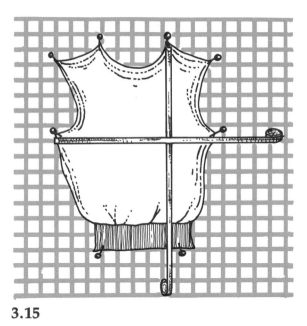

3.15

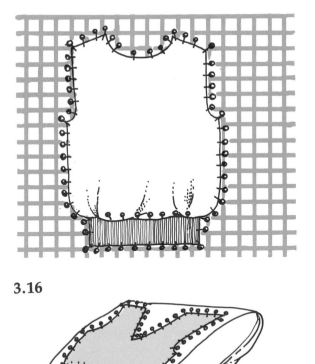

3.16

3.17

direction, or work the border separately and **graft** the two sections.

The pieces of a sweater to be joined into a circular yoke, and any other similar cases, are also best blocked before joining. Totally **circular** and seamless projects should be sprayed thoroughly, then **dried** as explained in **Aftercare**.

Pleats should have the inner layers dampened before pinning.

Stretching with pins

Non-resilient yarns should be stretched, to avoid them going out of shape later on. Stretch evenly in all directions (Fig 3.18).

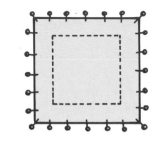

3.18

Slippery yarns, and fabrics expected to droop, should be stretched sideways but kept short (Fig 3.19). Once hanged they will adopt the intended shape.

Lace and some other **openwork** patterns are the main candidates for stretching. **Long-chain cast-off** and **picot selvedges** are often used in lace to make stretching easier.

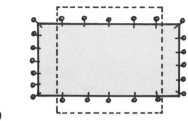

3.19

Squares and rectangles can be stretched on a checked cloth:

a Use 4 pins to mark the 2 axis lines, and 4 more to mark the 4 corners (Fig 3.20).

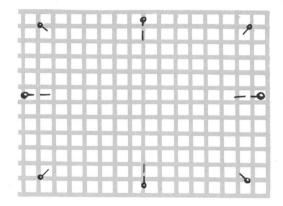

3.20

b Pin the corners and the centre-point of each side of the knitting (Fig 3.21).

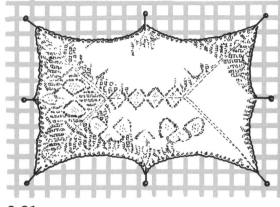

3.21

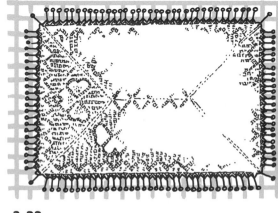

3.22

c Pin each loop, following a totally straight line and keeping the spacing regular (Fig 3.22).

An alternative is to thread fine knitting needles through all the loops of each side, and keep the needles in position with a few pins on the side of the knitting. A strong, thin white cord could also be used. This should first be tensioned, then kept in position (Fig 3.23). If using this method, you could pin the lace on a pegboard and keep the cords or needles in place with pegs without going through the lace.

3.24

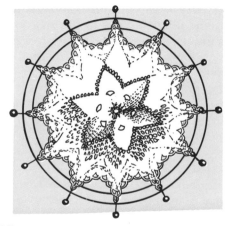

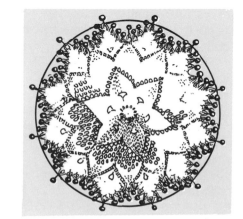

3.25

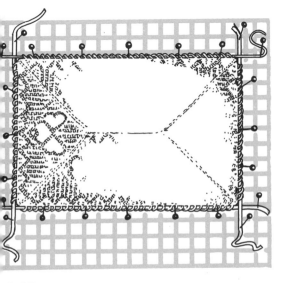

3.23

For **circular shapes**:

a Attach a pen to the end of a tape measure, or of a piece of string, and draw a circle to exactly fit the medallion to be blocked.

b Mark the points of the medallion at regular intervals.

c Draw a second circle if the edge is scalloped (Fig 3.24).

d Pin centre and main points of medallion (Fig 3.25).

e Pin remaining loops (Fig 3.26).

You can draw the shape on the back of tracing or greaseproof paper, or see-through thick plastic, and place this on top of the pinning surface. Or, if you want a more durable

3.26

shape pattern, machine-stitch the outline on a stable piece of cloth, or draw it on a wooden board and hammer in a little brass nail for every loop. This last method is time consuming in the first instance, but it is extremely strong.

Fine woollen lace should not be stretched too drastically, because the loops could break. Cotton lace is more sturdy. It is often **starched**, sometimes quite heavily. Woollen lace is sometimes starched, if it lacks body, but only lightly.

Some people prefer stretching wet, rather than dry, items. And, of course, if something is being re-stretched as part of its **Aftercare**, it will have been washed and it then makes sense to stretch it wet. After a few hours of drying check whether re-tensioning is necessary; some fibres become longer when they dry. If uncertain about whether to stretch before or after wetting, try both methods on **samples.**

Knitting which has been stretched wet can be dried upright. Knitting sprayed after stretching must be dried flat, so that the moisture permeates the fabric.

Stretching without pins

(See also **miscellaneous moulds** below)
This makes use of one of the adhesive sprays used by photographers and graphic artists. Make sure to buy the type that allows for re-positioning without time limits, and check that it says 'non-staining'.

Results are quite acceptable, especially if the project does not require great sharpness of corners. Watch that the edges do not lift after dampening.

a Draw shape (see **stretching with pins** above) on card, thick plastic, floor tile, melamine board, etc. Or, draw on paper and place behind piece of glass or window pane.

b Spray surface with adhesive strictly as directed by manufacturers.

c Place dry knitting on top and ease into shape with the help of a pin or **cable needle**. Lift and reposition as required, keep-

ing in place with one hand and pressing down with the other.

d **Spray** with water or starch. Allow to dry.

e Carefully peel off knitting.

If the blocking surface is not a disposable piece of card or plastic, either clean as indicated on spray can or leave as it is for future use.

Frames and moulds

The following are some of the contraptions that can be used to help shaping:

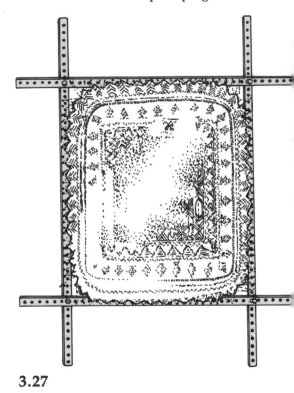

3.27

● **Shawl frames**   As used in the Shetlands (Fig 3.27). Four long timber sections, with holes every 2.5cm (1in), approximately. The sections are pegged so that they make a frame of the required size for the shawl. More pegs secure a thread passed through the points of the shawl, which dries quickly because air circulates freely through.

● **Sweater frames,** or boards (Fig 3.28). Another Shetland device, to counter the tendency of the local wool to 'plump up' and

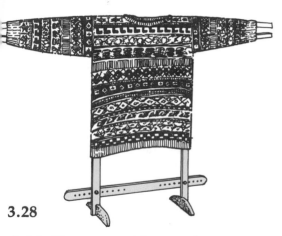

3.28

shrink. They are good for stretching T-shape sweaters, but not for raglan or set-in sleeves, unless they are specially adapted. Ribbings have to be steamed back into shape, because they stretch.

● **Hat moulds** Hats that fit round the skull can be shaped over a pudding basin or mixing bowl. (Fig 3.29). Berets can have a plate put inside (Fig 3.30).

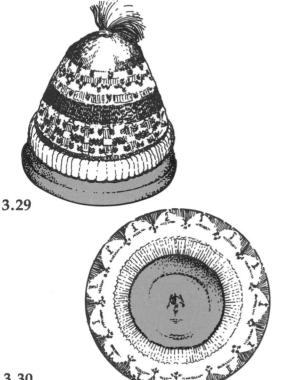

3.29

3.30

● **Glove, and other boards** Again from the Shetlands. Wooden shapes to make sure that the wool does not matt whilst drying.

● **Collar moulds** Collars can be successfully shaped over an upturned mixing bowl, with the outer edge pinned to a flat surface. The bowl is placed off-centre of the edge circle (Fig 3.31). See **Addresses** for a **collar shaping guide**.

3.31

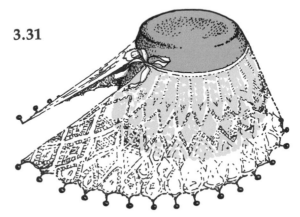

3.32

● **Miscellaneous moulds** Small items can be shaped over dishes, glasses or bowls – either wet (or starched) or dry if using adhesive spray as in **stretching without pins** (Fig 3.32). Larger pieces can be placed around cushions, bolsters, tailor's hams, folded towels, sofa arms. **Hoods, tunnels, sculptured knitting** and anything else that is hollow underneath can be temporarily stuffed with cotton wool, little yarn balls, buttons, beads, bits of fabric, or anything that fits the shape.

Improving fabric

The three golden rules are: BLOCK FLAWS OUT, BLOCK TEXTURE IN, BE CRISP.

- Stretch edges that are pulling.
- Make sure that rows and vertical lines of stitches are absolutely straight.
- Make **tight stitches** larger by drawing yarn from a couple of stitches at either side. Use a **cable**, or **sewing, needle**.
- Make **larger stitches** smaller by easing up the side stitches.
- Straighten up the loops in rows that have become lopsided after being too long on the needles. Use a cable, or sewing, needle.

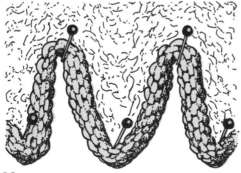

3.33

- Draw out points and secure with a pin at the tip. Draw in corners and keep in place with a pin on the outside (Fig 3.33). Points and corners should be made as sharp as possible without distorting, whether they define a neckline, a lace edging or a **chevron** fabric edge.
- Draw the sides of **slits** and **buttonholes** to-

gether and keep in position with as many pins as required.
- Draw back and pin any strand that obscures what should be a neat line or a hole. If an **eyelet**, for instance, is totally obscured because it has been worked in bouclé yarn, use as many as half a dozen pins to make it round (Fig 3.34). As with corners, the pin should push the strand or fabric back, but should not go through it.

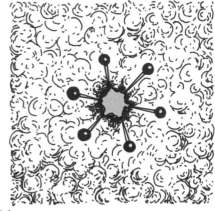

3.34

- Push pins down to their heads to flatten raised stitches that should be flat.
- Use devious ways to emphasise the texture of a pattern. Shape **welts** and **flutings** with your fingers; use **moulds** to keep hollow raised areas in position; run a finger or a pen-cap along grooves, to lower them; spear rows of lifted stitches with a knitting needle (Fig 3.35), raise the needle a few times and then withdraw.

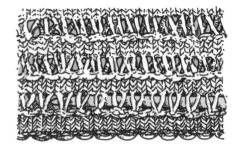

3.35

After sewing

Seams do not always need blocking, but when they do the difference really shows.

As far as possible, block seams unfolded, otherwise a crease can form. If an unavoidable crease bothers you, block seam again, unpinned, around a convenient **mould**. It is often possible to block one or more seams unfolded, if one last seam has not yet been sewn. This last seam is later blocked folded.

● To block **unfolded seams**, push many pins at either side of the seam line, down to their heads. The pins should be on top of the fabric taken in by the seam, on the **wrong side**, and they may need to be nearly touching (Fig 3.36). In **folded seams**, there is only room for one row of pins (Fig 3.37), on the **right side**. Wet the seam very well, spraying cold water from a distance of only 3–4cm (1½in). Allow to dry.

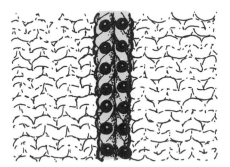

3.36

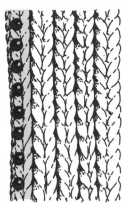

3.37

Cutting

(See also **Making up**)

In general, it is safer to cut knitting after **blocking**. Once the yarn has 'set', it does not **ladder** so easily. **Twice-knit knitting** is an exception that will not ladder at any stage.

Cutting may play a big role in the **tailoring** approach to knitting. It is also used for restyling, adapting to size, changing damaged areas and providing openings in **circular knitting** (see **bridges**).

Horizontal cuts are made by **pulling a thread**. Cuts in all other directions are made by the **cut and sew** method.

PRACTICE WITH SAMPLES, worked in the appropriate stitch pattern and preferably the same yarn.

Pulling a thread

This is based on the idea that rows are interlocked yarn waves (see **the knitted stitch**). Cutting a row at the two ends, and then pulling the thread, frees the crest of the wave below and the trough of the wave above.

Notice that the unlocked crest shows a row of real stitches, and can be **unravelled**. The unlocked trough, on the other hand, cannot be unravelled, although it can **ladder**. In **stocking stitch**, the waves are very clear. In other patterns they may be far less so. Usually, the trough has one loop less than the crest.

Having cut the fabric, thread a fine needle through the free loops. You can then do a number of things:

• Unravel part of the lower section, and **graft** what is left to the top section.

• Add rows to the lower section, and graft to the top section.

• Discard one of the sections and **cast off** or add rows to the other one. You can do this to the troughs of the top section, as well as to the crests of the lower section, but only **stocking stitch** will look unbroken – except for a half-stitch kink at the edges. Changing stitch pattern gets over this problem.

gathers towards the right, find the new yarn end and continue pulling in stages. If the pattern is very awkward, unpick the row stitch by stitch.

If worried about the idea of cutting, or if working with a **slippery yarn**, thread a contrast thread through the rows above and below the one to be cut, before starting.

Cut and sew

Or, rather, 'sew, cut and sew'. Some cuts can be planned ahead (see **bridges**).

a Tack the cutting line in contrast thread.

b Work 2 lines of **close stitching** (see below) on the inside of the cutting line, almost touching each other, in matching thread.

c Repeat **b** about 0.5cm (¼in) further in, if working with **slippery yarns**.

d Cut along tacking (Fig 3.39).

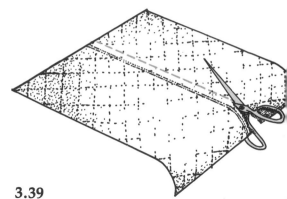

3.39

3.38

To cut (Fig 3.38):

a Snip a st some 5cm (2in) away from left edge.

b Pull right-edge st of same row, first with a needle, then with your fingers. The fabric will gather.

c Once the gathers reach the cut st, smooth them towards the left and continue pulling the thread until the cut end reaches the right edge.

d Unpick the sts remaining at the left edge.

Some yarns and patterns are easier to pull than others. If the yarn breaks, smooth the

The best **close stitching** is done by machine. Try on **samples** first; you may need a fairly loose setting. If the fabric is very thick and gets caught, try placing tissue paper on top of it; this can easily be removed afterwards. Be careful not to stretch the fabric. To close-stitch by hand, use a very small and tight **backstitch**.

Do not be surprised to find a wavy edge after cutting.

Binding

Although cut edges of out-of-sight seams are often left alone, cut edges always look much neater if they are bound. Use bias-binding tape, knitted **bias bands**, or:

● on free edges, **pick up** and work a strip at the edge fold. Cast off, turn in and secure with a **slip stitch** (Fig 3.40);

● on any edge, place an independent piece of knitting under the edge (this could be a **border** on a free edge, or a larger, uncut piece of knitting on a seam – such as the cast-off top of a sleeve could be placed under a cut armhole). Secure with **fake grafting** to the edge fold, and with **slip stitch** to the wrong side (Fig 3.41). This is a variation of **flat-felled seam** (see also **facings** and **reinforced buttonholes**).

Block well, as explained in **after sewing**.

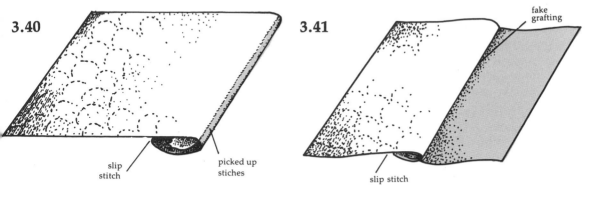

3.40 slip stitch — picked up stiches

3.41 fake grafting — slip stitch

Grafting

(See also **Making up**, and seams under **choosing seams – loop edges**)

Grafting (or **weaving**, or **Kitchener stitch**) is a way of joining two pieces of knitting with an imitation row. The join is done with a **sewing needle**, but looks knitted.

Although real grafting is done between two sets of free loops, rows of free loops can be grafted to solid rows or edges. **Fake grafting** uses the same technique but with solid rows and edges, rather than free loops, on both sides.

Knit stitches are the easiest to graft. **Stocking stitch** is the easiest fabric, and the only one that will not betray two sections knitted in opposite directions, except for a half-stitch kink at the edges. All other fabrics will only graft successfully if the two sections are worked in the same direction.

Grafting at a change-of-pattern line is likely to disguise changes in fabric direction, will make a different **tension** in the grafting row less noticeable, and may allow you to join two complex patterns with simple **knit grafting**.

Grafting is easier to understand when the stitches are off the needles, as in the illustrations. In real life, drop them off the needles one at a time, as you need them. To practise, however, try this:

a Work 2 **st st** samples in very thick yarn. Do not cast off.

b Pin them as for **blocking**. Remove needles and keep each free loop in place with a pin.

c Spray well with **starch**, and allow to dry.

d Graft with a yarn of similar thickness but of contrast colour.

Starching is also a good idea for fiddly work with very fine cotton.

For best results:

• Work flat on a table, or over a cushion placed on your lap. DO NOT keep the two needles together in your left hand with the knitting back to back.

• Check that the tips of both needles are pointing to the right. Transfer to spare needles if necessary.

• Use, in preference, yarn coming out of one of the two rows to be grafted. You will need about four times the width of the rows.

• Keep **tension** even or, if not even, keep it loose and later ease all the excess yarn towards the left edge with a **cable**, or **sewing**, **needle**. The grafted row must not look different from the rest.

• If one needle has more stitches than the other, work together two stitches of the longer row at regular intervals.

Knit grafting

Fig 3.42.

a Insert needle UP 1st lower loop.

b Insert needle DOWN 1st upper loop, then UP 2nd upper loop.

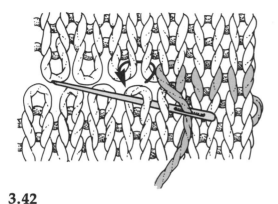

3.42

c Insert needle DOWN 1st lower loop, then UP 2nd lower loop.

Repeat **b** and **c**, always going DOWN on the loop you have already gone UP. If the two sections were worked in opposite directions, you will have to go 'UP the 1st upper loop only' the first time you work **b**.

Purl grafting

If the whole row is purl, turn the work and **knit graft** from the other side.

In purl grafting the needle works in an up-and-down movement (Fig 3.43):

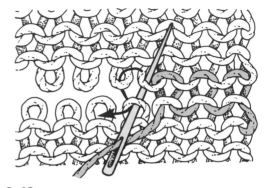

3.43

a Insert needle DOWN 1st lower loop, then UP 1st upper loop.

b Insert needle DOWN 2nd upper loop, then UP 1st upper loop.

Repeat **a** and **b**. You will be going first DOWN a new loop, then UP a loop you have already been through.

Garter-stitch grafting

To keep the pattern unbroken, the lower section must show the purl side of the stitch, and the upper section the knit side (see **the knitted stitch**).

The grafting movement is a combination of **knit grafting** on the lower loops, and **purl grafting** on the upper loops (Fig 3.44):

a Insert needle UP 1st lower loop.

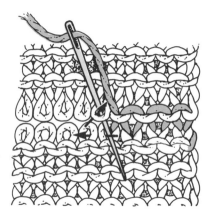

3.44

b Insert needle UP 1st upper loop.
c Insert needle DOWN 2nd upper loop.
d Insert needle DOWN 1st lower loop, then
   UP 2nd lower loop.
Repeat **b** to **d**.

Ribbing grafting

Another combination of **knit** and **purl**
grafting.

Single rib

Assuming that the first stitch is a knit (Fig
3.45):
a Insert needle UP 1st lower loop.
b Insert needle DOWN 1st upper loop, then
   UP 2nd upper loop.
c Insert needle DOWN 1st and 2nd lower
   loops.

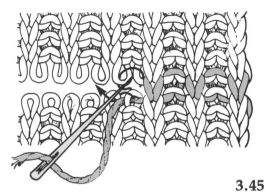

3.45

d Insert needle UP 2nd upper loop, then
   DOWN 3rd upper loop.
e Insert needle UP 2nd and 3rd lower loops.
Repeat **b** to **e**.

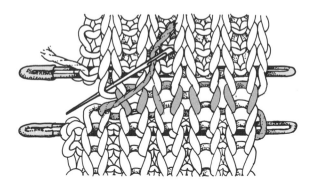

3.46

Single rib worked in opposite directions
(such as the two sides of a cardigan
neckband joining at back of neck) can be
joined by **knit grafting** (Fig 3.46). The result
is not elastic, but quite adequate for situations like the one just mentioned.
a **Sl** the **k** sts of one side onto a needle, and
   the **p** sts onto a **holder**.
b Repeat with the other side.
c **Knit graft** the sts on the needles.
d Turn work, transfer the remaining sts
   onto the needles and **knit graft**.

Other ribs

Work as for **single rib**, changing to **knit** or
purl grafting as suggested by the knit and
purl sequence.

Grafting to stitch lines

This is often done to an edge (such as the last
row of a sleeve being grafted to an armhole),
but could be done to any other line of
stitches.
a **Pin** the edges with safety pins, without
   overlapping the fabric if grafting to an
   edge. Gather one of the sides if you want
   to. Count stitches and rows to find the

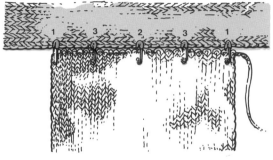

3.47

centre line and insert another pin. Add more pins to divide into quarters, then eighths, and so on until there is a pin every 5cm (2in) or so (Fig 3.47).

b **Knit graft** (or graft as suggested by the free loops), taking as much or as little of the top fabric as required to keep the join flat (Fig 3.48). Make sure you follow a straight stitch line. If gathering one side, take more from that side than from the other.

3.48

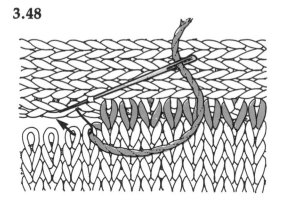

Grafting to rows

Pinning, as in **grafting to stitch lines**, is only necessary when either the numbers of stitches or the widths of the two sections are different.

To graft a knit row to a knit background, proceed as for **knit grafting**, but catch a top stitch instead of a top loop (Fig 3.49).

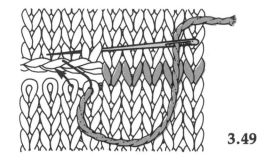

3.49

To graft a knit row to a purl background (which could easily be the case in **hems**), proceed as for **garter-stitch grafting**, again catching a top stitch instead of a loop (Fig 3.50).

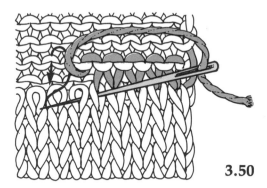

3.50

Seams and joins

(See also **Making up**, **Edges and selvedges** and **Grafting**)

Looking at illustrations of some of the seams described as 'neat', 'professional' or 'almost invisible', makes you wonder how many people are in bad need of a good pair of glasses. Take the **garter selvedge/edge-to-edge seam** combination so popular in British publications. It runs through most stitch patterns, including the archetypal **stocking stitch** of the illustrations, with the subtlety of a motorway dashing across a meadow. No wonder sewing has a bad press!

Neat, even invisible, seams are possible and not difficult. To be fair, quite a number of these can be found in British books, alongside the eyesores previously mentioned. And often these are eyesores only because they are used wrongly.

The big error is to assume that all projects need flat seams. If you are working a bedspread with two hundred diamonds, yes, you do want flat seams. But, then, you will work special edges and integrate the seams into the design. If you are working back and front of a sweater separately, you want the side seams to be undetectable. Your best bet is to hide the edges inside the seam, not to display them for everyone to see.

General rules

The number of seams in a project depends very much on which of the **three approaches** to knitting has been adopted. Whatever the approach, however, the following steps will ensure good results:

a **Plan seams** to fit in with the pattern. They are not afterthoughts, but part of the global idea.

b **Choose seams** carefully and allow for the appropriate **selvedge** from the moment you **cast on**.

c Use the right **sewing yarn**, in the correct way.

d **Block** seams that bulge or make the fabric curl the wrong way (see **after sewing** in **Blocking**).

Remember, also, that:

● Straight lines should be straight. Stitches and rows are often of help. If necessary, mark them beforehand with a running contrast thread.

● Matching sides should be joined accurately. Count stitches or rows rather than rely on a tape measure. Use **fabric markers**.

● Quite a number of seams do not need tacking or **pinning**. If pinning, use either safety or long glass-headed pins. Follow the sequence explained in **grafting to stitch lines** (Fig 3.47).

● Anything to be turned back (cuffs, hat brims etc) must have the turnover section, plus another 1.5cm (½in), seamed from the opposite side to the rest of the seam. If there is a **selvedge**, it should ideally be **cast off** at the appropriate place, then **cast on** again on the next row.

● It is easier to sew flat pieces than tubes (Figs 3.1 and 3.2).

● Shapings worked two or three stitches in from the edge do not interfere with sewing, but are not always desirable. If sewing across an **increase** or **decrease** simply remember to take the seam gradually over it and not to leave any holes.

● Loose cast-on or cast-off loops by a seam edge can be neatened when sewing. Secure them onto the seam, or twist them as shown in Fig 3.4.

● Light colours need more care than dark ones. They show more clearly any attempts at cheating.

Planning for seams

A seam, or join, has to fit in with the overall design. It can play a decorative role, a functional one, or both. In each case it has to relate to the adjoining stitch pattern(s). In merely functional seams, the fabric should look unbroken. Add **selvedge** stitches, and plan the pattern **repeats** to match once the selvedges have been taken in by the seam.

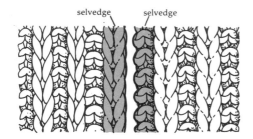

selvedge   selvedge

3.51

Ribbings, because they are so often used, are a good illustration.

● A **single rib** join should have one side ending in knit and the other in purl (Fig 3.51). A sweater back, for example, requires an odd number of stitches, starting and ending with a knit stitch. The front must start and end with a purl stitch. Cuffs, being round, need an even number of stitches.

● A **double rib** join should have three knit

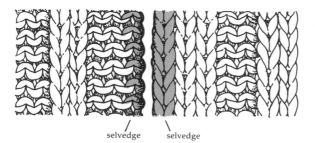

selvedge   selvedge

3.52

stitches at one side and three purl stitches at the other (Fig 3.52). This makes sweater fronts and backs multiples of four stitches, and cuffs multiples of four stitches plus two. Notice that the double-rib seam lies at the meeting point of knit and purl, taking advantage of fabric texture to 'hide'. In broader patterns, consider making the front larger than the back, and adjusting the stitch difference at the armholes. For optical reasons, the join shows less behind a raised line, such as that provided by knit stitches in ribbings, than in front of a raised line.

Choosing seams

Remember, this must be done at planning stage, so that the appropriate selvedges can be allowed for.

If all you require is something as inconspicuous as possible, go for **ladder stitch**. For more elaborate seams it is best to experiment in advance. Either incorporate different **selvedges** into the **tension samples**, or work narrow strips (half a dozen stitches may be enough) for the sole purpose of trying seams. Look also at the list below where seams within each category are given in the order in which they appear in the book.

If you like the concept of a fully knitted project, use **knitting on**, and see also **seam cast-off** and **Grafting**. For seams that are not knitted or sewn, see **crochet joins**.

Some seams can only be used along rows, some only along selvedges; but most seams can be used in either situation, or even to join a row to a selvedge.

ORDINARY EDGES
ladder stitch
backstitch
slip-stitch crochet

BORDERS, knitted separately
(See also **decorative seams** and **edgings** below, **knitted-in borders**, **tubular borders** and **picked-up borders**)
Attaching a row:
free-loop backstitch from **right side**

free-loop slip stitch
free-loop crochet
(grafting to stitch lines or **to rows)**

Attaching a selvedge:
ladder-stitch variation
edge to edge
knitting on
lifted ladder

CUT AND SEW
slip stitch to tidy up

DECORATIVE SEAMS
slip stitch if sewing under a decorative selvedge
flat-felled seam
overcasting from **right side**
fishbone stitch
knitted stitch
alternate free loop (rows only)
knitting on
slip-stitch crochet, or other **crochet** stitches, from **right side**

EDGINGS
If they cover the fabric's edge, **slip stitch** from **wrong side**; otherwise, see **borders** above.

HEMS
Horizontal:
free-loop backstitch
slip stitch if the edge is **cast-on** or **cast-off**
free-loop slip stitch
(grafting to rows)

Vertical:
lifted ladder

FLAT SEAMS
flat-felled seam
edge to edge
overcasting
fishbone stitch
knitted stitch
alternate free loop
lifted ladder

LOOP EDGES
Loop edge over solid fabric:
free-loop backstitch
free-loop slip stitch
(grafting to stitch lines or **to rows)**

Two loop edges:
edge to edge
overcasting
fishbone stitch
alternate free loop
free-loop crochet
(see also **seam cast-off**)

OVERLAPS
slip stitch from **wrong side**

PATCH POCKETS
slip stitch
ladder stitch
pick up stitches around edge and **free-loop backstitch** (or **graft to lines of stitches** or **to rows**)

POCKET LININGS
slip stitch

RECYCLING EXPECTED
crochet joins

REINFORCED SEAMS
backstitch
knitting on
slip-stitch crochet

REVERSIBLE PROJECTS
flat-felled seam
The other **flat seams** above may also be adequate, depending on fabric texture.

Sewing yarn
In general, the yarn used for knitting is the best for sewing. Its thickness matches that of the fabric and gives just the right strength.
If you cannot use matching yarn because its lack of **twist** makes it break, or its texture is too knobby, find a plain one in matching colour, or a shade darker. Make sure that it can

be **cleaned** in the same way as the main yarn, and that it will not shrink. As far as possible, use the same fibre you used for knitting.

If you know that you will want to **recycle** the project, use a contrast colour for sewing. It will be easier to unpick.

Use **vertical darning** to anchor new yarn to the selvedge, if this is to be taken in by the seam. Repeat on the taken-in selvedge when yarn is running out (Fig 3.53). In all other cases, try to keep selvedges as neat as possible; anchor the yarn wherever it will show least.

If using the same yarn, try to leave long tails in strategic places as you knit, and tie them in **little bundles** (Fig 3.54). Using long tails will encourage you to start seaming from the

lower, or the top, edge (rather than, say, from the underarm). This is excellent, because it makes it easier to leave a smooth edge, without 'steps'. To avoid the gap that often forms at the start of a seam, use a **figure of eight** (Fig 3.55). Repeat, if required, until the edge is totally smooth.

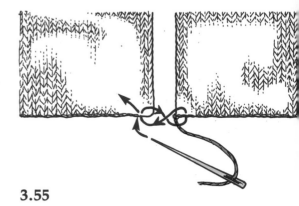

3.55

Ladder stitch   E

Also called **mattress stitch, invisible seam, weaving** and **vertical grafting**.

One selvedge stitch is taken in from each side except in **garter stitch** (see below). Some people take in only half a stitch to diminish bulk, but this often makes the seam more noticeable on the right side. Use, in preference, a **no-selvedge selvedge**.

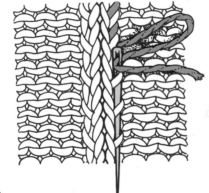

3.53

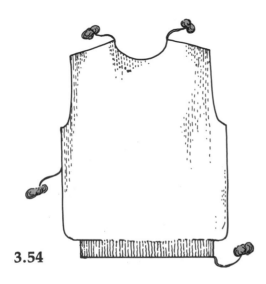

3.54

3.56

a Make a **figure of eight**.
b Place the two pieces in left hand, without overlapping, and with the two **right sides** facing you.

c Pick up strand between 1st and 2nd sts on top piece. Pull yarn.

d Repeat with lower piece.

Repeat **c** and **d** (Fig 3.56).

There is no need to tack the seam, but both sides must have the same number of rows unless you are gathering one of the sides, or they are in different patterns, or a side selvedge is being sewn to a cast-on or cast-off edge. In these cases, pick two strands instead of one from the appropriate side at regular intervals. **Pinning** may be advisable (Fig 3.47).

The shape of the strand being picked up depends on the pattern. In **reverse stocking stitch** and in **garter stitch** it is a 'bump'. Reverse stocking stitch should alternate one lower strand with one upper strand (Fig 3.57). So should **garter stitch**, but this time closer to the edge to make the seam flat (Fig 3.58). With other patterns proceed in the way that gives the less noticeable result.

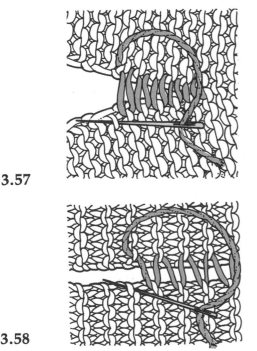

3.57

3.58

Cast-off edges can be sewn in the same way, taking one stitch (half if the stitch is large) instead of one strand. If the yarn is not pulled tight, a row of knit stitches appears – **fake grafting** (Fig 3.59).

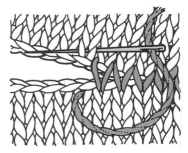

3.59

Variations

A variation, useful for carefully designed, well-integrated seams (perhaps for a **border** join) makes a half-flat seam. One side (the border's) needs a **garter** or **slipped garter selvedge**; the other side needs a **chain selvedge**. Alternate one garter-selvedge 'bump' with the strands attaching one of the chains (Fig 3.60). This leaves a very near chain on the **wrong side.**

Another variation, leaving a double chain, uses a chain selvedge on both sides.

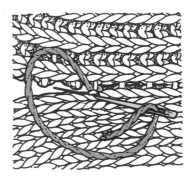

3.60

Backstitch   U

A strong seam, worked from the **wrong side.** One selvedge stitch is taken in from each side. The selvedge that helps best to keep a straight line and to match the two sides (provided they have the same number of rows), is **chain selvedge**. This leaves a very neat pair of chains on the wrong side, but shows more on the right side when the fabric is pulled apart. **Cast-off** edges and **no-selvedge selvedges** can equally be used.

a Make a **figure of eight**.

b Place the two pieces together in left hand, **right sides** against each other.

c Insert needle UP between 1st and 2nd row. Pull yarn.

d Insert needle DOWN between 1st row and **cast-on**, then UP between 2nd and 3rd row. Pull yarn.

Repeat **d**, always going DOWN where you first went UP, and UP one row further to the left (Fig 3.61).

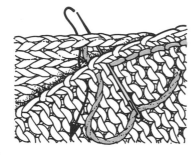

3.61

If using chain selvedges, insert the needle between the main fabric and the two strands of each chain.

Except with chain selvedges, tack before starting to sew. **Blocking** will probably be necessary.

Free-loop backstitch S

Used mainly for attaching separately knitted **borders**, or **hems**, from the **right side**.

The border or hem is either started with a **provisional cast-on**, or finished with two additional rows, in contrast **slippery yarn**.

a **Block** the edge, so that row to be sewn 'sets'.

b **Pin** or tack in position.

c **Unravel** slippery yarn, st by st, and work a **backstitch** on the newly freed loops (Fig 3.62).

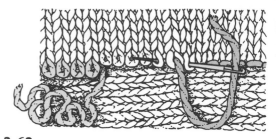

3.62

If you prefer, work the backstitch without unpicking the slippery yarn. In this case there is no need to block, but be careful not to catch the contrast yarn – you could have trouble when unravelling it later.

You can also consider omitting the extra rows and working the stitches straight off the needles.

In some countries, this is a popular way of joining **ribbed** neckbands.

Slip stitch U

Good for **pocket linings**, for neatening **cut and sew** edges, sundry odds and ends, and for joining two pieces when one slides underneath the other – perhaps because the top one is making a flap, or has a **slip-cord**, or other decorative **selvedge** or **edging**, that covers the seam.

Work with the two **wrong sides** facing you.

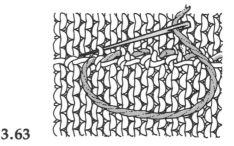

3.63

a Tack or pin the edge to be sewn onto the main fabric.

b Catch one or two strands from main fabric, then a couple of strands from the edge (Fig 3.63). Do not pull yarn too tight.

Flat-felled seam   S

Good use of **slip stitch** for reversible projects, or to make a decorative thick line.

The two sides should have selvedges appropriate to **free edges**, and all **darning** should be restricted to the seam overlap. If the project is reversible, avoid darning at mid-rows.

You will lose the width of the overlap, counted only once, from the overall fabric width.

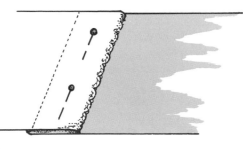

3.64

a Place one edge on top of the other. Pin or tack (Fig 3.64).

b Sew one of the edges with a **slip stitch**, taking care that the sts remain hidden. Instead of catching a couple of strands right at the edge, catch them from under the edge or edging. One strand may be enough.

c Repeat with the other edge, working from the other side.

Free-loop slip stitch   S

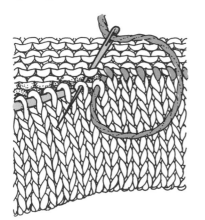

3.65

Mainly used for **horizontal hems**.

Work a **slip stitch**, catching one strand from main fabric and one stitch from needle (Fig 3.65).

Edge to edge   S

The fateful 'flat seam' that has disfigured so much British knitting because of its indiscriminate use.

There are two versions, neither of which takes in any fabric. The first is like a **ladder stitch** worked at the very edge, from the **wrong** or the **right side**. The second places the two pieces together as for **backstitch**, then merely takes the yarn from one side to the other, without ever going back (Fig 3.66).

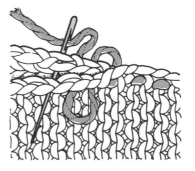

3.66

The only place for this seam is in carefully designed, fully integrated situations, for example:

● the ladder-stitch version joining two **picot selvedges**;

● the same version joining two contrast patterns (one perhaps a **border**), when both sides have **garter** or **slipped garter selvedges**. Try **samples**.

There should be no **darning** right at the edges.

Overcasting

Another edge-to-edge seam often used in the wrong situation with blatantly poor results.

Generally worked from the **wrong side**, with

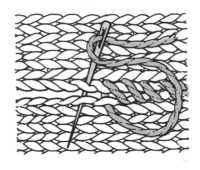

3.67

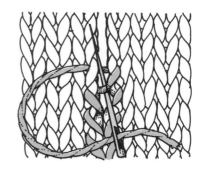

3.69

the two right sides against each other, as for **backstitch**.

• The needle is always inserted UP, from back of work, and moves one row at a time. Another version works from the **right side** with the two pieces side by side (Fig 3.67).

The second version, using thick contrast yarn, can be used for **decorative seams**. The yarn must be thick enough to hide the edges, unless these have been worked neatly like **free edges**.

Fishbone stitch

Similar uses to the second version of **overcasting**.

• The needle is inserted UP on both top and lower edges (Fig 3.68).

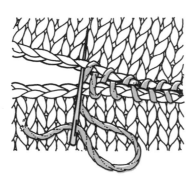

3.68

Knitted stitch

An imitation line of knit stitches, based on **Swiss embroidery** (Fig 3.69). Slightly raised. Could be worked in contrast for a decorative effect.

Alternate free loop   U

Decorative and simple, but only of use with two open rows.

a Place one piece above the other, needles touching and both pointing towards the right. Preferably have one strand hanging from the right and the other from the left.

b Thread right strand through all the sts, alternating one from each needle, and removing the needles as you work.

c Repeat with the left strand in the opposite direction (Fig 3.70), or with the first strand starting on 2nd st.

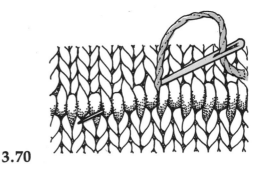

3.70

Knitting on   S

A very strong and decorative join, with a great number of variations. One piece is knitted first, and the second joined to it on alternate rows (Fig 3.71).

a Work 1st piece with a **chain selvedge**. Other selvedges could be used, but this is the most convenient and neatest.

b Work 1st row of 2nd piece to last st.

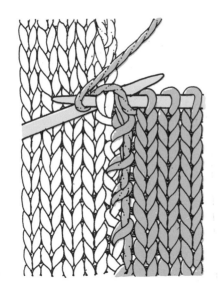

3.71

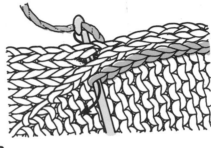

3.72

c Work together last st with the two strands of the chain selvedge. You can choose between **k** or **p**, taking first the st or first the chain.

d Work 2nd row in usual way.

Repeat **b** to **d**.

You can also work the selvedge by itself, and knit or purl together the first 2 sts of the 2nd row (or, indeed, the 2 sts before the selvedge on the 1st row). And you can also knit-on to the centre of work, in which case the selvedge is obviously immaterial.

Crochet joins

The beauty of most crochet joins is the speed at which they can be unravelled, which makes them ideal if you plan to **recycle** a project.

Some are also very decorative and, being worked with a hook, they all tend to appeal to knitters who hate sewing.

Slip-stitch crochet   U

Same **selvedge** comments and fabric position as for **backstitch**. Then:

a Insert hook DOWN through both layers of fabric.

b Catch yarn and draw a loop through the fabric and through loop already on hook. Repeat **a** and **b** (Fig 3.72).

It is not as neat as **ladder stitch**; and it needs careful **blocking**, making sure that there are no strands showing on the **right side**. The chain is also quite bulky. Finer yarn makes it less so, but this obviously makes a weaker seam.

An alternative is to work it from the **right side** as a decorative seam. Selvedges should then be as for **free edges**, with no **darning**.

Free-loop crochet   S

Can be applied to any situation where there are two rows of loops to be joined: open rows, **picot selvedges** (try making them rather large), **fur stitch** rows, **fringe selvedges** etc.

• The easiest version is to take alternately one loop from each side and draw it through loop on hook (Fig 3.73). Variations include a number of crochet stitches that pick up, alternately, one or more loops from each side.

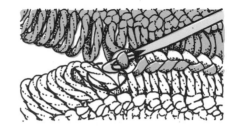

3.73

Shaped edges can be joined in this way if the shapings are worked two or three stitches in from the edge.

Keep loops on needles or holders if worried about not working them in the correct order.

Lifted ladder U

A good join, slightly raised, reversible in some fabrics.

One side needs a one-stitch **fringe selvedge**. The other may have a **no-selvedge selvedge**, a **free edge** selvedge, or an **edging**. Or it could be joined away from the edge, as in **vertical hems**.

a Place knitting flat, with the two **right sides** facing you. Keep fringe on a needle

3.74

or holder if worried about not working the loops in the correct order.

b Insert hook DOWN into 1st row of main fabric – on the selvedge, between free-edge selvedge or edging and 1st pattern st, or at appropriate place in hems.

c Catch 1st rung of ladder and draw through.

d Insert hook DOWN into 2nd row.

e Catch 2nd rung of ladder and draw through fabric and through loop on hook.

Repeat **d** and **e** (Fig 3.74).

Machine stitching S

Not something I would recommend. It has to be done very carefully, tacking very close to the edges and making sure that no loops are caught or distorted and that the edge does not wave.

Mistakes may not be easy to unpick. In the end, machine stitching may take longer than sewing by hand.

A straight stitch, even if long and worked at a loose tension, may break. A narrow zigzag, again at a loose tension, 'gives' more, but is less continuous. A stretch stitch is best, but practise beforehand because it may take you a while to control.

Edgings

(See also **decorative cast-ons**, **decorative cast-offs**, **loop buttonholes**, **ruffles** and **free-edge selvedges**)

Edgings are finishes given to an edge, be this a **cast-on**, a **cast-off**, or a **selvedge edge**. They can play a very powerful decorative role, or a very understated one. But they always have a clear, functional purpose – to control the edge, so that it does not stretch.

Additionally, edgings may reinforce the edge, to stop it fraying.

In order to control the edge (especially in **stretched edges**) all edgings must be worked, or joined, SLIGHTLY SLIGHTLY tight. Only slightly, or the edging will pull. **Block,** pinning the edging carefully so that it reaches the full length of the edge. After blocking it should feel firm, but not pull.

Depending on the type of edging, use one of the following methods to assess the correct degree of tightness:

• In **embroidered** and **fringed** edgings, find out a rule of thumb (for instance 'every stitch', 'every other row') by experimenting on the **tension samples**.

• In **crochet** edgings, if you have a little experience, work a small section and check tightness. Unravel and try again if it feels wrong. If you have no experience, try on samples.

• In **knitted edgings**, work roughly the length that you expect to need, but do not **cast off** or cut any strands. **Pin** (Fig 3.47), starting at the **cast-on** end. Adjust length once the edging has been **joined**, and its tightness checked.

Continuous edgings

Edgings that make a closed circuit around a project must, if possible, disguise the start-and-end point. This may require careful spacing of repeats, **grafting**, **ladder-stitch seams** etc. Avoid overlapping.

Corners

Turn corners carefully. The outside of a curve is longer than the inside. The outside of an angle must be sharp and not pull. Therefore, the edging must be shaped to fit the corner.

• **Knitted edgings** may require **mitred corners**.

• **Crochet** and **embroidered edgings** may require several stitches worked over the same spot.

• **Cords** and **skeins** may require some strands to be pulled more than others.

Forward planning

Try to decide on the edgings before you start to knit, so that you can allow for any special **selvedges**.

Knitted edgings

(See also **Edges and selvedges** and **Picking up stitches**, especially **knitted-in, tubular** and **picked-up borders**.

There are infinite possibilities, many of which can be found in good pattern dictionaries (see **Books**). Before working the edging, think of how it is going to be attached to the edge, and work the appropriate **selvedge** if necessary (see **Seams and joins**).

Separate borders

• Work a narrow band in any **flat pattern**, and sew to the edge of the main fabric. Fig 3.60 shows one possible **seam**.

If the band is to be buttoned up (a band going up one side of a jacket front and down the other, for instance), start with the **buttonhole** end; otherwise, the buttonhole arrangement could be spoiled when adjusting the length (see above).

Bias bands

They adapt well to curves and are also good for **cut and sew**.

• Strips of **flat, bias knitting** can be attached directly to the edge. **Curly** fabrics, such as **stocking stitch**, should be folded over the edge and sewn separately on both sides (Fig 3.75). The **wrong side** is sewn with a **slip stitch**. The **right side**, which is normally joined first, can be sewn similarly if the **selvedge** is good enough to show. Otherwise, use a **ladder stitch**, turning the selvedge in. **Block** flat if the work looks too bulky.

3.75

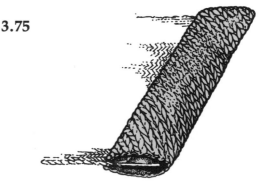

Double-fold bands

Fig 3.76.

● Work a wide band, either lengthwise, widthwise, or on the **bias**. **Join** or **graft** the two long sides. Fold in two, without pressing the edges flat, so that the join falls at the centre line. Sew to the edge.

3.76

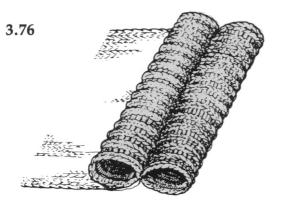

Cords

● Attach one of the knitted cords explained under **Cords and belts** to fabric edge with a hidden **slip stitch**, or with one of the methods suggested for **skeins**.

Figure 3.78 shows a large **plait** made out of three strips of **stocking stitch**. Fig 3.79 shows a **slip cord** sewn in a squiggle.

3.78

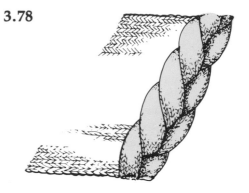

Lace edgings

By far, best worked in fine yarns. They may be sewn flat, or frilled. Watch the **cast-on** and **cast-off** ends because they could be far from straight.

A traditional use for very fine cotton lace, such as in Fig 3.77, is to edge cloth – mats, pillowcases, blouses etc.

● Work edging separately and carefully **slip stitch** to a hemmed cloth (right at the edge or under a small tuck), or work it from stitches **picked up from the cloth**.

3.79

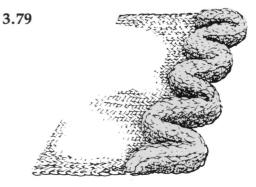

Cast-off edgings

● Simply **pick up stitches** all around the edge (with a **circular needle** or several **double-pointed needles**, if necessary), and work a **decorative cast-off**.

Fringes

Choosing a cast-on and **choosing a cast-off** give methods that make it easier to add fringes. A **picot selvedge** would serve a similar purpose on a vertical edge, or you could

3.77

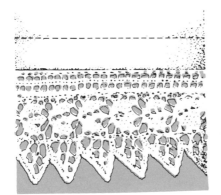

go as far as working a **fringe selvedge** – the knitted-in version of **loop fringe** below. **Samples** are advisable, because all these methods give a soft edge for attaching the fringe, and in some cases you may want a harder one.

Common fringe

Fig 3.80.

a Wrap yarn around a book or picture frame and cut at one end. This should give you a pile of strands somewhat longer than twice the fringe depth (knotting has a shortening effect).

b Take a few strands, and fold in two. How many depends on how thick you want the fringe and how close together the knots are.

c Insert a crochet hook UP, and draw the strands through the fabric, by the fold line. The fabric should be **right side** up.

d Pass the ends of the strands through the loop, again with the hook, and fasten.

e When all the knots are done, tidy them carefully to make them look alike, and trim the ends straight.

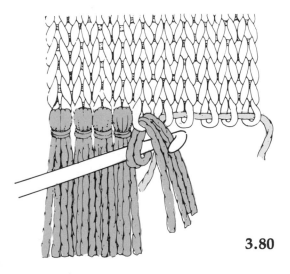

3.80

The knots should be evenly and thoughtfully spaced. A few strands too wide apart will look straggly, too many strands too close will make the edge wave.

Tufted fringe

Work a **common fringe**, then brush firmly with a **teasel** (Fig 3.81).

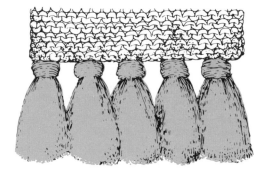

3.81

Knotted fringe

Fig 3.82.

a Work a **common fringe** with longer strands.

b Pin the fabric to a cushion.

c Take half the strands from one knot, and half from the next knot, and make a new knot. Use a pin to draw the knot up to the required position.

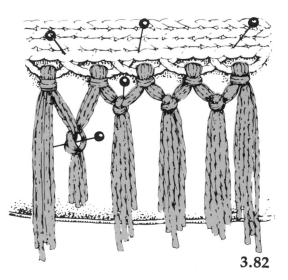

3.82

You can make as many rows of knots as you like, but remember that each row will take up yarn.

If you feel adventurous, you could try some macramé knotting instead.

Loop fringe

Fig 3.83.

Work as for **fringe selvedge** on just a few stitches. The stitches not to be unravelled should be in a **flat** pattern (**k1, over, k2 tog** in illustration). Compare the length of the fringe with that of the area not yet unravelled in Fig 3.83.

The loops tend to be rather curly. To straighten them, thread a needle or cord through them, so that you can tension them when **blocking** – rather like in Fig 3.23.

You could omit the flat pattern altogether if you used a **knitting-on join**. Remember to cast off the joining stitch and to secure the last yarn tail.

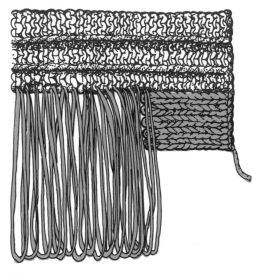

3.83

Curlicue fringe

(See also **curlicues**)

Like **loop fringe** it can be worked separately, with a **flat** base (Fig 3.84), or it can be **knitted onto** an edge.

a Having worked the base, or knitting-on st, **buttonhole cast-on** a few sts.

b Turn. **Double knit-and-purl increase** into each of the new sts, whilst **basic casting-off** each new st as soon as you make it.

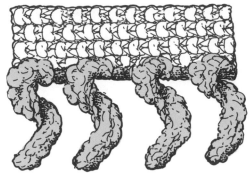

3.84

Do not space too closely. If worked with a flat base, you will probably require a few rows between curlicues.

To **block**, shape each curlicue into a good spiral and pin end in place.

Picot-point fringe

(See **picot-point knitting**)

Like **curlicue fringe**, but work picot-points instead of curlicues.

The picot-points can take different forms, apart from the usual one. Fig 3.85 shows a **double-chain cord**:

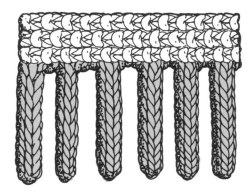

3.85

a **Cast-off cast-on** sts required for fringe.

b Turn and **basic cast-off** all the new sts. **Sl** 1st st to give a rounded edge; **k** all the others.

Picot-points can be spaced closer than curlicues, perhaps leaving only a couple of rows in between.

Embroidered edgings

Apart from the rather uninspiring basic blanket stitch (a **buttonhole stitch** with wide gaps), there are many ways of finishing an edge with embroidery. To show at its best, the edging needs to be done in contrast yarn, but there are cases in which the same yarn used for knitting may be more appropriate – for example, to give just a hint of texture to a very delicate project.

Take great care of the spacing. Work, for instance, into every edge stitch of every second row, or into every stitch along the cast-on row.

Make sure the yarn is suitable. Very textured yarns may prove difficult to work with. **Darn** the ends very carefully, making sure they do not show on the **right side**.

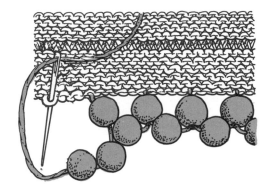

3.88

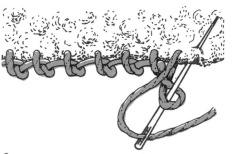

3.86

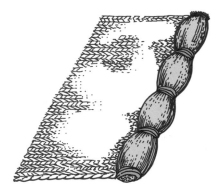

3.89

3.89), binding a **hem** with ribbon (Fig 3.90) and scalloping a fabric **roll** with whipping (Fig 3.91).

When using ribbon, **eyelets** may be necessary if the ribbon is wide and the fabric very solid.

3.87

Two good edging stitches are **Antwerp stitch** (Fig 3.86) and **Armenian stitch** (Fig 3.87). A **bead edging** (Fig 3.88) is another possibility. Other approaches would include attaching a cut **skein** to an edge with regularly spaced whipping (**overcasting** without gaps – Fig

3.90

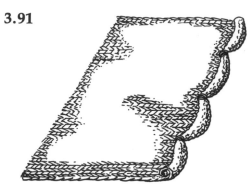

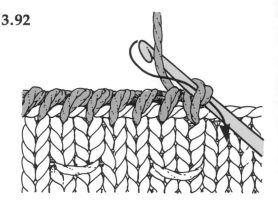

Crochet edgings

These are great favourites with some people, but I rarely find them satisfactory. The structure is quite different from knitting, and the two do not always blend well – crochet adding unwanted stiffness, and quite often looking too fussy.

You may entirely disagree – if so, you will find many edgings in crochet books. I shall only mention two here. One, because it is useful and blends in very well with knitting. The other because, despite being a very unsatisfactory way of dealing with **stretched edges** (they should not be tightened, but avoided in the first place), it may occasionally get you out of trouble.
Chain selvedges are advisable.

Crab stitch

Also called **corded edging** (Fig 3.92). It is like **double crochet** but worked from left to right.

a Insert hook DOWN into fabric edge, at least two strands in. **Chain selvedges, chain cast-off** and **cast-off cast-on** chains make this easy.

b Draw a loop through fabric.

c Catch yarn and draw a new loop through loop on hook.

d Insert hook DOWN into next st, catch yarn and draw a new loop through fabric.

e Catch yarn and draw a new loop through the two loops on hook.

Repeat **d** and **e**.

For a dramatic effect, use several strands together.

Slip stitch

Use to tighten edges, or when you have forgotten to work a **chain selvedge**.

With **right-side** facing (Fig 3.93):

a Insert hook DOWN catching one or two edge strands.

b Catch yarn and draw a loop through the fabric and through loop on hook.

Repeat **a** and **b**.

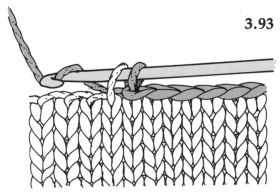

Fastenings

Often left as afterthoughts, yet fastenings can make or break a project. Think of them in the early stages – to find the perfect buttons could take you even longer than the actual knitting!

Button up

Buttonholes, both **slit** and **loop** types, have been dealt with in **Slits and buttonholes**. Here, just a few words on how to strengthen them, and a look at their inseparable companions – buttons.

Reinforced buttonholes

As previously said, if a strong buttonhole is chosen there is absolutely no need to do anything to it. However, if you are reading that advice too late or are working a **cut buttonhole**, you may be glad of some rescue measures.

The more usual way of reinforcing buttonholes is with **buttonhole stitch** (Fig 3.94). This looks very neat on a drawing, but it can be quite bulky in reality. If the yarn is very thick, split and twist well, or use matching thread. Work the stitches fairly close to-

gether, but not so close that they get overcrowded and stretch the edge. Make sure the stitching does not pull and make the hole smaller.

Another device is to add a pre-shrunk, grosgrain ribbon **facing** to the wrong side. Each buttonhole is carefully cut on the facing, then **buttonhole stitched** to the knitted buttonhole. This may be used in **cut-and-sew** projects, but in general it should be quite unnecessary. If your buttonbands stretch, you have knitted them too loosely. What they need is not facings, but finer needles!

Buying buttons

Buttons should be chosen before knitting the buttonholes, so that these can be made to the exact size.

Selecting buttons is an art in itself. They must fit in within the overall picture. Sometimes this calls for very unobtrusive buttons, sometimes it demands that the buttons be the main feature.

- **Size** Tiny buttons on chunky, adult jackets look lost. They may be chosen in the belief that they will not distract attention from the star of the show – the knitting. But they often distract more; being out of scale, they throw the whole project off balance.
- **Colour** A contrast may be better than a half-match.
- **Material** A cheap plastic button will make pure silk look inferior. A hand-carved wooden button may make an inexpensive acrylic look out of this world. In general, try to emphasise the character of the yarn. Shiny yarns should have shiny buttons; harsh oiled yarns should not. (This is, of course, a general rule that experienced designers may well be capable of breaking very successfully.)

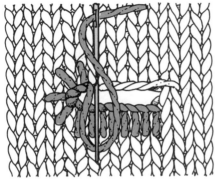

3.94

- **Holes** If possible, buy buttons with shanks, or buttons with holes large enough for a needle, threaded with the same yarn used for knitting, to go through.
- **Weight** Because knitting is elastic, heavy buttons can cause sagging. Use only on sturdy fabrics.

If good buttons seem impossible to find, if you like the totally hand-made look, or if you just want to have extra fun, why not make your own?

Making buttons

There are several approaches:

- Buy a button-covering kit. Cover with cloth or leather to match the colour of the yarn.

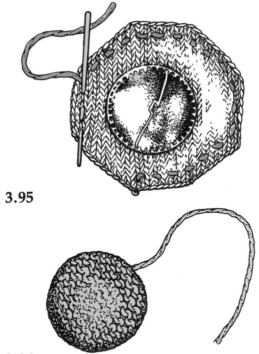

3.95

3.96

- Buy a kit but cover with a stretched, knitted **octagon**; the kit will tell you the size. Unless the knitting is very fine, the back plate will not snap on; ignore it. Work a **running stitch** all around the edge with the cast-off

tail (Fig 3.95), pull tight and secure with a few stitches. Leave a long tail for sewing (Fig 3.96). A fabric backing is often necessary to stop the mould showing through the knitting, especially if it is in shiny metal. Work the octagon quite tightly, on fine needles, in **rows** or **rounds**.

- Use old buttons, upside down, instead of buying a kit. Or, **stuff** the octagon as explained in **Miscellaneous Finishes**.
- Cover a ring with **crab stitch** and work a

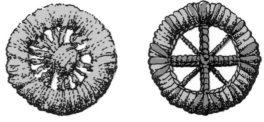

3.97   **3.98**

decorative centre with a **sewing needle** (Fig 3.97). Or, cover the ring with **buttonhole stitch**, turn the ridge to the inside of the ring, then fill the centre (Fig 3.98).

- Make a **drawstring ball** and **stuff** it.
- Make a small **coil**.
- Paint wooden buttons with acrylic or pva paints, mixed with painting medium if desired. Or use any other waterproof crafts paint, or varnish – varnish can be bought in very small amounts from modelling shops.

Sewing buttons

Buttons with a shank can be sewn with thread in matching colour, or a shade darker.

Buttons with holes need a thread-shank made to them (Fig 3.99), otherwise they will pull the fabric or even come undone:

a Insert a **cable needle**, thin pen etc, between button and sewing yarn. The extra length must match the thickness of the buttonhole.

b Sew the button in the usual way.

c Remove the needle or pen, pull the button up and wind yarn around shank to strengthen it.

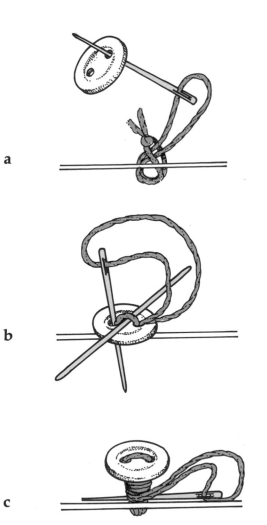

a

b

c

3.99

3.100

To position buttons correctly before sewing, count rows or stitches between buttonholes. If the button area is worked at the same time as the buttonhole area, use **fabric markers** to highlight button position every time you work a buttonhole.

Zips

Try to avoid zips. Their stiffness does not mix well with an elastic fabric such as knitting. Additional problems are:
• They remain at a constant length, whilst the knitting may stretch or shrink – even if only slightly.
• A good colour match may be impossible. If necessary, go for a darker colour.
• The wrong side never looks very neat, unless the zip is concealed inside a double layer

As far as possible, attach the buttons with the yarn used for knitting (split if necessary). Place needle at mid-point, to obtain double thickness. Try to anchor without resorting to knots, or catch knot as in illustration, so that it remains between button and fabric.

Buttons with four holes can be sewn in a number of ways (Fig 3.100). Try to reflect fabric texture.

If the fabric does not offer a very good base for sewing buttons, consider placing a very small button, or special disc, on the **wrong side**, and sewing the two buttons together through the fabric (see also **facings**).

3.101

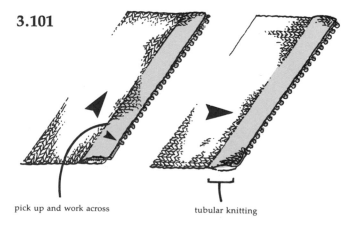

pick up and work across   tubular knitting

(Fig 3.101). This can be worked from **picked-up stitches**, or in **tubular knitting** (**cast off** the two layers separately).

• Finding the exact length may also be a problem. Buy the zip whilst you are knitting, so that you can add or omit a few rows if necessary. Do not cast off until the zip has been fixed in position.

If you still insist on having zips, consider three types (Fig 3.102):

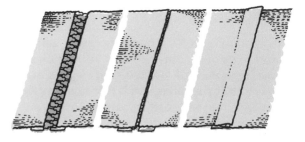

3.102

• **Visible zips** The fabric just reaches the inside of the teeth. There should be a **flat border** or a **free-edge selvedge** at either side of the zip.

• **Concealed zips** Same borders or selvedges, but the fabric is sewn so that the two edges meet once the zip is fastened; in other words, the fabric reaches the outside of the teeth.

• **Concealed zips with flap** One side is sewn as for **visible zips**, but the other covers the zip and goes beyond it. If the flap runs in a central position, the zip needs to be sewn off-centre.

To fit a zip (Fig 3.103):

a Tack a strip of fine, stable cloth to each of the two edges, on the **right side**. The edges must be totally flat, and have identical lengths. The cloth will prevent stretching whilst sewing the zip, and consequent buckling.

b Tack the fastened, pre-shrunk zip to the **wrong side**, first one edge and then the other.

c Open the zip and **backstitch** next to the teeth with two strands of sewing thread. This must not show on the right side.

d **Slip stitch** the edge of the tape.

Cord fastenings

Drawstrings

Easily made, but avoid too much bulkiness. If the fabric is very thick, or if there is a lot of it, results may look clumsy – experiment.

A simple drawstring is made by running a **cord** or ribbon through a line of **eyelets** (Fig 2.184). The eyelets should be evenly spaced, along a row, or following a vertical stitch line. There should be an even number of them, so that the cord starts and ends on the right side. In **openwork** fabrics, or if the cord is not very thick, eyelets may not be necessary. Space eyelets close together for shallow folds, far apart for deep folds. To avoid bulk when much fullness is required, place the eyelets within a gathering strip of fabric. In horizontal arrangements, **decrease** right across fabric a couple of rows before the eyelets; **increase** in a similar, or different, sequence a couple of rows after the eyelets (Fig 3.104). In vertical arrangements, use

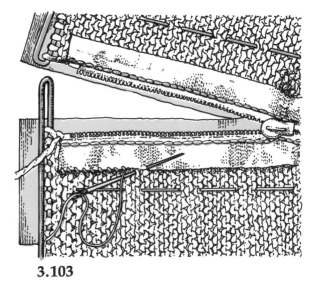

3.103

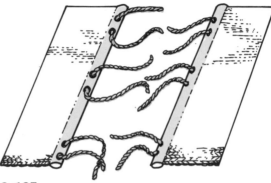

3.104

3.105

short rows to increase the length of the fabric at either side of the eyelet strip.

Another possibility is to make a **hem** or **casing** and thread a cord or ribbon through it. **Tubular hems** worked on the same number of stitches as the rest of the fabric are likely to have an often welcome, gathering effect (Fig 2.393).

Ties

Two short lengths of cord, attached to the edges to be fastened. To avoid bulky joins:

• **Pick up stitches** from, or thread lengths of yarn through, the edge of the fabric. Work the cords from these.

• Work a **tubular cast-off** edge, leaving small holes by taking a couple of stitches together with sewing needle, first on one side and then on the other. Make double ties by threading lengths of cord, in one hole and out the next (Fig 3.105).

• Work pairs of **eyelets** near the edge, one above the other. Thread cords as just explained.

Lacings

A further use for **eyelets** (Fig 3.106), although **openwork** fabrics may not need them.

If you want a horizontal bar at the top, as in illustration, you will need an even number of eyelets.

Lacings are good as permanent or adjustable fastenings. They are not a good idea for, say, jacket fronts.

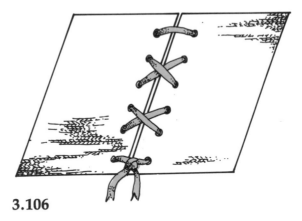

3.106

Elastic

Although elastic can have very valid uses, such as holding the waistband of a skirt in place, it is often used as a rescue measure. It may then be very welcome, but results are rarely as good as they would be without elastic.

Elastic on surface

A good, non-bulky way of attaching wide elastics, when there are no objections to their showing on the wrong side. It is more suited to holding in place a **border** or area that is already roughly the right width, than to gather large amounts of fabric. It is therefore ideal for waistbands.

A zigzag of **crochet chains**, attached to the fabric above and below the elastic, is sometimes used as a casing. This is a bulkier method than the one shown in Fig 3.107:

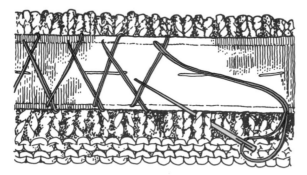

3.107

a Cut pre-shrunk elastic to required length plus about 2.5cm (1in). For waistbands, pin it and wear it for a while, before cutting, to check its comfort.
b For a closed elastic, overlap the extra length, **overcast** top and bottom edges, and **slip stitch** the ends (Fig 3.108). For an open elastic, fold under half the extra length at each end, and **slip stitch** in position.
c Pin both fabric and elastic, first at midpoint, then at quarter points. Pin elastic to fabric at these points exactly, then pin at intermediate points, always slightly away from fabric edge.
d Tack.
e **Herringbone stitch** as shown in illustration with two strands of matching thread, catching the edges of the elastic. Avoid splitting the rubbery threads.

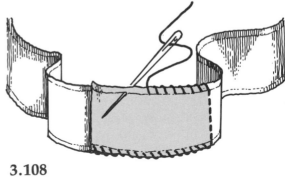

3.108

The elastic generally needs to be kept stretched whilst tacking and sewing. Pinning the right end to a stiff cushion or mattress helps to control it.

Catching the edges of the elastic with herringbone stitch gives an even distribution of gathers. However, if you want to be able to adjust length, do not catch. In this case, you could use matching yarn for sewing if not worried about the extra bulk.

Elastic in casing

For heavy gathers, or when the wrong side needs to be as tidy as the right side. The elastic is drawn through a **hem** or **casing** with the help of a bodkin or safety pin.
● For an open elastic, fold under about 1cm (½in) at each end and anchor to fabric. **Slip stitch** the two fabric layers to close the casing. For a closed elastic, overlap the ends (as explained in **b** above) after threading. The gap that was left in the casing for threading is then closed in the most appropriate way.

Shirring elastic

Used to rescue ribbings that have gone astray or, intentionally, to add elasticity to areas such as tops of socks. It is now being superseded by **knitting-in elastic**.
One big problem is to find a colour that blends in with the yarn. Another is that the elastic tends to have a shorter life than the yarn, and may need replacing.
● Intentional elastic is **woven in** on the **wrong side**, as in **jacquard**. Rescue elastic is threaded later with a **running stitch**, also on the wrong side. Thread on every row, on alternate rows (Fig 3.109), or less frequently. Make sure that all threads are kept to the same tension.

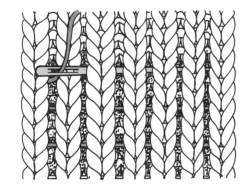

3.109

Knitting-in elastic

A very fine elastic made of the same elastane fibre used in bathing suits and bras. It has incredible stretch and either comes in its natural state (see-through, rather shiny), or covered with a coloured thread. It shows slightly, but far less than shirring elastic.
● Work it together with the knitting yarn, just as if you were using two balls at the same time.

Cloth additions

A mixture of good ideas, unnecessary techniques and rescue measures.
Always check that cleaning instructions are compatible. Pre-shrink cloth, or cloth and knitting if not sure about the knitting.

Fabric mix

Cloth and knitting are used to enhance one another. In all the other techniques in this chapter, cloth is a behind-the-scenes tidy-upper. In **fabric mix** it is an equal partner.

Edgings
Knitted edgings are often added to cloth (Fig 3.77).
Cloth edgings are less often added to knitting, but can be extremely effective.
Bias bands (Fig 3.75), for instance, can be

made of cloth. Work top stitching first, right sides of both knitting and cloth against each other and wrong side of cloth facing you, with a **backstitch**. Turn the band over the knitted edge, fold under its raw edge, tack and **slip stitch** to the wrong side of the knitting.

Or, add some ready-frilled satin ribbon (Fig 3.110).

3.110

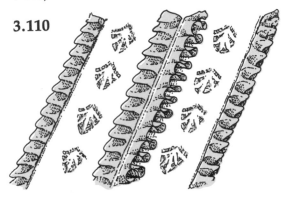

Half-and-half

A combination of large areas of cloth and large areas of knitting.

The characteristics of the two fabrics must be weighed very carefully, so that they do not work against each other.

To add knitting to cloth, see **picking up stitches from cloth**.

To add cloth to knitting:

a Draw two threads, as for adding knitting to cloth, one to give a straight cutting line, the other a straight working line. This time, the hem can be as wide as you like.

b Work a **hemstitch** on the wrong side (Fig 3.111) catching both the hem and the knitting – a **chain selvedge**, the free loops of the last row, or the free loops of a **provisional cast-on**.

3.111

The **right side** shows a clean line of short stitches. If working with a loosely woven cloth you may be able to use matching yarn to hemstitch (Fig 3.112).

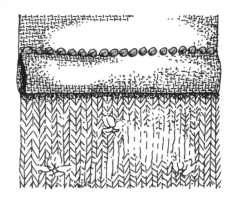

3.112

If you are adventurous, draw many more threads and indulge in some drawn-thread embroidery.

Conventional **seams** and **crochet joins** are, of course, also possible.

Backing

A contrast-colour cloth placed behind knitted **openwork**, especially **lace**, outlines every little detail.

Do not use indiscriminately. A lace shawl with backing would lose its softness and draping qualities. But cushions or see-through dresses may benefit; better to see the backing than certain types of underwear! Stretch knitting, then relax for a couple of days before backing it. Work on a hard, flat surface. On dresses, curtains, and anything that hangs, attach at the top and leave the bottom loose. Sometimes, even the sides are best left unattached. The idea is to give knitting a backdrop, not to force it into a corset as **lining** might do.

Lining

As opposed to **backing**, lining is designed to neaten the wrong side (rather than to enhance the right side) and to help knitting 'keep its shape better'. In the process, it makes it lose its elasticity, snugness and comfort.

Certain skirts can take a loose lining, attached only at the waist, and there are probably one or two other exceptions. But, in general, there is only one thing to do with linings – AVOID THEM.

If you work everything at the correct **tension**, know better than have never-ending **jacquard floats**, and work heavy items such as coats in **flat** patterns (allowing for a certain amount of sagging), you will never need any linings.

Binding

(See also **bias bands** above and under **Edgings**, and **binding** under **Cutting**)

May be used in **cut and sew** to hide untidy edges. It is also recommended to keep shoulder seams, back of necklines, and other lines of stress under control. In most cases, if the **tension** is correct there is absolutely no need for it, but there may be the odd exception.

● To tidy edges, **slip stitch** the two edges of a pre-shrunk binding tape, or bias, so that the edge is fully covered (Fig 3.75). To strengthen **seams**, use the same method, or

backstitch the centre line of a narrow tape over the seam (or over the stress line).

Facings

Another addition best avoided, unless using **cut and sew**.

Mainly used to reinforce **buttonhole** and **button** bands, so that they do not stretch. The best insurance against stretching is to knit them at the correct **tension**, in a **flat pattern**!

Use soft pre-shrunk, grosgrain ribbon – the one with ridges that comes in several widths and many colours (Fig 3.113):

a Tack the ribbon on the **wrong side**, working on a hard, flat surface. It must be the exact length of the edge, when flat.

b With matching thread, **slip stitch** first one side, then the other.

c Cut and stitch buttonholes, if any.

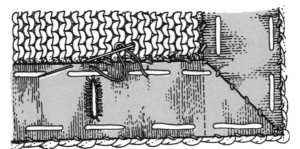

3.113

Cords

Belts, **edging cast-ons, fastenings, edgings** (with or without **loop buttonholes**), **appliqué**, loops for hanging – these are just a few possible applications for cords. Allow plenty of yarn. Cords often take up tremendous amounts.

Because of yarn and structure, cords often stretch if subjected to any tension, as for instance in belts or fastenings. Cords, therefore, should be **blocked** stretched before use:

● Keeping the cord dead straight, pin the

two ends and spray well; allow to dry.

Tubular and **crochet** cords to be used for hanging a substantial weight can be **stuffed** with petersham, grosgrain ribbon or piping cord (Fig 3.147).

Be bold and let your imagination run free. Use as many strands together as you fancy. A one-strand, knitted cord may be perfect if you require something very small and subtle, or if you are using many of them, side by side. But in most cases it will just look undernourished.

To cut many equal strands, wrap the yarn around two upside-down clamps, set at the edge of a table (Fig 3.114). If the clamps are the required yarn length apart, cut the strands at both ends. If they are half that distance apart, cut at one end only.

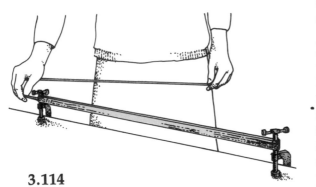

3.114

Experiment with colours and textures. Try, for instance, mixing several, slightly different shades of the same colour, in three or four different textures.

Cords are often powerful decorative elements; perhaps the only decorative element of a plain project. Have fun with them.

Knitted cords

Unless working purely decorative cords that will not undergo any stretch, work tightly.

Flat-pattern cords

Wide, flat cords, obtained by two methods:

- **Cast on** just a few stitches (could be as few as 3), and work on a **flat** pattern for required length. Fig 3.115 shows a 5-stitch **moss stitch** cord.
- **Cast on** as many stitches as required to obtain length, work a few rows in a flat pattern and cast off. Length is not so easy to adjust as in the first method.

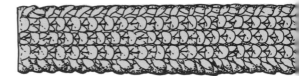

3.115

Patterns that look alike on both sides are the most successful. Try matching the cord to a flat-pattern **border**.

Roll cords

- Work as before but in a very **curly** pattern. Pull the ends to straighten, and run the fingers along to make a smooth roll. **Slip stitch** along the edge if desired.

Stocking stitch (see **border** illustrated in Fig 2.318) is an obvious pattern choice. Fig 3.116 shows a more unusual cord in a basketweave pattern made up entirely of **cross stitches**. Because of the curl, at least about three times the required width has to be knitted.

3.116

Cast-on cast-off cords

- Simply **cast on** the amount of stitches required to obtain length, and **cast off** on the following row.

There are innumerable variations – just think of combining all the casting on, and off, methods explained in this book!

An interesting combination is **cast-off cast-on** with **basic cast-off.** This gives a

double-chain cord – two chains travelling in opposite directions, making a fairly triangular section (used in **picot-point fringe**, Fig 3.85). For two chains pointing the same way and a flat cord, work a knit row after casting on (Fig 3.117).

3.117

Tubular cords
(See also **tubular selvedges**)
These can be worked in a variety of ways. All can be **stuffed** if extra strength is required (Fig 3.147).
Wider, flat cords are made by working a long strip of **tubular knitting**. Decoration can be added with **Swiss darning** (Fig 3.118). Or you could work the cord in **double-sided jacquard**.

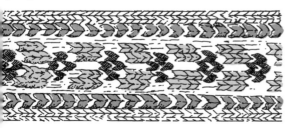

3.118

The **slip cord** is a piece of **circular knitting** worked on, say, 3 to 6 stitches, with **double-pointed needles**. It is also called **idiot-cord** or, more politely, **I-cord** (Fig 3.119):
a **Cast on** and **k** 1 row.
b Without turning the work, push the sts to the other end of the needle.
c **K**, pulling the yarn tight when working 1st st.
Repeat **b** and **c**. To end, work a **double** or **multiple decrease**.
Another way of making these cords is with **bobbin knitting** (also called **French knit-**

3.119

ting). It is a more laborious way if you stick to the spool with nails at the top that children play with (Fig 3.120). If you can find a **knitting mill**, however, you will make metres and metres in next to no time, although you will be restricted to four stitches and medium-thick yarn.

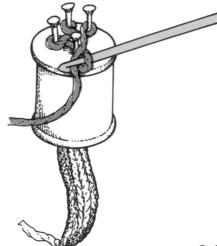

3.120

Picot cord
A fairly lacy cord. Good for projects with **picot** or **double-picot selvedges**.
a **Cast on** 2 sts. Turn work.
b **Selvedge over, slip** 1 **pwise, k1, psso** (Fig 3.121). Turn work.

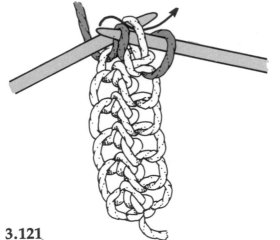

3.121

Half the illustration is worked taking both sides of each chain (the one at the top of the stitch) with the hook. In the other half, only the back side of the chain is taken. This makes a thinner, less sturdy cord.

Twisted cord

Everybody's idea of a cord (Fig 3.124).

Repeat **b**. **Selvedge over** as in Fig 2.204.

Faggot cord
Very springy (Fig 3.122)
a **Cast on** 2 sts. Turn work.
b **Selvedge over, p2 tog.**
Repeat **b**. **Selvedge over** as in Fig 2.205.

3.122

Crochet cord

Very strong. Fig 3.123 shows it over four stitches, but the number could be adjusted. It can be **stuffed**.

3.123

a Crochet a 4-link **chain** (Fig 2.51).
b **Double crochet** into 1st chain to close circle.
c Work round and round in double crochet.

3.124

a Cut several strands of yarn, three times the desired length of cord.
b Knot the two ends, keeping the strands at an even tension.
c Hook or pin one end and insert a knitting needle through the other.
d Turn needle over and over, until the strands are well twisted.
e Fold in half, keeping the cord taut to avoid tangling.
f Knot the two ends together, let the cord twist, and even out the turns.

3.125  **3.126**

Work from two balls of yarn, or from a length (about eight times the required length) of another cord.

a Either knot the 2 strands of yarn, or fold the cord in half.

b Take one strand in each hand, keeping knot between left thumb and middle finger.

c Lift left yarn with left index finger.

d With right index finger, draw right strand through left loop (Fig 3.127).

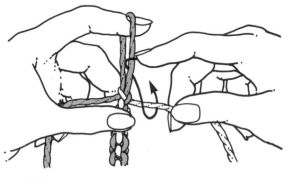

3.127

Plaited cords

Any cord, indeed any yarn or strip of knitting, can be plaited.

For an ordinary, three-strand plait (Fig 3.125):

a Cut 3 strands, or bunches of strands, 1½ times desired length of cord.

b Knot them at one end, and hook or pin this end.

c Take, alternately, right strand over centre strand, then left strand over centre strand, until strands run out.

d Knot the strand ends.

More strands can be plaited in a number of ways. Fig 3.126 shows an easy way with four strands.

Finger cord

Also called **finger crochet**. Not one little tool required – great fun.

e Take knot into right hand, and pull left strand with left hand (Fig 3.128).

Repeat **d** and **e**, alternating hands.

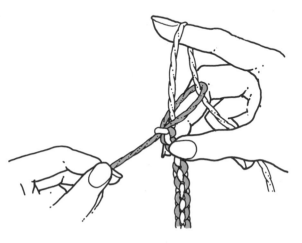

3.128

Wiggle-woggles

Things that dangle are even more fun than **Cords**.

Again, let your imagination run riot, experiment and allow for masses of yarn.

Tassels

Fig 3.129.

a Wrap yarn loosely around a book, or piece of cardboard.

b Thread a strand (or more) of yarn through the top and tie firmly, with a **square knot**, leaving a long end for later winding and sewing.

c Cut the strands at the bottom.

d Hide the knot, and the short end left from tying it, under the folded strands.

e Wind the long strand a few times, to secure the folded end, then thread it through, so that it comes out at the top.

f Trim ends.

You could also attach the tassel directly to a cord by tying the tassel and the end of a cord together at **b**. Two or more strands would be advisable. The long strand should later be secured back and forth across the tied area, and trimmed.

Pompoms

Fig 3.130. They are often used in isolation, but large arrangements can be tremendously effective.

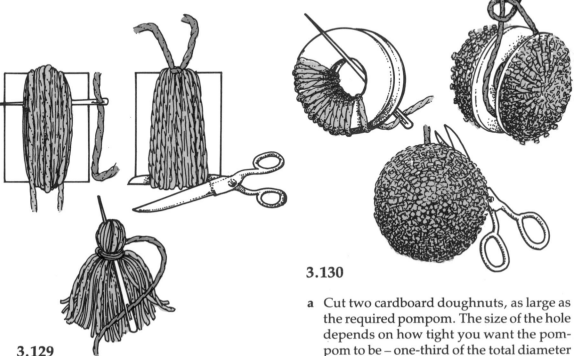

3.129

3.130

a Cut two cardboard doughnuts, as large as the required pompom. The size of the hole depends on how tight you want the pompom to be – one-third of the total diameter gives a medium pompom, half the diameter gives a very compact one.

b Wrap yarn around the two cards until the hole is full. Use several strands together. Do not worry if the yarn keeps running out. Add new yarn and leave tails dangling on the outside.

c Cut around edge, a few layers of yarn at a time, until you reach the cardboard.

d Pull cards a little apart, wrap yarn a few times around the strands, and tie tightly with a **square knot**. Leave one or two long ends for later sewing.

e Discard cards, fluff up and trim.

Pompoms can be worked in several colours. Wrap them together for a speckled effect; one after the other for stripes; in blocks for a random, perhaps marbled, effect.

Curlicues

For those who like the unexpected.

A helix is made by keeping one edge tight and the other three (or more) times longer. Two approaches: **cast on, increase, cast off,** and **cast on, decrease, cast off.**

Smooth curlicue

The first approach gives a smooth edge (Fig 3.131). Length cannot be adjusted. It can have a knitted row between cast-on and cast-off, as in illustration; several rows (each one increasing further); or no rows at all. The last is useful when the yarn needs to go back to the original position, as in **curlicue fringe**, or when making bunches of curlicues. The increases are then cast off as soon as they are worked.

a **Cast on** as many sts as you want, to form the core. Use one of the methods recommended for **ordinary** or **reinforced edges** – it must be firm but not bulky.

b Turn. Work a **double increase** on each st, for instance **double knit-and-purl**.

c Turn. **Cast off** loosely – a tight cast-off would defeat the purpose of the increases.

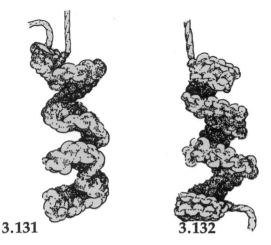

3.131   **3.132**

If making bunches, you may need to cast on as for **end of rows**.

Sawtooth curlicue

The second approach gives a stepped edge (Fig 3.132). The depth of the knitted strip cannot be altered, but the length of the curlicue can. In fact, length can be decided as you go along.

a **Cast on** 8 sts as suggested for **lace edges**. This time the cast-on must be soft, and the cast-off firm.

b Turn. **K2 tog** 4 times. **Cast on** 8.

c Turn. **K8, k2 tog, k3 tog.**

d Turn. **K2 tog** 5 times. **Cast on** 8.

Repeat **c** and **d**. To end (after **c**):

d Turn. **K2 tog, k3 tog.** Turn. **K2 tog** and pull thread.

Curlicues can be left as they are, joined into circles, untwisted and then joined into circles, or **blocked** with a stretched core. Play with them for a while and you will get a surprise or two.

Drawstring balls

They can be made in any pattern and any size. **Stuffed**, they make good **buttons**.

The instructions are for fourteen stitches and **stocking stitch** (Fig 3.133). If you change the number of stitches, or the pattern, alter the rows accordingly.

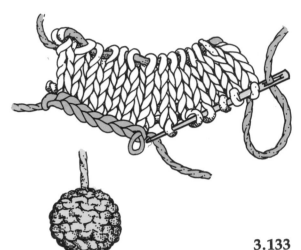

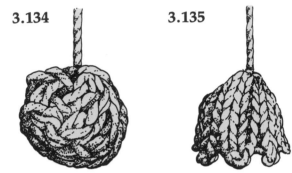

3.134   3.135

3.133

Bells

A clever use of a **horizontal hem**. Try working the two layers in different colours, or change the stitch pattern, or work the top layer in **jacquard**.

Use two sets of needles, one about three sizes finer than the other.

Fig 3.135 shows a fourteen-stitch bell in **stocking stitch**. If you change the number of stitches, or the pattern, alter the rows accordingly.

a **Provisional cast-on** 14 sts with finer needles.

b Work 6 rows in **st st**, leaving a tail long enough for later sewing.

c Work a row of **eyelets**, next to each other, to make a picot edge.

d Change to thicker needles and work 7 rows in **st st**.

e Unravel contrast yarn and place free loops on a spare needle – pointing in the same direction as the needle at the other end.

f Change to thinner needles again, and work 2 more rows in **st st**. On 1st row, work together 1 st from each needle (Fig 2.391).

g **Provisional cast-off**, leaving not too short a tail.

h With cast-on tail, **ladder-stitch seam** the side edges. **Darn** the tail.

i Thread cast-off tail through free loops again, in the same direction, to close the circle. Pull tight.

a **Provisional cast-on** 14 sts, leaving a 15–20cm (6–8in) tail. If **looping cast-on**, use 2 strands of the main yarn.

b Work 5 rows in **st st**.

c **Provisional cast-off**.

d Unpick contrast cast-on yarn, and thread the yarn tail through the free loops. (Omit if **looping cast-on**.)

e Thread yarn again through both cast-on and cast-off loops, in the same direction as before, closing the circle.

f Pull threads tight, **stuff** if desired, and **seam** the edges.

Coils

Slip cord, faggot cord, picot cord and narrow **flat-pattern cords** can be shaped into flat, or dome-shaped coils. Fig 3.134 shows a dome-shaped, faggot-cord coil.

a Work a short length of cord, just long enough to turn a circle.

b Curl the cord clockwise and attach the cast-on end to the last row with a **knitting-on join**.

c Continue working short lengths of cord, and joining to the budding coil.

Embroidery

(See also **embroidered edgings**)

Knitting makes a good fabric for embroidery because the stitches give you a grid. This is not so relevant when working free-flowing arrangements, but is wonderful for **cross stitch, smocking** and **running stitch** for instance, or for using these or other stitches to enhance the knitted fabric.

The scope is vast, and there is only room here to outline some of the most popular stitches.

For best results:

• Use a soft yarn. It must not be thinner than the knitting yarn, but it could be slightly thicker if you want it to cover the knitted stitches completely. Too thick, though, it will stretch the fabric.

• Choose colours carefully. As well as knitting yarns, embroidery threads and crewel, tapestry or Persian wools can be used, provided they are compatible for **cleaning** purposes. These have the advantages of being sold in very small amounts, and of coming in vast colour ranges – some in as many as 400 different shades. The slight drawback is that you may need several strands to match the thickness of the knitting yarn.

• Do not pull tight.

• When embroidering large areas, consider outlining different sections with tacking, perhaps in several colours.

• If working from **charts**, allow for the knitted stitches perhaps not being square. If necessary, transfer the chart to **ratio graph paper**, and correct it (see **stitch shape**).

• Make the most of the knitted fabric. Work with it, not against it.

• If the embroidery does not cross any **seams**, work it after **blocking** and before sewing up.

• Re-**block** after embroidering.

Swiss darning

Also called **embroidered jacquard** and **duplicate stitch**. As the last two names imply, it imitates the **knit stitch**.

Traditional Swiss darning is used for motifs similar to those used in **jacquard**. It works better than jacquard when there are long gaps between stitches of the same colour in one row, and for vertical lines set widely apart. The two techniques can be combined, but expect the embroidered stitches to look slightly larger, and somewhat raised.

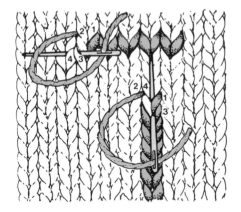

3.136

• Work in Vs, as shown in Fig 3.136, from right to left. When working blocks of stitches, work to the end of the first row, then turn the work upside down so that the second row also goes from right to left, after an initial half-stitch.

Chain stitch

Blends in very well, because chains are also achieved by knitting (Fig 3.137). Use, for instance, to outline changes in pattern, perhaps from a knit to a purl background.

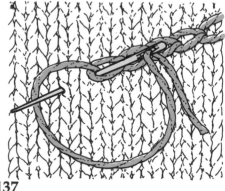

3.137

It could be used instead of **Swiss darning** for vertical, one-stitch lines. The result is somewhat more raised, because the yarn stays on the **right side** all the time.

Crochet chain stitch

Another way of working chain stitch is with a **crochet hook** (Fig 3.138). Keep the yarn on the wrong side and the hook on the right side. Work a **crochet chain**, inserting the hook through the fabric.

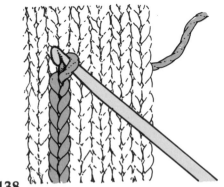

3.138

Daisy stitch

Single chain stitches arranged forming a circle, make a daisy. Daisies can have five, eight

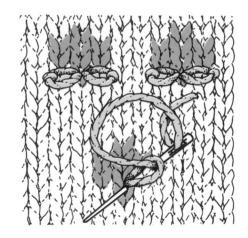

3.139

or more stitches, but there is no reason why you could not use just a couple of them (Fig 3.139).

Cross stitch

There are several ways of working cross stitch. Fig 3.140 shows two methods, travelling in opposite directions.

3.140

Long rows of cross stitch can also be worked in two stages – first all the strands in one direction, then all the strands in the other direction.

Whichever way you prefer to work, make sure that all the top strands go the same way.

Stem stitch

Very versatile. Try outlining changes in pattern by, for instance, picking up the heads of

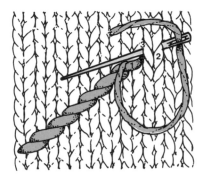

3.141

lines of purl stitches on a knit background or working diagonal lines by moving one stitch and one row away on every stitch (Fig 3.141).

Running stitch

One of the simplest stitches – the needle just goes in and out of the fabric.

It can be used to imitate **knitweave**, to highlight the top of raised patterns (such as narrow **cables**), to draw strands of yarn or ribbons through **eyelets** etc.

It blends extremely well with **moss stitch**. Either cover a whole project, fill in small geometric shapes, or play games such as shown in Fig 3.142.

Be careful not to pull tight, especially on moss stitch.

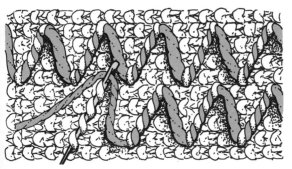

3.142

Smocking

A very effective way of gathering fabric, perhaps for a yoke, or to create very thick,

springy areas.

It can be worked on **stocking stitch**, rather as done on cloth. On **ribbings**, however, it is especially effective because it takes advantage of fabric curl.

The ribs are usually **irregular**: 1 (sometimes 2) **k**, and 3 or more **p**. The more purl stitches, the deeper the honeycomb, and the greater the gathering.

• All the **k** stitches of one row are joined in pairs with a couple of anchoring stitches. A few rows down, the process is repeated, alternating the rhythm. The row distance must be proportionate to the number of purl stitches. If the embroidered rows are too close, the knit stitches will pull. As a rule, the distance between rows should be equal to, or greater than, the distance between stitches when measured with a ruler.

If worried about catching the wrong row, or if working on **stocking stitch** or other smooth pattern, highlight the relevant stitches with horizontal lines of tacking.

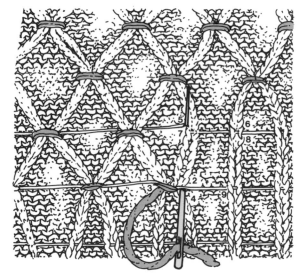

3.143

Fig 3.143 shows a **k**1, **p**4 rib, stitched on every 7th row. Progress is made on 2 rows at the same time, to avoid awkward strands on the wrong side.

For more decorative effects, make the yarn

move from one row to the other on the **right side**, and/or vary the distance between rows, perhaps even keeping the pairing arrangement unchanged between some of the rows.

Appliqué

(See also **patch pockets**)

Many things have been applied to knitted fabrics, including felt, leather, suede, cloth and fur. This may produce stunning results but is not always successful because of two problems. First, the **cleaning** processes are often incompatible. Secondly, if the stiffness of the appliqué materials is not taken into account at design stage, the knitted fabric may well get pulled and distorted.

Far fewer problems appear if applying knitting (or, at least, something made out of yarn) onto knitting. This offers quite a number of interesting possibilities, such as:

3.144

● **Cords**, either sewn with a **backstitch** (or two lines of **slip stitch**) or **knitted on** to the background fabric. Fig 3.144 shows a **plait** of **slip cords** half-covering a seam.

● **Skeins**, rather like the ones used for **Edgings**, attached every so often with **whipping**, so that they resemble strings of sausages.

● **Wiggle-woggles**, sewn dangling or flat depending on shape and intention.

● **Medallions**, attached with invisible stitches. Perhaps **lace** ones, in contrast colour.

● Fancy shapes, sewn flat or raised (Fig 3.145).

● Geometric patches, sewn as **applied patch pockets**.

● **Knitted-on** geometric patches. Work as suggested for **picked-up patch pockets**, then **graft** the last row.

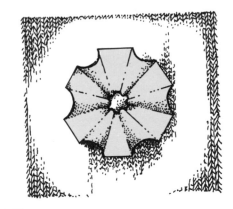

3.145

Sometimes, appliqué is lightly **stuffed** with wadding or finely cut yarn scraps.

Miscellaneous finishes

Padding

Pads for moulding certain areas can easily be knitted. Work out the shape you require and knit it on very thick needles and several strands of yarn. Use **garter stitch**, or any other thick, flexible pattern – preferably a **flat** one, unless special circumstances recommend a **curly** pattern.

To add thickness to centre area, work a second, smaller pad and sew it to first pad.

To add thickness to one side, make that side larger than it needs to be and fold it over, as in the shoulder pad shown in Fig 3.146.

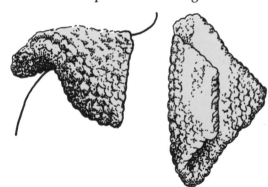

3.146

To make a really thick pad, work two identical ones, join the edges together except for an opening, **stuff** with wadding, and finish sewing.

If the padding is to be **washed**, a light, non-shrink, fast-drying yarn may be advisable.

Stuffing

(See also **blind objects** and **Books**)
Hard moulds to be covered with knitting can be made out of plaster of Paris, or papier mâché.

Tubular pockets, drawstring balls and other small areas can be filled with finely cut yarn scraps, unspun wool, shredded old tights, wadding, foam chips or other materials.

Appliqué can be lightly stuffed with wadding or yarn scraps.

Large projects can be stuffed with foam rubber, wood wool or kapok.

Small projects that are to 'sit' and/or change shape, can be stuffed with dried beans or lentils.

In all these cases, excepting the hard moulds, small amounts of stuffing are gently pushed into the cavity with the help of a knitting needle, wooden-spoon handle etc. Be careful not to overstuff.

Cords

Tubular and **crochet cords** can also be stuffed. A suitably shaped core (petersham, grosgrain ribbon, piping cord, candlewick cotton), is driven from one end to the other with the help of a bodkin or safety pin (Fig 3.147). The stuffing must fill the cavity, but not so tightly that progress is difficult.

Whatever stuffing you decide to use, make sure it cannot stain the knitting, and that **cleaning** methods are compatible.

3.147

Wiring

Wire of different thickness can be used to keep pieces of knitting taut and stiff (Fig 3.148), or to make them bend in certain shapes (Fig 3.149, where the stiffening is achieved by **starching**).

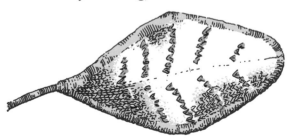

3.148

3.149

The leaf has its edge **overcast** over a rather rigid, medium-thick wire. The flower has the three petals, and the stamens, attached to a soft wire by means of a tightly wrapped silk thread. Each petal has the finest of cotton-covered wires **slip stitched** on the, wrong side, along the centre-line.

Brushing

This is done to improve the lift of **brushed yarns**, or to raise hairs on yarns that have not been brushed at the mill.

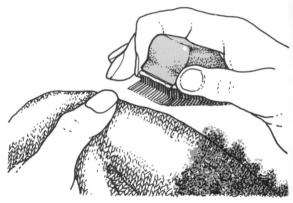

3.150

It should be done after sewing, to make sure that no hairs are trapped when seaming.

Work lightly with a **teasel** (Fig 3.150). If the yarn has not been previously brushed, take great care not to damage it – too much brushing can create holes. Plan ahead, and knit at a fairly tight **tension**, on a dense pattern.

Brush slowly, gently dabbing the knitted surface with a steady lifting or pulling action, until it is all equally fluffy.

Try first on a **tension sample**, both to learn the technique and to make sure that the teasel is clean, and free from hairs from other yarns.

Fulling

The process of intentional controlled felting, or matting, of wool fabric.

Short-fibre and softly spun wools full more easily. All wools full quicker at high temperatures, but tepid water gives better control. The latter is essential, because the process is totally irreversible.

The amount of shrinkage varies, but is always quite noticeable. If planning ahead, work a few **samples**. Outline them on a piece of paper, or photocopy them, and keep accurate records of **needles, tension** etc. Check new size and tension after fulling at different water temperatures, soap amounts and time. Take note of everything.

Base your calculations on the tension of the preferred fulled sample, but knit at the tension it had before fulling. Once the project is finished, full it according to the sample. However, fulling being a very experimental art, do not expect a large item to behave exactly like a sample. It may shrink the same percentage horizontally, but not vertically, or vice versa.

By hand

Fulling by hand is time-consuming and rather hard work, but gives greatest control:

a Rinse the knitting in lukewarm water, squeeze excess water and spread out.

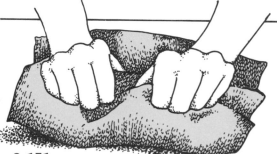

3.151

b Mix pure soap flakes (not ordinary washing powder) with a little water, to make a thin paste. Spread soap paste over the knitting and work in well, kneading and rubbing until the desired effect is achieved (Fig 3.151). A rolling pin might be useful.
c Rinse, squeeze excess water, roll in a towel and leave for a quarter of an hour.
d Shape on a flat surface, and allow to dry (see **drying**).
e Brush.

In multicolour projects, check at sample stage that they do not run.

By machine

The process can also be done in a washing machine. This must be full, perhaps with other items to be fulled, because friction is important. Start your experiments at the shortest cycle. Keep checking every few minutes if you want to retain control; with an automatic machine, this may be awkward.

Painting

Painting with special textile paints can be done on knitting as well as on any other fab-

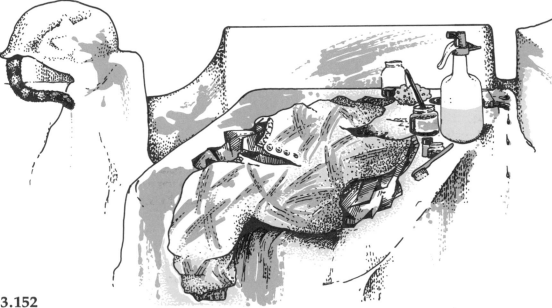

3.152

ric. Follow strictly the manufacturer's instructions, but be careful not to flatten the texture if they call for **pressing** with a hot iron.

The usual background fabric is **stocking stitch**, but others can be used. Tools vary from watercolour to decorator's brushes, cut potatoes, sprayers, afro-style combs, wire screens, washing-up brushes and sponges.

Different fibres react to paint in different ways. Blends may well give patchy results, but pure fibres (be they natural or man-made) will not. Try first on **samples**; with some techniques the patchy effect may even be an advantage.

Protect the working area and yourself well, to avoid paint covering the wrong things. Keep the knitting as flat and crease-free as possible. If it is made up, line with polythene to prevent colours seeping through (Fig 3.152).

See **Addresses** for more information, and have fun – the possibilities are certainly there.

PART FOUR
PATTERN INSTRUCTIONS

Row by row

(See also **Abbreviations** at start of **Part Two** and **adapting instructions**)

To knit, you do not necessarily need to follow someone else's instructions. Designing a project is not all that difficult once you try it (see **Books**). Whichever your choice, however, your project will have to be described in some way. This will normally take one of two forms: **row by row** (this chapter) or **charts and diagrams** (next chapter).

Both **stitch patterns** and **garments**, or other projects, can be described with one of these two methods. In Britain the first one is the most popular – although charts are often, if unfortunately not always, used for **colour knitting.** It is a cumbersome approach, that encourages mindless copying rather than clear understanding, especially when applied to garments without adding diagrams. On the other hand, some stitch patterns are easier to follow when written row-by-row. Ideally, it would be nice to have both versions when neither is totally satisfactory.

Stitch pattern instructions

Row-by-row instructions describe how to work every stitch of every row. Good instructions state whether the first row is a right-side or a wrong-side row. If nothing is said, it is likely to be a **right-side** row, but check it. In instructions for **circular knitting**, all rounds are right-side ones unless otherwise specified (wrong-side rounds are very rare, but not impossible).

Instructions assume that you have a needle full of stitches – if you are starting a fresh piece of work, **cast** them **on**. In any case, make sure that your total number of stitches

is compatible with the pattern (see **pattern repeats** and **number of stitches** below).

Some patterns include a **selvedge** stitch. If you do not want it, omit the first and last stitches of each row. If you would like a different selvedge, change the first and last stitches accordingly. Depending on the selvedge, more stitches may be required; patterns with selvedges often start and end each row with **k**1. If you want a selvedge and this is not included, add (an) extra stitch(es) at each end.

Lengthy instructions are not necessarily difficult. A simple **k**4, **p**4 arrangement travelling one stitch to right or left on alternate rows could be presented as an overwhelming 16-row pattern. From a **chart** its simplicity would be obvious.

For ease:

● Place a **fabric maker** on **right side**, or make a note of whether the **cast-on** tail is on the right or the left edge when working a right-side row.

● Transcribe (or **chart**) instructions when they are difficult to read or when you do not like the **abbreviations** used.

● In lengthy instructions, use **fabric markers** every time you reach the last row.

● Use a **row counter** (or one of its alternatives).

● Use a **line finder** (or one of its alternatives).

● Develop a rhythm that you can sing to yourself as you work – knit 1, slip 1, purl 2, would make a 1-2-3 beat.

Pattern repeats

When the same action is repeated on every stitch of a row, the pattern can be worked on any number of stitches. **Stocking stitch** is a good example. When the action keeps changing in a regular way, groups of stitches to be repeated will either appear in **brackets** ( ) or have an **asterisk** (*) at the start, and possibly another one at the end.

Usually, the group of stitches that forms a complete pattern repeat is pinpointed by asterisks. Smaller groups of stitches, within this large group, may appear in brackets if a working sequence is to be repeated two or three times. Example:

Row 1 (wrong side): p1; *ssk, (yo, slip 1) twice, k2 tog, p1*; repeat from * to * to last 2 sts; k2.

Number of stitches

Instructions for repeat patterns only work if the total number of stitches is a multiple of a certain figure, usually the number of stitches between asterisks. In **flat knitting**, a few extra stitches may need to be added to this figure to produce convenient edges. The example would need a stitch total multiple of 7 sts plus 3 sts (10, 17, 24, 31, 38, 45 . . . sts). Note that **decreases** count as one stitch only, and that **overs** and **slip stitches** count as worked stitches; in other words, what matters is the number of resulting loops, regardless of how they are achieved.

With the exception of some fairly rare patterns that change stitch total from row to row, the number of stitches between asterisks and the number of odd stitches will remain constant. Distribution, however, may vary: although the total of odd stitches does not change, the way they are split at either side of the asterisks can change. Sometimes, a whole pattern repeat is added to this number:

Row 4: k1, p4; *k2, p4, k1*; repeat from * to * to last 5 sts; k2, p3.

The resulting multiple of 7 plus 10 sts, can obviously be taken as multiple of 7 plus 3 sts. Knowing these rules, it is often possible to work out the pattern repeat figures when these are not given, as can happen in **garment instructions**. You can then use flat-knitting instructions for circular knitting (see **adapting instructions**).

Garment instructions

Commonly known as **patterns**, but not to be confused with **stitch patterns**.

In Britain, scaled, dimensioned **diagrams** of each piece to be knitted are only exceptionally included. Without these diagrams it is practically impossible to **measure** and **block** accurately. British knitters should decidedly revolt against this situation, and demand the type of instructions with diagrams found in so many other countries (see **garment diagrams**). Magazines and spinners beginning to adapt this approach should be warmly congratulated and encouraged. Let's hope that many more will join them soon.

Another badly needed change in British patterns is the abolition of the 'sleeve seam' measurement as the only indication of sleeve length. This varies so tremendously from style to style as to make comparison impossible.

Format

Patterns describe how to knit a garment, piece by piece, and how to put it together. A photograph or artist's impression, materials required, overall measurements, **tension**, list of abbreviations, **stitch pattern instructions** and any special features are also included.

Double and treble **asterisks** (**, ***) may be used to pinpoint sections to be repeated, if single asterisks are being used for the stitch pattern. They could be used, say, for a sequence of raglan shapings on the back, when this is to be repeated on the sleeves.

Square brackets [ ] may be used in multi-size patterns when several options are given: **cast on** 85[91;97;105] sts.

Writing and checking patterns is tremendously complex. Despite all efforts, mistakes do sometimes escape attention. If you think you have found one, tell your retailer or write to the publisher.

Pitfalls

Beware of:

- Recommendations to change needles to obtain different sizes (see **tension** below).
- Patterns that do not indicate 'actual width'. You should know exactly what to expect, because your idea of 'to fit size **x**' may not be the same as the designer's.
- One-size patterns 'to fit the average figure', either meaning 'to fit a designer's dream' or 'the design is awkward to adapt to other sizes, but fits nicely into this one – whatever this one happens to be'.
- 'Sleeve seam' measurements (see above).
- 'Knit it tonight, wear it tomorrow' (and throw away the day after!) patterns based on an extremely loose **tension**, without any tightening stitches or areas. Sweaters soon grow into maternity dresses.

Checklist

For good results:

- CHECK WHAT SIZE YOU NEED. Do not rely on your wearing size **x** dresses. Check actual width with a similar garment.
- USE THE RECOMMENDED YARN. If that is impossible to find, see introduction to **Yarns** and **yarn thickness**.
- DO NOT IGNORE TENSION WARNINGS (see **tension** below).
- INSIST ON DIAGRAMS.
- Choose exciting designs that are not too difficult for your present abilities.
- Read the instructions carefully before you start, to get the general idea.
- As work progresses, read each step again with even greater care.
- Check whether **selvedges** for **seams** or **free edges** have been allowed for. If necessary, add them or alter them.
- Check whether the stitch pattern and the **ribbings**, if any, will flow continuously across **seams**, once the **selvedges** have been taken in (see **planning for seams**). Alter the stitch total if not satisfied.
- Check whether the correct **selvedge** has been given to edges from which stitches are to be **picked up**.
- Check the look of the **ribbings** in the photograph. If they look too loose, **cast on** fewer stitches and adjust stitch total before starting main pattern, or work with finer needles. The section of ribbing directly under a **cable** always needs fewer stitches than the cable – otherwise it buckles.
- **Measure** work accurately and frequently.
- When working symmetrical pieces, remember to **pair** the **increases** and **decreases**. **Cast off** right-edge shapings from the **right side**, and left-edge shapings from the **wrong side**. Instructions for symmetrical pieces may be given as 'work as for first side, reversing all shapings', 'work to match' or 'work to correspond'. Consider working the two pieces at the same time (Fig 1.35).
- Use **needle** and/or **fabric markers** as required.
- Highlight relevant information (such as the stitches for your own size) with a fluorescent pen. To avoid damaging the original, either photocopy it or place it inside a plastic folder.
- Use a **line finder** (or one of its alternatives).
- Transcribe instructions that are difficult to read.

Tension

(See also **stitch size**)

Instructions only give a needle size as guidance for you to work your first **sample**. YOUR ONLY GUARANTEE THAT RESULTS WILL NOT BE TOO SMALL (Fig 4.1) OR TOO LARGE (Fig 4.2), BUT JUST RIGHT (Fig 4.3), IS TO OBTAIN THE STATED, COMPULSORY TENSION. Remember that tension samples MUST be measured away from the edges. If you need 28 sts in 10cm (4in), work a sample not smaller than 32 sts in the correct stitch pattern and with the yarn and colour you intend to use (see **yarn thickness**).

A **tight tension** causes garments to matt and to stiffen. A **loose tension** makes them grow and lose their shape. This is why you should

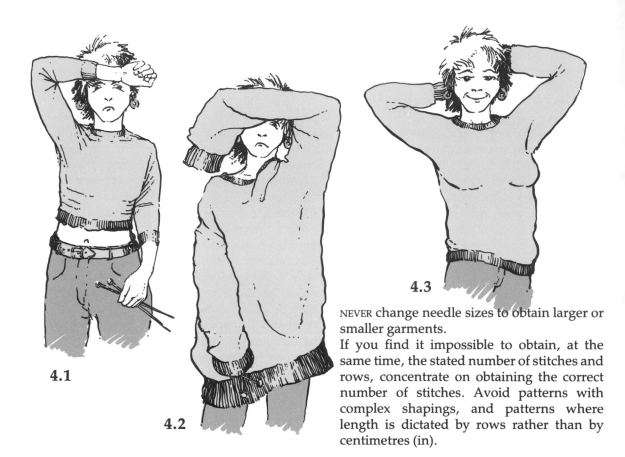

4.1

4.2

4.3

NEVER change needle sizes to obtain larger or smaller garments.

If you find it impossible to obtain, at the same time, the stated number of stitches and rows, concentrate on obtaining the correct number of stitches. Avoid patterns with complex shapings, and patterns where length is dictated by rows rather than by centimetres (in).

Charts and diagrams

Charts and diagrams have a number of advantages over **row-by-row** instructions:
- you can see at a glance what is to be done;
- you learn to think and judge;
- at the end of the day, your understanding is increased, and you feel more encouraged to continue knitting.

Charts

These are representations on **graph paper** of a piece of knitted fabric. Ideally, only **ratio** **graph paper** should be used, reflecting true **stitch shape**. When squared paper is used, allowance must be made for the knitted results probably being squatter than the chart (see **stitch shape**).

Each square or rectangle represents a stitch, and each horizontal line represents a row or round (in good charts these are numbered). Charts are always read from the bottom up, normally starting at the lower right-hand corner. In **flat knitting**, right-side rows are read from right to left and wrong-side rows from left to right (Fig 4.4). In **circular knit-**

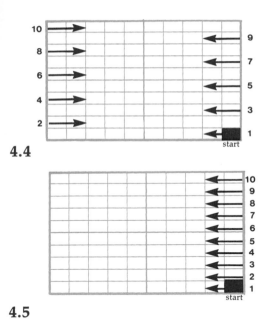

4.4

4.5

ting, all rounds are read from right to left (Fig 4.5).

Single motifs are usually shown in the centre of a chart. **Repeat patterns** are often shown from edge to edge. The repeat is highlighted by strong vertical lines – the chart equivalent to asterisks. In flat knitting only, there may be odd stitches at either side of the repeat. On **right-side rows**, work the stitches on the right edge once, then the repeat as many times as necessary, and finally the stitches on the left edge once. On **wrong-side rows**, do the same but in the opposite direction.

Multi-size **garment patterns** may have more than one set of edge stitches (Fig 4.6). Read instructions carefully, and work the set intended for the size you are knitting. To save space, these patterns sometimes use the same chart for different purposes: one part of the garment is explained at the bottom, another at the top. In Fig 4.6 the bottom instructions are for front and back, the top instructions are for the sleeves.

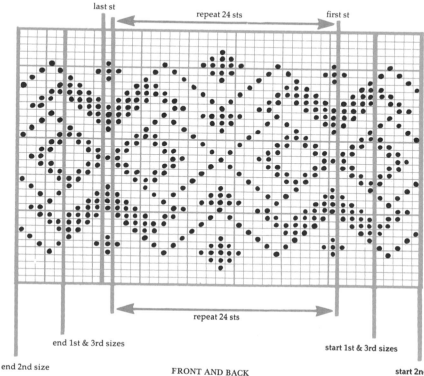

SLEEVES

last st   repeat 24 sts   first st

repeat 24 sts

end 1st & 3rd sizes   start 1st & 3rd sizes

4.6   end 2nd size   FRONT AND BACK   start 2nd size

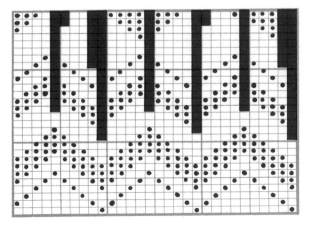

4.7

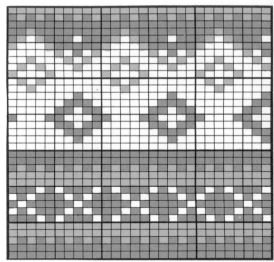

4.8

Charts must allow empty squares for stitches to be **increased**, or for stitches that have been **decreased**. Fig 4.7 shows such a chart for a round yoke. Paint the non-stitch squares in black if the chart has used another symbol. (Sometimes the missing stitches are put together at one edge, so as not to break the pattern – the chart then looks like a pyramid.)

Reading a chart is not difficult, but requires concentration. A **line finder** is invaluable, even if you have to settle for an **alternative**. If using a proper one, place it just above the line you are knitting, so that you can see the area you have already worked. Checking for mistakes will then be easier.

To make small-square charts easier to read, get an enlarged photocopy, or transcribe onto large graph paper.

Charts are extremely versatile. **Brocade, eyelet, two-strand, colour** or **bead knitting** charts, and **cross-stitch** or other **embroidery** charts might be interchangeable. With any adaptation, however, remember that each technique has its own rules. Do not expect all charts to be good for everything.

Colour charts

Most colour charts are intended for **stocking-stitch jacquard** and show the **right side** of work.

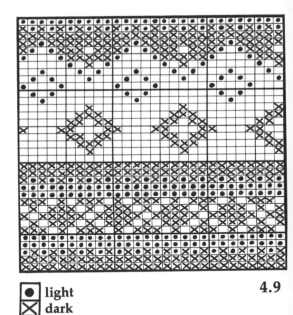

|⬤| light |
|✕| dark |

4.9

The colour pattern is shown either in colour (Fig 4.8) or in black and white (Fig 4.9). In the second case, a list of symbols is given. The background colour is generally left blank, especially in black-and-white charts. Confusing black-and-white charts come to life if each colour is painted over with an appropriate colour pen.

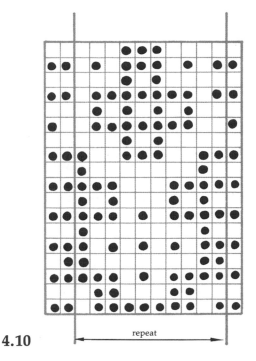

4.10

repeat

Knit stitches are possibly clearer if left blank. Stitches that only appear in some rows, because of **increases** or **decreases**, are clearer if shown as black squares in all the other rows. Each square represents a new loop. **Decreases**, therefore, take up only one square. When every other row or round is either all knit or all purl, the chart often shows only the patterned rows or rounds. Charts for flat knitting sometimes have shaded wrong-side rows.

Some patterns translate extremely successfully into charts. **Brocades** (Fig 2.101), **cables** (Fig 4.11) and **lace** (Fig 4.12) are good examples.

Bead knitting uses this type of chart. **Mosaic knitting**, however, is charted on square paper; each line represents two rows instead of the usual one (Fig 4.10).

Stitch pattern charts

Usually, these charts show the stitches from the **right side**, but occasionally charts for **flat knitting** show the **wrong-side rows** as they are worked. The first type of chart is much clearer visually, but in flat knitting you must remember to work all the stitches (including **increases** and **decreases**) from the other side – purl for knit, knit for purl etc.

Symbols are far from standard. The best symbols are those that clearly reflect texture, such as:

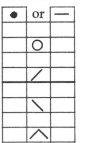

● or —		**purl**
	○	**over**
	/	**k2 tog**
	\	**ssk**
	⋀	**double slip decrease**

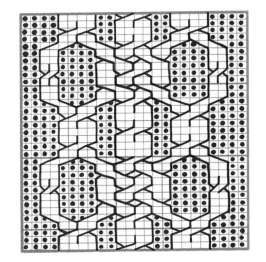

4.11

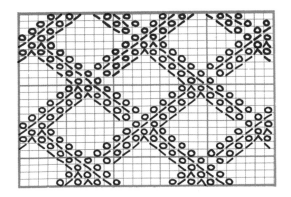

4.12

Garment charts

Whole garment pieces can be shown in chart form, often combined with **colour** or **stitch pattern charts** (Fig 4.13).

The charts clearly show all the shapings and exact position of **pockets, buttonholes** etc.

Unless they are drawn on a small grid, these charts can become annoyingly large. Sometimes only half the back or half the front is shown.

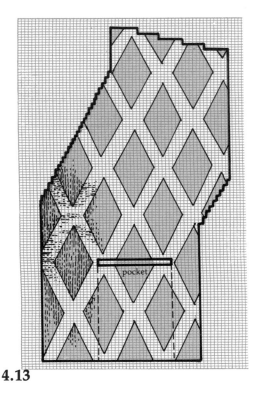

4.13

Garment diagrams

In many countries it would be totally inconceivable to produce a knitting pattern without diagrams. Until the time comes when they are fully adopted in Britain, make a point of showing your disbelief at their absence every time you buy a new pattern that does not include them.

With diagrams such as those in Fig 4.14 you have a perfectly clear idea of what each piece is going to look like, and a true guide for **measuring** and **blocking**. And you need

much shorter instructions – because you see what shape you are building, you do not need to be spoon-fed.

In addition you can, if you want to, cut a full-size **paper pattern** against which to check work progress, or embark on alterations.

The pieces used to make a knitted garment are very similar to those used in dressmaking. Not to show them in patterns is like telling a dressmaker: 'cut 50cm horizontally; turn a right angle to the left and cut 45cm vertically; turn a 38° angle to the right and cut 10cm . . .' Would any dressmaker stand for that?

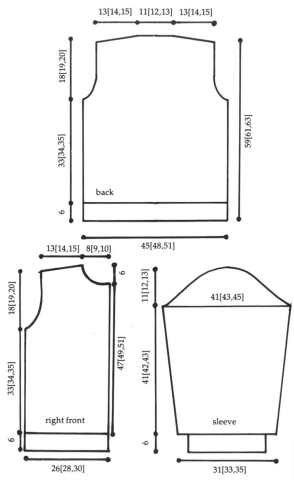

4.14

PART FIVE

HELP!

Mishaps

Errors and accidents can happen to anyone. DO NOT PANIC. If you keep a cool, clear head, you will almost certainly put things right.

Dropped stitches

New knitters, **slack knitters**, and knitters not keeping a good grasp (see **Holding the work**), tend to be prone to drop stitches. Which is not to say that all other knitters are immune to this problem. If you are working on your first project, or if your stitches drop like ripe apples in the wind, inspect every row before you start on the next.

Always:

● Stop free loop with right or left needle as soon as you spot it.
● Keep safety pins at hand. A dropped stitch will go no further if caught with one.
● Keep stitches close together. Pulling the fabric sideways to get a clearer view of the problem will cause more laddering.
● Relax. Clutching the work may cause more stitches to drop.

If you spot the free loop only after leaving it **a few rows down**, rescuing it will make the fabric tighter than it would otherwise be. Place one or more **fabric markers** to highlight the area, and correct it as well as you can when **blocking**.

On row being worked

Unravel row back to free loop, if necessary.
● Put stitch back on left needle, making sure it is not **twisted** (see **stitch and needle**). If it is twisted, work it through the **back**. Or, insert right needle into it as if to **knit-back** (Fig 2.87), take it off left needle and return to left needle in the correct position.

On row below

To correct a KNIT stitch:

a Insert right needle into free loop and under strand above it, from the **front**. Notice that strand is behind st.
b Insert left needle into dropped st, from the **back** (Fig 5.1), and **basic cast-off** the strand.
c Place new st on left needle.

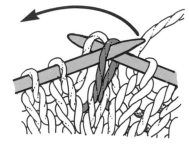

5.1

To correct a PURL stitch:

a Insert right needle into free loop and under strand above it, from the **back**. Notice that strand is in front of st.
b Insert left needle into dropped st, from the **front** (Fig 5.2), and **basic cast-off** the strand.
c Place new st on left needle.

5.2

A few rows down

A ladder will have formed. Make sure to

work up the rungs of the ladder in the correct order.

Either repeat the instructions just given for every row, or use a **crochet hook**, finer than the knitting needles, and work as follows.

To correct a KNIT ladder:

a Insert hook into free loop, from the **front**.

b With hook pointing up, catch 1st strand of ladder, from below (Fig 5.3).

c Draw strand through loop.

Repeat **b** and **c**.

5.3

To correct a PURL ladder, turn work to obtain a KNIT ladder, or:

a Insert hook into free loop, from the **back**.

b With hook pointing down, catch 1st strand of ladder, from above (Fig 5.4).

c Draw strand through loop.

d The hook is now inserted into new st from the **front**. Remove it, and reinsert it from the **back**.

Repeat **b** to **d**.

5.4

On other fabrics, keep turning work to face always knit stitches, or alternate knit and purl actions as required. In complex fabrics, either **unravel** or try to find your way up the ladder keeping the pattern correct. Whether you succeed or not, your understanding of knitting will benefit no end. If forced to admit defeat, unravel.

Several stitches

● If you drop several consecutive stitches, stop them all with one **safety pin**. Then, release them, one by one, and proceed as for single stitches.

You might have to ease the yarn across the stitches, either now or when **blocking**, because the first one is likely to be very loose and the last one very tight. In fine cotton lace, if you find the work too fiddly, try **starching** the ladder area.

Too late for rescue

If you only discover a dropped stitch after **casting off** and **darning** the yarn ends, work the free loop up the ladder if it has run and/or secure it at **back of work** with matching thread.

Small errors

Extra stitches, split-yarn stitches, twisted stitches, mistakes in pattern, can all be corrected. If only one stitch is involved:

a Work to the st on the present row just above the error.

b Drop this st and ladder it down to the row below the error.

c Proceed as for **dropped stitches a few rows down**.

If you had a stitch too many, the new stitches will be **larger** than they should. Distribute the extra yarn on the adjoining stitches, either now or when **blocking**.

When several stitches are involved, you can drop them all, ladder them, put them on a safety pin or holder, and retrace the ladder up stitch by stitch. By clever use of safety pins and short, perhaps double-pointed needle(s), plus a crochet hook, you can correct glaring mistakes this way. A fairly straightforward case would be to reverse a **cable** twist, but complex **lace** and other patterns can often, if not always, be equally tackled. Straighten up the new fabric either now or when **blocking**. As with **a few rows down** above, even if you have to admit defeat you will learn a lot about fabric structure.

Sometimes, especially when the wrong stitches are all on the same row of a knit-and-purl pattern, it is speedier to cut the yarn at mid-error, and unravel the row as for **cut horizontal slits** (Fig 2.364). The free loops can then be **grafted** in the correct pattern with a new length of yarn.

Major errors

When none of the previous methods work, or when you have actually missed one or more rows, there is only one possible remedy – **unravelling**, the most heartbreaking of all knitting techniques.

You may be tempted to say that 'it will not show'. Do not kid yourself. It will and, knowing that it is there, you might even draw people's attention to it!

Unravelling a single row

Best done stitch by stitch. Keep the yarn in your usual hand. If this is the right hand, unravel from left to right. If it is the left hand, unravel from right to left.

On **knit**:

5.5

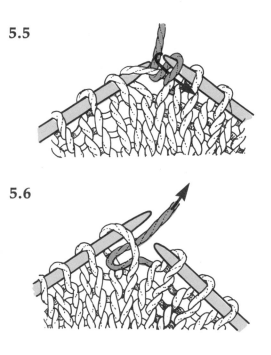

5.6

a Assuming st to be unravelled is on right needle, insert left needle into st below, from the **front** (Fig 5.5).
b Drop st off right needle.
c Pull yarn (Fig 5.6).
Repeat **a** to **c**.

On **purl**:
Proceed as for **knit** (Fig 5.7). The yarn is now

5.7

in front, but the technique is otherwise unchanged.

Unravelling several rows

You could repeat the **single-row** procedure, but if many rows are involved it would be long and tedious.

The fast method is to take the work off the needles and pull the yarn. Keep the work gathered in the hand that is not pulling, to avoid laddering. Pull firmly, but with care; with hairy yarns or intricate stitch patterns you could create tight spots if you pulled too firmly. (See Fig 5.11 under **pull away**.)

As a safety measure, especially with silky, **slippery yarns**, you can thread one of the following through the first good row, before starting to unravel:

- a fine knitting needle;
- a length of fine yarn;
- a length of sewing thread.

No stitch will then drop beyond this row.

Or, you could pull all the rows except the last one, and do this one slowly. Pull half a dozen stitches at a time, and thread the needle through them before pulling any more. A fine needle will be easier to thread, but remember to change it back to the correct size after the first row.

When threading the needle, the stitches often seem easier to catch from the **back**, but this twists them. It is up to you to decide whether to catch them the easy way and work them through the back of the loop on the next row, or to catch them through the **front** in the correct manner (Figs 5.8 and 5.9).

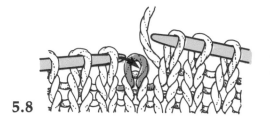

5.8

5.9

Recycling

You may think of recycling because of hardship or from being tired of seeing a brand new piece of knitting unworn. Whatever your reasons, it is comforting to know that yarn need never be wasted.

Pull away

The first thing to do is to **unravel** the work. This usually starts with some rather tedious preparatory work. Do not try to hurry through it, because you could well make the task much longer.

Work in a quiet area, away from children and pets. Make a pile of yarn on the floor or inside a very large box. Left undisturbed, the yarn will not get tangled. Short lengths can be tied together, until you have roughly the equivalent of one of the original balls. Leave the last end clear of the pile (Fig 5.10). Make a **skein**, then continue pulling.

Discard worn or very short lengths of yarn.

Tight stitches are made worse by hard pulling. They are often caused by hairs getting tangled. Gentle tugging will generally free them. **Brushed** and **hairy** yarns may become so tangled as to make work very difficult.

Slightly felted knitting may need dusting with talcum powder. Very felted knitting may not unravel at all.

a Unpick any **seams**, being careful not to snip the fabric. Loosening the stitches, one by one, with a blunt sewing needle is best. If not sure whether a loop belongs to the seam or to the fabric, pull it to see what other loops follow.

b Unpick **darning** to free the yarn ends.

c Unfasten last **cast-off stitch**. Unravelling from the cast-on end is impossible.

d Gather fabric in one hand and, carefully, pull yarn with the other hand to the bitter end (Fig 5.11).

5.10

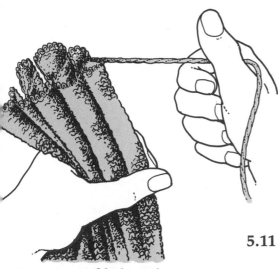

fibres can be steamed, I find washing preferable – obviously provided that the yarn is washable. If it is not, you may not be able to steam it either.

a **Wash** hanks as appropriate, and rinse well.

b Still soaking wet, hang them to dry, away from direct heat and direct sun. Peg one of the ties, but not the yarn (Fig 5.13).

c Although the dripping water will get rid of most of the crinkling, attach a small weight to the tie at the bottom of the hank for best results, especially if drying in the wind.

The dry yarn should be put back around the picture frame or chair back, and wound into loose balls (see **skeins**).

• • •

Now you are ready to start knitting all over again. So, what about going back to Part Two and trying one of the more unusual ways of **casting on**?

5.11

Re-conditioning

Because of **blocking** or **washing**, the unravelled yarn will be very crinkly. To re-condition it is a two-step job.

Skeining

a Wind the yarn around a board, picture frame, chair back, or whatever you have at hand.

b Tie the two ends in an obvious knot.

c Tie the skein with very strong yarn, tape or strips of fabric in three or four places (Fig 5.12). If the skeins are very thick, tie into a figure-of-eight loop so as to split the skein.

Straightening

Although **wool** and some other natural

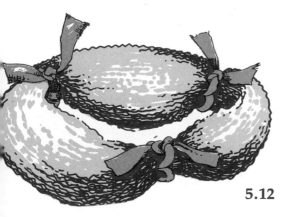

5.12

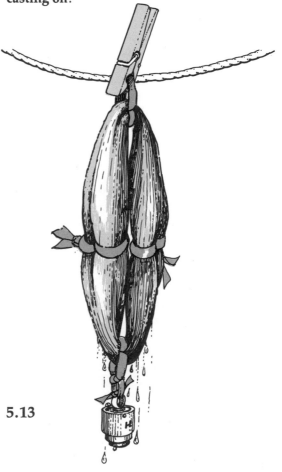

5.13

Publications

Books

New books appear all the time, and there are so many on hand knitting that a full list would take many pages. What follows is a selection of classic, specialist and innovative titles, plus odd ones from other fields; no compilations of instructions for sweaters and other projects have been included. If you cannot find a title through your local shop or library, see list of new and secondhand **booksellers** under **Addresses**.

For a thorough bibliography of books in English, send £1 plus a large (A4) sae to the Knitting and Crochet Guild (see **Addresses**).

Colour theory

Johannes Itten, **Art of Colour, New Edition**, Van Nostrand Reinhold, New York, 1973. 'The' book. There is an abridged version, edited and evaluated by Faber Birren: **The Elements of Colour**, same publishers, 1970.

Design

Montse Stanley, **Knitting: Your Own Designs for a Perfect Fit**, David & Charles, Newton Abbot, 1982, 1985 (revised). Made-to-measure knitting explained in full detail. With many sketches to spark-off ideas and a complete set of ratio graph papers.

Dyeing and painting

See **Addresses** for booksellers, associations and general suppliers catering for dyers.

Dylon International Ltd, Lower Sydenham, London SE26 5HD publishes excellent free leaflets on dyeing and painting fabrics. Some of the imaginative (and fun) special effects can be applied to knitting. Send A5 sae.

Handicapped knitters

Mary Konior, **Knitting and Crochet with One Hand**, Philip & Tacey Ltd, North Way, Andover, Hants, 1986. Marvellous.

Shelagh Hollingworth, **Knitting and Crochet for the Physically Handicapped and Elderly**, Batsford, London, 1981.

Audrie Stratford, **Better Knitting Made Easier**. Five 60-min cassettes for visually handicapped knitters, plus companion book for sighted helpers. Cassettes available on loan from Communications Department, Jewish Blind Society, 91 Stamford Hill, London N16 5TP, Tel 01-800 5672 to registered blind or partially sighted. Also from Calibre, Aylesbury, Bucks HP20 1HU, Tel 0296-32339/81211 – to join this free library send doctor's certificate stating you cannot read ordinary print. Book available from the author, The Bennals, 13 Chase Avenue, King's Lynn, Norfolk.

Braille patterns may be obtained from The Royal National Institute for the Blind (RNIB), 224 Great Portland Street, London W1N 6AA, Tel 01-388 1266, and Moon patterns from The RNIB, Moon Branch, Holmesdale Road, Reigate, Surrey RH2 0BA, Tel 07372-46333. Both braille and Moon patterns and braille instructions on learning to knit can be borrowed from the National Library for the Blind, Cromwell Road, Bredbury, Stockport SK6 2SG, Tel 061-494 0217.

In Touch, BBC Publications, London, 1983. A most comprehensive book on aids and services for visual handicaps, including all types of low-vision aids – from simple magnifiers to closed-circuit TV. New edition in late 1986, hopefully to be updated annually.

Left-handed knitters

Regina Hurlburt, **Left-Handed Knitting**, Van Nostrand Reinhold, New York, 1977. Elementary, but tackles the question head on.

Stain removal

Good Housekeeping, **How to Remove Stains**, Ebury Press, London, 1979. All you will ever need.

Stitch-pattern dictionaries

Nobody has surpassed Barbara G. Walker's work in this area. She has given us mosaic knitting and created many cable combinations, apart from collecting hundreds of patterns of all types and presenting such brilliant techniques as slip-slip-knit decrease, one-row buttonhole and reinforced-eyelet buttonhole. All her books are published by Charles Scribner's Sons, New York; the first two have very good lace sections:
A Treasury of Knitting Patterns, 1968 and later editions. **A Second Treasury of Knitting Patterns**, 1970 and later editions. **Charted Knitting Designs: A Third Treasury of Knitting Patterns**, 1972. **Sampler Knitting**, 1973.

Not to be compared with Barbara Walker's, but quite adequate for ordinary needs:
Anne Matthews, **Vogue Dictionary of Knitting Stitches**, David & Charles, Newton Abbot, 1984. Useful French, German, Italian and Spanish terminologies.
The Harmony Guide to Knitting Stitches, Lyric Books, London 1983. Good value.

Technique and structure

The 'bible' for British knitters are the two books by Mary Thomas, both published by Hodder & Stoughton, London, and reprinted as paperbacks in 1985:
Mary Thomas's Knitting Book, 1938.
Mary Thomas's Book of Knitting Patterns, 1943.
Maggie Righetti, **Knitting in Plain English**, St Martin's Press, New York, 1986. Designed to be used as a class textbook or as a reference guide. Eminently practical and no-nonsense, based on the author's long experience as 'the knitting lady' in several woolshops. I owe her large-eyelet buttonhole.
Audrie Stratford, **Introducing Knitting**, Batsford, London, 1972. Knitting approached with the well-trained, enquiring mind of the scientist, asking for the why as well as the how. Techniques later developed by the author include bead markers and helix stripes. She also carried out the research into length of 3-ply yarns mentioned in Yarn Thickness.
Elizabeth Zimmermann, **Knitting Without Tears**, Charles Scribner's Sons, New York, 1971. Wit, fun, common sense and tricks from one of circular knitting's greatest advocates. She has 'unvented', amongst others, seam cast-off, outline cast-off and many of the slip cord (which she calls I-cord – from its other name of idiot cord!) applications.

More specialized titles:
Lee Gilchrist, **Twice-Knit Knitting**, Grosset & Dunlap, New York, 1970. Technique and patterns for this unusual way of knitting.
Jane F. Neighbors, **Reversible Two-Colour Knitting**, Charles Scribner's Sons, New York, 1974. Double-sided tubular jacquard and multicolour slip stitch theory and patterns.
Mary Walker Phillips, **Creative Knitting: A New Art Form**, Van Nostrand Reinhold, New York, 1971. Technique and inspiration for large decorative work, by the master of the subject.
Elyse and Mike Sommer, **A New Look at Knitting**, Crown Publishers Inc, New York, 1977. A playful approach, full of unexpected ideas.

Yarns

For lists of books on yarn spinning, see **booksellers** under **Addresses**.
Tessa Lorant, **Yarns for the Knitter**. The Thorn Press, 1980. A small book on yarn types and properties, systems of measuring

thickness and hints on buying and using yarns.

Tessa Lorant, **The Good Yarn Guide**. The Thorn Press, 1985. Directory of UK suppliers, plus a glossary of technical yarn terms.

Tessa Lorant has written several other books. I owe her collar moulds and some of the miscellaneous moulds, stretching without pins and three-loop crochet join.

Maggie Righetti, **Universal Yarn Finder**, Vol II, Maggie Righetti Designs, Atlanta, 1983. Vol III to be published in March 1987 by Prentice-Hall, New York. A marvellous source of information on 1400 yarns available in America (many also in Britain). An excellent tool for substituting yarns.

My Valuable Yarn Guide and **Valuable Knitting Information**, Knitting-Information, Richmond, U.S.A. The first title, for consumers, covers over 2000 yarns. The second, for retailers, covers 6500. Less information on each yarn than previous title, but probably easier to use and updated every 6 months.

Magazines

Apart from the many magazines regularly available from newsagents, and those published by **organisations**, the following might be of interest.

Knitters. Golden Fleece Publications, 126 South Phillips Avenue, Sioux Falls, SD 57102, USA. Six-monthly. Each issue looks deeply into one subject, including technique and some patterns. Scaled diagrams.

Labores del Hogar. Aribau 28 entlo, 08011-Barcelona, Spain. Monthly knitting and needlecrafts. Scale diagrams.

Mille Idee. Rizzoli Editore, Via Angelo Rizzoli 2, 20132 Milano, Italy. Monthly. Italian fashion. Scaled diagrams.

Rakam. Rusconi Editore, Via Vitruvio 43, 20124 Milano, Italy. Monthly. Fashion plus home furnishings in knitting and other needlecrafts. Scaled diagrams.

Threads. The Taunton Press, 63 South Main Street, Box 355, Newtown, CT 06470, USA. Bi-monthly. Intelligent articles on all thread crafts. No patterns.

Vogue Knitting. Vogue Pattern Service, New Lane, Havant, Hants PO9 2ND. The British version is available through main newsagents. Six-monthly. Stylish fashion and some excellent articles. Scaled diagrams.

Addresses

Organisations

When requesting information, always send a largish (A5) sae.

The Knitting Craft Group, PO Box 6, Thirsk, North Yorks YO7 1TA.

Resources, advice and courses for teachers. 'Knitterbugs', yarn packs for children. 'Soft options', video for teenagers.

The Knitting and Crochet Guild, Elizabeth Gillett, Membership Secretary, 5 Roman Mount, Roundhay, Leeds, West Yorks LS8 2DP.

For those who want to share their interest in hand/machine knitting or crochet. Small library, competitions, local groups, magazine 'Slip Knot'.

The Edinburgh Knitting and Crochet Guild, Julie Matthews, Secretary, 9 Lennie Cottages, Craigs Road, Edinburgh EH12 0BB.

A more local guild. Regular lectures and workshops, library, exhibitions, magazine

'Hook and Needle'.

Association of the Guilds of Weavers, Spinners and Dyers, The Secretary, BCM 963, London WC1N 3XX.
Many local Guilds. Activities both at local and national level. Courses. 10-day summer school on alternate years. Exhibitions. Journal.

Needle Crafts Club, The Old Vicarage, Haley Hill, Halifax HX3 6DR.
Sponsored by the British Needlecraft Council, the club embraces all kinds of needlework. Product information, courses, competitions, visits, regional and national events, magazine 'Needle Crafts'.

The Textile Society, Barbara Ingram, Membership Secretary, 19 Ty Mynydd Close, Radyr, Cardiff CF4 8AS.
For the study of all types of textile art, design and history. Newsletter. Fascinating visits and events.

Disabled Living Foundation, 380-384 Harrow Road, London W9 2HU, Tel 01-289 6111.
Help with all kinds of disabilities, multiple handicaps and infirmities of age. Information service. Aids and equipment centre where a variety of aids (not for sale) can be seen – visits by appointment.

The Society of Teachers of the Alexander Technique, 10 London House, 266 Fulham Road, London SW10 9EL.
List of qualified teachers for those who want to learn to use their body correctly.

Booksellers

When requesting information always send a large (A4) sae.

New books

Most booksellers will take orders for titles in print not currently in their stock.

Bayswater Books, 21 Gwendolen Avenue, London SW15 6ET. Tel 01-788 4029.
Mail order; callers by appointment only. Catalogue of knitting, spinning, dyeing and weaving books.

Fibrecrafts (see **general suppliers**).
Knitting, spinning, dyeing and weaving books. Magazines.

R. D. Franks Ltd, Kent House, Market Place, Oxford Circus, London W1N 8EJ. Tel 01-636 1244/5/6.
'The' bookshop for the fashion trade. Open Monday to Friday, plus mail order. Credit cards. Catalogue. Subscriptions to foreign magazines.

The Textile Bookshop, Tynwald Mills, St John's, Isle of Man. Tel 0624-71213.
Mail order; callers by appointment only. Credit cards. Two catalogues – one on knitting; one on spinning, dyeing and weaving. Magazines.

The Thorn Press (see **general suppliers**).
Own imprint books by Tessa Lorant.

Antiquarian and secondhand books

The following will all search for specific titles.

Black Cat Books, 1 Granby Road, Edinburgh EH16 5NH. Tel 031-667 6341.
Mail order; callers by appointment only. Catalogue of needlework, cookery and household books.

Faith Legg, The Guildhall Bookroom, Church Street, Eye, Suffolk. Tel 0379-870193.
Mail order. Shop open Fridays and Saturdays, or by appointment. No catalogue, but knitting books always in stock.

Judith Mansfield, 60A Dornton Road, London SW12 9NE. Tel 01-673 6635.
Mail order; callers by appointment only. Catalogue of textile books, including knitting.

Sacketts, 34 Dorset Street, Blandford Forum, Dorset, Tel 0258-53837.
Mail order only. Catalogue of knitting, weaving, textiles and embroidery titles. All books sent on approval.

Felicity J. Warnes, 82 Merryhills Drive, Enfield, Middlesex, EN2 7PD. Tel 01-367 1661.
Mail order; callers by appointment only. Catalogue of costume and fashion books, including knitting and needlecraft.

General suppliers

When requesting information always send a sae – small unless otherwise indicated.

Albion Botanicals Ltd, High Street, Coton, Cambridge CB3 7PL.
Herbal moth deterrents and dried dyeplants. Wholesale only.

Len Crisp, 39 Borrowdale Drive, Norwich NR1 4LY.
Mail order only. Wooden knitting sheaths.

Fencraft Products Ltd, P.O. Box IW6, Leeds LS16 7SS, Tel 0532-676093.
Mail order. 'Knitters Friend' – stand for holding patterns up to A4. Includes a sliding, magnifying ruler.

Fibrecrafts, Style Cottage, Lower Eashing, Godalming, Surrey GU7 2QD. Tel 04868-21853. Also under **booksellers**. A4 sae.
Mail order; callers by appointment only. Credit cards. Needles, ball winders, swifts, jumbo cherry-wood sewing needles, herbal moth deterrents. Also spinning, dyeing and weaving supplies. 'True Knit' ratio graph papers.

Goodlad and Goodlad, 147 Commercial Street, Lerwick, Shetland. Tel 0595-3797.
Shop and mail order. Leather knitting belts.

Mary Gostelow, 43 Milton Abbas, Blandford, Dorset DT11 0BP.
Mail order. Magnetic line finders.

Homecraft Supplies Ltd, 27 Trinity Road, London SW17 7SF, Tel 01-672 7070/1789.
Mail order. Needle holder for knitters who can only use one hand.

Machine Knitting and Design Centre, High Cross House, High Cross, Aldenham, Watford, Herts WD2 8BN. Tel 09276-3095.
Kamalini Trentham's tension gauge.

H. McMorran, 103 Meigle Street, Galashiels TD1 1LW.
Mail order only. 'The McMorran Yarn Balance'. A clever instrument to determine how many yards in 1 lb of yarn (order yd/lb beam), or exact count in one of the more sophisticated systems of measuring thickness (order appropriate beam for system required).

H. W. Peel & Co. Ltd, Norwester House, Fairway Drive, Greenford, Middlesex UB6 8PW, Tel 01-578 6861.
Manufacurers of 'True Knit' ratio graph papers. Trade and wholesale only.

Spinners, Fakenham Road, Beetley, Dereham, Norfolk NR20 4BT. Tel 0362-860194.
Shop open Friday and Saturday or by appointment. Mail order. Swifts, ball winders, blocking pins, sheaths and other hard-to-find items. Wooden buttons, spinning supplies, herbal moth deterrents. 'True Knit' ratio graph papers.

Hugh Steeper (Roehampton) Ltd, 59 North Worple Way, Mortlake, London SW14 8PS, Tel 01-878 8633.
Showroom and mail order. Needle holder for knitters who can only use one hand.

Stove and Smith, 98 Commercial Street, Lerwick, Shetland ZE1 0EX. Tel 0595-3383.
Shop and mail order. Long double-pointed steel knitting needles up to old British size 16.

The Textile Bookshop (see **booksellers**)
'True Knit' ratio graph papers.

The Thorn Press, The Old Vicarage, Godney, Wells, Somerset BA5 1RX. Tel 0458-32225. Also under **booksellers**.
Mail order; callers by appointment only. Short double-pointed steel knitting needles in old British sizes 15 and 16. Tessa Lorant's special accessories: yarn gauges, tension gauges, strip line finders (locators), collar shaping guides.

Index

American terms in **bold**. When several page numbers are given, main entries also in **bold**.